COVERT PLANTS

Before you start to read this book, take this moment to think about making a donation to punctum books, an independent non-profit press,

@ https://punctumbooks.com/support/

If you're reading the e-book, you can click on the image below to go directly to our donations site. Any amount, no matter the size, is appreciated and will help us to keep our ship of fools afloat. Contributions from dedicated readers will also help us to keep our commons open and to cultivate new work that can't find a welcoming port elsewhere. Our adventure is not possible without your support.

Vive la open-access.

Fig. 1. Hieronymus Bosch, Ship of Fools (1490–1500)

Covert Plants

Vegetal Consciousness and Agency in an Anthropocentric World

Edited by Prudence Gibson
& Baylee Brits

Brainstorm Books
Santa Barbara, California

brainstorm books

First published in 2018 by Brainstorm Books
A division of punctum books, Earth, Milky Way
www.punctumbooks.com

ISBN-13: 978-1-947447-69-1 (print)
ISBN-13: 978-1-947447-70-7 (epdf)

LCCN: 2018948912
Library of Congress Cataloging Data is available from the Library of Congress

Interior design: Vincent W.J. van Gerven Oei
Cover art: Jackie Cavallaro
Cover design: Shant Rising

Contents

≈

Part II — Thinking Plants

Baylee Brits
Brain Trees:

Dalia Nassar
Metaphoric Plants:
Goethe's *Metamorphosis of Plants* and the

Tamryn Bennett

Ben Woodard
Continuous Green Abstraction:

Lisa Dowdall

≈

Part III — Political Landscapes

Prudence Gibson

Monica Gagliano
Persons as Plants:

Justin Clemens

૨૭

Introduction: Covert Plants

Baylee Brits and Prudence Gibson

Covert Plants: Vegetal Consciousness and Agency in an Anthropocentric World is an anthology of interdisciplinary essays and creative works, which charts the transformation in the conceptual and ethical status of plants in an era of changing climates. It presents a range of academic and creative perspectives from evolutionary biology to literary theory, from philosophy to poetry, at a time when a call for restorative care and reparative action has been sounded for the environment. The anthology contributes to the emerging field of Critical Plant Studies, at the crossover of plants and philosophy,[1] literature,[2] and arts,[3] with a focus on the non-human components of our world.[4] The essays in this anthology engage with new discoveries in plant science and evaluate how these changes affect the humanities and the arts. Art, literature, and philosophy have the capacity to mediate difficult issues of climate change and present a new perspective on human–plant interactions, just as new plant science transforms these practices and disciplines.

Plants are often considered of secondary importance to animal or even insect species, even though they are equally threatened by rising temperatures and changing ecologies and function

1 Luce Irigaray and Michael Marder, *Through Vegetal Being* (New York: Columbia University Press, 2016).
2 Randy Laist, *Plants and Literature* (Boston: Brill-Rodopi, 2013).
3 Prudence Gibson, *The Plant Contract* (Boston: Brill-Rodopi, 2018).
4 Richard Grusan, *The Non Human Turn* (Massachusetts: University of Minnesotta, 2015).

as cornerstones of any given ecology. Plants are vital resources for understanding current and future ecologies, and our parallel human culture and society. We hope to contribute to the revaluation of the significance of plant life through foregrounding the importance of vegetal life for humanistic enquiry across disciplines. This requires updating our perception and understanding of plant life, by keeping abreast of ongoing discoveries in plant science and registering the philosophical effects of knowledge. The conceptual regimes that dictate the relations between objects, subjects, and the 'natural world' have stifled a vocabulary and theoretical apparatus that might emerge from the vegetal world. We need to develop strategies to think, speak, and write about plant life without falling into human–nature dyads, or without tumbling into reductive theoretical notions about relations between cognition and action, identity and value, subject and object.

Although the humanities have had a close historical link with the representation of vegetal life, this has frequently involved harnessing plant analogies to sustain an intellectual position, often obscuring the diversity and nuance of plant behaviour and the implications of vegetal life for thought. We hope that the essays gathered in this anthology begin to mitigate this through their interdisciplinary approach. We believe it is critical to respond to and express Critical Plant issues through cross-disciplinary scholarly and creative praxes. These kinds of interventions into conventional scholarly writing are a risky and provocative means of interrogating the effects of new plant discoveries.

Goethe's 1790 *Metamorphosis of Plants* is a search for an *Urpflanze*, one archetypal pattern in nature from which all vegetal matter springs. In many ways, this volume attempts the opposite. We are instead discovering the multiple tendrils of vegetal being that have emerged from new knowledge that plants have greater sensory capacities than previously thought. While these concepts have precedents in the past, recent scientific developments allow them a new valency in terms of distributed thought and as non-human actors. Each of the contributors to this volume addresses vegetal life to better comprehend their own artistic and academic genres. Although we can't 'speak plant,' we can seize the opportunity to interrogate the absence of an appropriate lexicon to discuss the vegetal world. We can envisage a future where plants lead us to new models of thinking, better solutions, better collaborations and better adaptive potentials. As Michael Marder and Luce Irigaray suggest in their 2016 book *Through Vegetal Being,* we can give our writing back to plants.[5] This is plant writing: an openness to sentience, sapience, and forms of life that are distinctly botanical.

The aim of this anthology is to contribute to discourse on the implications of new plant knowledge for the arts and culture. As such, a full view of this shifting perspective requires a 'stereoscopic' lens through which to view plants but also simultaneously to alter our human-centered viewpoint. Plants are no longer the passive object of contemplation, but are increasingly resembling 'subjects,' 'stakeholders,' or 'performers.' The plant now makes unprecedented demands upon the nature of contemplation itself. Moreover, the aesthetic, political, and legal implications of new knowledge regarding plants' ability to communicate, sense, and learn require investigation so that we can intervene in current attitudes to climate change and sustainability, and to revise human philosophies to account for a better plan–thuman relational model. The ethics and aesthetics of plant life are also affected by new plant knowledge, because we now must ask: how should we alter our approach to farming, conservation, cultivation, and consumption based on new information about plants' sensory reactions? The critical work of this anthology's chapters seeks to re-orient human relationships with plants and to redress their relationship to the law, theories of agency, and intelligence, and the role of aesthetics for these ecologies.

Michael Marder, responding to Prudence Gibson's questions in the interview in this volume, suggests that new aesthetic engagements with plants are better thought of in terms of 'expression' rather than 'representation.' Unlike representation, expression implies a projection, discarding the subject–object divide inherent in representation. Expression, for Marder, then allows for a 'decentering' of the 'vegetal' work done by the arts, whereby the object is not totalised by the subject position that renders it

5   Luce Irigaray and Michael Marder, *Through Vegetal Being* (New York: Columbia University Press, 2016).

visible. Instead, the artist expands, extends, or exports their object, taking it outside itself, but not necessarily making it a possession or a secondary effect of a subject position.

In Section 1 of this volume, *Express, Present and Represent,* the interview with Michael Marder and the ensuing essays tackle the difficult issue of environmental aesthetics. How do we engage with the plant world without being reductive, without diminishing the status of plants to mere object, there for the aesthetic pleasure of the human subject? We cannot move outside our human condition, but we can consider ways to represent or to present or to express (the latter term is posited by Marder) the dark inner workings of the plant. Stephen Muecke writes in this volume about the agency of the Gadgur tree. He turns to the Goolarabooloo people of the West Kimberley in Australia to pose different relations between human and environment. The Goolarabooloo sustain a cosmos of networked connections among humans, plants, animals, and earth formations. Humans in this community play their part in enlivening the dreaming law. The Gadgur tree is cut and its parts are used for the ceremony of the dreaming law. The Gadgur leaf and wood are associated with the 'making of men' and so must be protected: 'humans and trees are destined and designed to care for each other.'

Indigenous perspectives and popular culture are central to a new plant philosophy that delivers political as well as epistemological solutions to climate challenges. Matthew Hall quotes in *Plants as Persons* the words of Aboriginal elder Bill Neidjie, 'Tree....he watching you. You look at tree, he listen to you. He got no finger, he can't speak. But that leaf....he pumping, growing, growing in the night.'[6] Hall is drawing attention to an ancient and sensory approach to the world, where all species are kin and where humans are not privileged as innately superior. Jeffrey Nealon's plant theory toys with the popular culture chestnut that 'plants are the new animal.' His proposal is the connective and transitioning role of plants in the biopolitics of life.[7] Plants, Nealon believes, are the linchpin of 'life' as they point to 'imagining

---

6   Hall, *Plants as Persons,* 108.
7   Jeffrey Nealon, *Plant Theory: Biopower and Vegetable Life* (Stanford: Stanford University Press, 2016), xiv.

possible futures.'⁸ Nealon suggests that humanist biopower, the human-centered habit of controlling the state and its resources, has consistently sidestepped the relevance of vegetal life, which is a misreading of Foucault's urging to curb such sovereignty over the natural world.

In Andrew Belletty's essay, 'An Ear to the Ground,' he shares his phenomenological journey to Country where he was led by a group of indigenous song custodians to a secret sacred place. There, as a cinematic sound recorder who has worked with Aboriginal people for over thirty years, he experienced and recorded the vibrations of the Desert Grevillia tree. His insights into the vibrations of relational natural ecological life is enriched by his discussion of the early recordings of Bengali physicist and botanist Jagadish Chandra Bose who created an apparatus, the crescograph, to record plant sounds. Poet Luke Fischer continues a sensory vegetal experience by presenting the inner life of plants. He does this through the use of conventional metaphorical techniques to align the ecological entanglement of plants and insects. Paul Dawson approaches the task of 'representing plants' via a fetishistic methodology, where 'interspecies love' might even extend to future copulations. In their writing, the poets were cognizant of the issues and philosophies surrounding new plant science, and are experimenting with new and traditional modes of poetic representation. Perhaps a better term for these poems is presentation — an award, a bestowal, a gift.

Tessa Laird also looks at representations of plants in the context of popular culture of the 1960s and '70s. Laird focuses on questions surrounding the value of plant life, as they relate to futuristic visions of the space age. She provides us with a fascinating history of the centrality and relevance of plants in imagining other sci-fi worlds, by looking at queer identities in fictional societies where the plant world holds dominion over the state.

In Section 2 of this volume, *Thinking Plants,* the chapters respond to the notion of 'plant thinking,' an issue that is key to Michael Marder's work. Marder writes of an allowance of continuous agile movement, a way of thinking that is not limited by closed networks of information nor by false perceptions of

8   Nealon, *Plant Theory*, xv.

how nature operates. Here, 'plant thinking' is a radical new term that describes a methodology for the humanities that is both adequate to and formally influenced by the possibility of plant intelligence. Plant thinking allows an exploration of the paradoxes of human exceptionalism, because it draws attention to a refocusing on nature as more than a backdrop to human action. Plant thinking refers to moving agency away from the human and towards vegetal life, which is the backbone of all ecosystems. It is an acknowledgement that discounting plant life is a grave ecological and philosophical error. Philosophers and theorists, from Goethe's 1817 theory of the 'super-sensuous plant archetype' that guides transformation, to Elaine Miller's seminal book documenting the relationship of plants, to figures such as Nietzsche, Derrida, and Irigaray, inform *Covert Plants*.

Three essays in this volume address 'plant thinking' and related questions regarding the relationship between language and modes of thought and cognition. Baylee Brits' essay, 'Brain Trees: Neuroscientific Metaphor and Botanical Thought,' takes up the use of the tree as one of the dominant metaphors in neuroscience. This investigation of trees as allegorical objects interrogates the purported representational task that they are allocated, arguing that the structure of the formal allegory of the brain, as tree, resembles the structure of thought that this metaphor is supposed to represent. This allegorical structure, far more akin to 'expression' rather than representation, allows for a closer relationship between ideas about the brain and new work done by evolutionary biologists on plant thought. A similar problem is tackled from the perspective of philosophy by Ben Woodard in his essay 'Continuous Green Abstraction: Embodied Knowledge, Intuition, and Metaphor.' Here, Woodard looks at the extent to which forms of human thought might 'map onto' the cognition of other species and the philosophical problems that attend this. Woodard asks how modes of thought, particularly '4E cognition' ('embodied, embedded, extended and enacted cognition') influence the ways that we conceive, of cognitive function and embodied cognition in other species. Plants, specifically, can function using extended or distributed information, via the communicative emission of gases and chemicals.

The issue of metaphor is addressed in Dalia Nassar's essay, 'Metaphoric Plants: Goethe's "Metamorphosis of Plants" and the Metaphors of Reason.' Nassar follows the transitions of metaphorical references to nature, as explications of reason. In particular, she traces Kant's determinate unity and Goethe's *Urpflanze* as a recasting of reason in terms of the plant. She asks how these metaphors influence our understanding of rationality, and Goethe's recognition of the continuum of the forms of the parts of plants is presented by Nassar as a dialogical emergence that ties into concepts of plant communication or story today. This anthology values the primacy of story-telling in new modes of plant thinking. Thus, Lisa Dowdall's text, 'Figures,' explores the storytelling of the 'Chthulucene,' a 'threshold at the edge of the present in which the monstrous, the chthonic, the tentacular, the horrific, and the weird abound.' Dowdall's fiction-essay also reflects Marder's substitution of expression for representation, exploring ideas like 'skin thinking' and the affective transformations of narrative to capture the 'entanglement' of plant and human life.

Marder's plant thinking extends to notions of excrescence and germination. These have perpetuated new critical thinking in related areas of the neglected status of plants, ecological ethics, and plant science. He leads a new field of Critical Plant Studies which encourages a shift in cultural attitudes away from the instrumental and towards the ethical. For instance, there is a groundswell of action and activism where the rights of plant life should be respected in order to protect significant tracts of ecologically significant lands, such as the Whanganui River in New Zealand which has the same legal rights in a court of law as humans, due to a 2014 constitutional change. These are political moves to grant ecological areas their own rights to be protected from harm, rather than only thinking of nature with regard to our instrumental usage, as food, shelter, shade, and medicine.

Poet Tamryn Bennett's 'Chanting Plants' plays with our biases towards plant life by focusing on language, both human and nonhuman. She does this to explore the relational ethics of plants and the psychic effects of plant matter and its ability to transform our perception of the world to a space at the periphery of the human. Whilst we cannot escape an anthropocentric ontology, Bennett's poetry pushes our understanding to the limits of the human.

In Section 3 of the volume, *Political Landscapes,* the writers address these political and ethical modalities of plant knowledge and plant aesthetics. In Prudence Gibson's essay 'The Colour Green,' she charts the course of the colour green, as an aesthetic, political, and cultural hue. Framed by the solastalgic effects of vegetal philosophy on our perceptions of nature, she reclaims the toxic emerald green pigment, the hallucinations of the psycho-active plant ayahuasca, the Medieval Green Man motif, and the colour green as a political story. This essay grapples with the impossibility of language-bound, perceptual blind spots between species. The ethics of being, and engaging with the vegetal, drives this search for the deepest and darkest of aesthetic ecologies: green. In this section, poet Justin Clemens uses sensual and erotic poetic devices in his poem 'Rooted' to move our understanding of plant life away from any delimiting literary structures and towards a fresh view of plant life, informed by new discoveries in plant science. His poem delves into the symbiosis and communication between trees, directly referencing new knowledge regarding sensory capacities of plants, whilst never losing the observational mode of the nature lover.

Jennifer Mae Hamilton, in her essay 'Planthropocenic Urbanism: Creating Different Relations Between Humans and Edible Plants in Sydney,' looks at the way Sydney-based artists, including Lisa Kelly, Dennis Tan Makeshift, Tessa Rappaport, Karl Logge, Lucas Ihlein, Diego Bonetto, Kirsten Bradley, Nick Ritar, and Sarah Newell, have experimented with plants and gardens. These case studies drive Hamilton's investigation of how we might 'materially create a world where one does not have to be on a meditation retreat to notice that a sunflower tracks the sun throughout the day and night.' These artists' projects do not seek to represent plants to us, so much as alter urban relations to plants, and the economic and imaginary systems that undergird these relations. These same issues are dealt with in Susie Pratt's interview with the artist Natalie Jeremijenko, whose artistic experiments seek to initiate inter-species contracts and agreements to alter our relation to public space and the green inhabitants of this space.

New visions in plant science and the bio-humanities see nature as an active informational biosphere. These visions involve new ways for humans to relate to plant life via aesthetic creativity that does not fall into the trap of limited representation. They raise awareness for plant relevance and ethics, and they draw attention to changing socio-cultural and bio-political relations between humans and plants. Changes in the production of food, food security, profit-driven agriculture, and even phyto-mining, where crops are grown to harvest minerals, have changed our perception of plants existing for human use or enjoyment alone. We reject this notion of plants existing only for human delectation, consumption, or reverie. Instead, plants produce the human and vice versa. In 'Agricultural Inventiveness: Beyond environmental Management,' Lucas Ilhein moves the discourse to the more practical human connection with plant life. He explores the active implementations of different agricultural techniques to minimize pollutant run-off from sugar cane farms onto the Great Barrier Reef. As a socially engaged artist, Ilhein collaborates with a sugar cane farmer via test cases, art events, and writing, to move beyond paternalistic discourses of environmental management and present more novel methods of working with invasive plants that threaten crops, to avoid conventions of weed distaste and to ensure human commercial interests do not destroy us.

Monica Gagliano's essay, 'Ecopsychology and the Return to the Dream of Nature,' looks at the aesthetic experience of philosophical reconceptualizations of plants as people. Of course, this latter statement, which comes from Matthew Hall's book, *Plants as Persons,*[9] is a deeply qualified one: plants do not resemble people, but new ecological work offers a way of approaching plant life in personal terms: through experience, relationality, perception, language and intelligence. Gagliano identifies the experiential reduction by which we demarcate plant life in opposition to human life: plant life does not involve the drama of human life. Without this drama of psychic experience, are plants really persons? This offers a fascinating insight into the regimes of knowledge by which we approach plant life, the key regime being

9   Matthew Hall, *Plants as Persons* (New York: State University of New York Press, 2011).

aesthetic. It is at this level — philosophy, narrative, imagination, reconfigurations of experience and intelligence — that the writing of this volume offers a 'way in' to reconfigurations of ecology.

As stated by Gagliano, Ryan, and Vieira in their introduction to *The Green Thread,* one of the major issues with new plant studies is language.[10] Plants remember, count, and craft algorithms in order to photosynthesize more efficiently, emit gases and chemicals to communicate, and have multiple sensing capacities beyond habituation. Yet, we are limited in our understanding of how that suggests a human-like intelligence because we can't move out of our own human habituation towards plants. In other words, humans are so used to or conditioned 'to know' plants, and claim to understand the exceptionalism of human cognition, that it becomes difficult to step back and consider there might be a non-human intelligence outside human understanding. Humans remain confined by the associative powers of linguistics, limiting our views of non-signifying or non-semiotic intelligences. We simply don't have the words to convey plant behaviour. This results in a kind of purposeful ignorance, and a claim to exceptionalism bound by the following logic: plants do not have brains, therefore they have no cognitive ability, therefore they are ontologically inferior.

Nature philosophies are embedded in literary and aesthetic traditions, such as Romanticism, where concepts of nature were developed, via the human subject communing with the natural world, or failing to do so. During this late 18th- and early 19th-century period, the South Pacific Antipodes offered writers and artists new flora which contravened European concepts of the natural world. Artists were dumbstruck by the bizarre range of flora. These new plant species put pressure on scientific taxonomy but also on imaginative apprehensions. Now, in a similar vein to these imperialist Australian times, as new scientific discoveries are emerging in the 21st century, we asked our contributors how we can reimagine the vegetal world. We were interested in com-

10 Patricia Vieira, Monica Gagliano, and John Ryan, eds, *The Green Thread: Dialogues with the Vegetal World* (London: Lexington Books, 2016), ix–xxvii.

missioning academics and poets, from this position, about what plant writing might be today.

In the interview in this volume, Michael Marder extends his established concept of philosophy as *sublimated plant thinking* into art as *sublimated plant sensing*. The writing in this volume seeks to probe the conditions of our relationship with plants that are conducive to survival for all. These essays contribute to constructing a plant imaginary, where readers can 'see' the value of plant life, beyond the obvious and instrumental capacities of plants as a source of food, agriculture, shelter, or medicine. These essays offer readers perspectives that defy images of the vegetal world draped in cliché or shrouded in myths of the inert 'thing.'

I

Express, Present, Represent

Interview with Michael Marder

Prudence Gibson

Re-presentation

PG: There are plant artists around the world who are using the eco-transmissions of roots or leaves to create sound artworks. Other plant artists unground natural species from the earth and bring them into the gallery space or create experiences that disrupt or intervene with an ecological state. These bodies of work develop from the history of botanical illustration, gardening, bonsai care, and other art-aesthetic preoccupations, even land art. However, contemporary plant art consistently highlights eco-ethics, those moral questions of how to relate to plants. New information in plant science informs our understanding of status and ethics, as you expound in your books. These ideas are being taken up by artists and presented as a means of advocacy as well as a continued creative representation. Can you respond to this new realm of representation, as both a conceptual artistic interpretation but also as a way of 'speaking for' plants?

MM: Although I am by no means a Kantian, I am a little nostalgic for the strict division between the questions of epistemology, practical ethics, and aesthetics, reflected in the three Critiques. The advantage of treating these issues separately is that they can be imbued with as much clarity as possible before being interrelated, amalgamated, mixed, etc. Let's take representation, for instance. Epistemologically, it refers to the framing of an object by a subject, using preexisting categories, schemas, and concepts. Ethically-politically, it means delegation (speaking on behalf of someone, as you

*note), the supplanting of one subject or a group of subjects by an-
other. Aesthetically, it implies a faithful recreation of a pre-given
reality in a work of art in which the depicted objects would be
recognizable as corresponding to a slice of the 'outside world.' So,
representation, an essentially modern philosophical and aesthetic
term, necessarily regulates the relation between subjects and objects
or among subjects. That is where my patience with Kantianism,
be it avowed or encrypted, runs out. I find the parameters of representation sorely deficient, especially with regard to plant life. I
much prefer expression, so long as we understand the literal sense
of this word —pressing outwards, albeit without the Romantic emphasis on interiority whence this movement proceeds —and detect
in it the growing activity of the plants themselves. Artists might
facilitate vegetal self-expression, or, at a certain meta-level, express
this expression with the vegetal world. Should they attempt to do
so, they would not run into the dead-end of 'speaking for' plants,
which, in the name of ethics, may turn out to be highly unethical,
precisely because the flora does not speak in anything like human
languages. The advantage of expression is that, thanks to its spatial
orientation (ex-, outwards), it can track the articulation of plants
and plant parts as material, embodied significations. I repeat: expression allows us to track the articulation of plants, becoming a
medium for their flourishing. And I'd love to see artists pick up
this vegetal idea of expression without a hidden inner core, without depth.*

A Terrible Mistake

PG: Staying with the idea of plant rights — while valid, are we
taking a risk? Are we mistakenly relegating plants to the realm
of mere innocents, as victims? How can we re-present plants and
re-perform them in an art context without falling into the representational wormholes of conventional aesthetics?

*MM: I would say that plants are beyond the categories of guilt
and innocence. These are but human feelings and constructs pro-
jected onto the world around us. You are right to recall, of course,
that conventionally, plants, especially flowers, served as the figures
of innocence. But, despite all that, in practice, they were never in-*

nocent enough: scapegoated, always burdened with our own guilt or with the task of symbolizing our emotions — be they grief or love. That is the logic of cuttability/culpability, signaled in Derrida's Glas. *Simply put, the presumably innocent flower had to be cut, culled, detached from its living source, and sacrificed to a reality higher than it. So, yes, in a sense, plants are the victims par excellence, the absolute 'bare life,' not even recognizable as living. In* The Philosopher's Plant, *I call their status* arbor sacra. *Now, when I invoke plant rights, I do so, on the one hand, to interrogate the very notion of rights and, on the other, to highlight the so-called 'moral considerability' of plants. If we insist on resorting to the discourse of rights with reference to people or animals, then plants should be definitely included. If not, then a different framework should be invented for regulating relations among living beings.*

Human-Plant Contradictions

PG: There are artists who hook up plants to all kinds of sensors (light, thermal, gas, liquid) in order to create artworks. The information measured by the sensors, for example, is then used to create sound or mobilise a tree in a gallery space or effect a dynamic change in the immediate environment or to stimulate audience participation. My question is whether there is a problem here, in treating plants as non-feeling subjects? Sticking probes into tree trunks or affixed onto leaves and roots can cause damage to the plants, perhaps even pain. Is it worth it? What are our moral obligations, as artists and writers, to show vegetal respect?

Well, obviously, there would be a huge public outcry if this sort of art was performed on a live rabbit or a dog, with electrodes attached to its head, measuring brain waves, or to the heart, registering cardiac rhythms. That it seems okay to subject plants to such a project is a sign of the insufficient change in our received ideas that view them as insensitive beings or 'non-feeling subjects' as you say. That is definitely an ethical problem. But I also see an epistemological problem here. The techniques you describe are predicated on a belief in the possibility of a global and universal translation. Everything can become meaningful only on our terms

27

and on our ground thanks to certain technological manipulations. The sensors attached to leaves, trunks, and roots definitely sense something, but, in the process, what vanishes is the sensing of the plants themselves. We can pat ourselves on our backs for deriving such 'information' from them, but as soon as it has become nothing but information, the plant has already disappeared. In a way, this is the general paradox of modern signification, where, unlike in expression, the signifier is ab initio *detached from the signified. Artists can either keep replaying this frustrating record of total loss, masquerading as total transparency, or they can imagine ways to see, listen to, be, and think with plants otherwise.*

Performativity

PG: The performativity of plants seems to refer to a state of being where they are not limited by functionality or utility. The attraction of a discourse in plant performativity is that it eschews conventions of immobility or inaction. It allows plant life a vitality, with or without human recording or observation. However, does this performativity of plants mark a slippage back into subject-object or human-plant dyads? What possibilities are there for a wider performativity where plant behaviour and conceptual art can meet on an equal plane?

MM: In a nutshell, the performativity of plants is their mode of being in the world — their affecting and being affected by the places of their growth. Plants are the artists of themselves: they create themselves and their environments all the time: losing parts and acquiring new ones, changing the landscape and the airscape, moulding themselves and their world through forms inseparable from vegetal matter. Though never complete so long as a plant is living and metamorphosing, this process has its intermediate 'products,' akin to stills taken from a film. These are the very identifiable self-expressions of vegetal life I have mentioned earlier. How can we approximate to, or resonate with, the moments of vegetal performativity? The possibilities are as numerous as they are still unexplored. For one, gesture can convey something of the language of plants, because it is an equally embodied and spatial kind of expression. For another — and I have written on this at length elsewhere — artists can attempt to perform growth, which is a formidable challenge, so much so that I have called it 'performing the unperformable.' The artist who, to my mind, comes closest to such a performance is Špela Petrič with her piece 'Confronting Vegetal Otherness,' in which for 12 hours a day she cast a shadow on germinating cress. I cannot see how there can be a 'slippage' into any traditional dyads here, or in any other exercises in vegetal performativity for that matter, given the irreducible time-lag between the human and the plant: the wildly different time scales of movements, behaviors, or responses. (Even with regard to ourselves, a certain time-lag applies, in that our 'involuntary' bodily activity operates at a different level from that of explicit consciousness.) So long as more than one temporality is at play, we are in a situation of an encounter — with the other.

Anti-Metaphysics

PG: With reference to the possibility of 'plant souls,' if plants do not have aspirations beyond nourishment, habituation, and survival, might there be a strong case that art should not have to produce transcendent possibilities either? Art has long endured that impossible criterion of judgment: truth. Could the anti-metaphysical qualities of plant behaviour inform our cultural attitudes to art creation and art appreciation?

MM: I like the implicit suggestion that not only should art engage with plants but that it might also be, at its core, vegetal. It is true that we customarily think of aesthetic creation as one of the highest endeavors of human spirituality, a largely ethereal activity on the par with religion and philosophy. Within such a framework, plants provide nothing but material support (recently I have also questioned this 'nothing but'; even the presumably dead plant-derived material support for art offers resistance and imposes on the artist an alien intentionality of its own) : in painting — pigments for various colors and the canvas itself; in earlier cinema and photography — celluloid film; in music — the wooden bodies of instruments, such as a cello or a violin. In Heidegger's terms, then, they often comprise the 'thing aspect' of the work of art, while the 'work aspect' is reserved for something other than vegetal creation. Your idea would mean that plants are the body and soul of an artwork, its form and content, the work and the thing. That would, indeed, be art at its most material, albeit not materialist, and at its most affirmative.

Three Axes

PG: In your essay in *The Green Thread,* you mention that there is a tendency in philosophy to ignore the outgoing in favour of the incoming (even when it is a non-arrival). When considering plants, there is not this cutting off or displacement from the source, but a continuous growing or possibility. Your three axes of the event unfolding are excrescence (how plants appear), expectation (waiting for germination), and exception (where seeds are extracted for the closed circuit of potentiality and are committed to chance). These three elements strike me as being useful vegetal processes to apply to the creation and experience of art. Artists create works or performances that are viewed (have an appearance), they await a response from the audience, or critics, or peers, in a state of hiatus. Finally artists' works are removed from the live experience or real appearance and can be re-performed or re-told or re-experienced via video documentation and reviews etc. This final phase of how the artworks can continue to grow falls into your final axis of becoming committed to chance. Can you comment on drawing a link between your concept of the three axes with art? Where might the act of creating art sit within the realm of plant life?

MM: Again, I agree with your extension of my vegetal thought to art. It is important to highlight here that we are circling back to the issue of expression as a pressing outwards characteristic of growth, or excrescence. Without a hint of idealism, expression is how artworks grow and make their appearance in the world. A spatial process, it requires time to unfold and mature (expectation). And, moreover, there is no 'cookie-cutter' recipe for a good or successful vegetal-artistic expression, because, in each case, its spatiality and temporality are singular (exceptional), as it hinges on who or what is growing in it. As for your broader question about the place of art, I would like to propose a variation on my defini-

tion of philosophy as 'sublimated plant-thinking.' Art, in turn, is sublimated plant-sensing. Aesthesis, at the root of sensation and aesthetics, is not the exclusive province of animals and humans; as we know, plants are highly receptive to a variety of environmental factors, from light and moisture gradients to vibrations. To be sure, plants neither think nor see in images, but this does not mean that they neither think nor see. The 'imageless presence' of music Adorno praised in his aesthetic theory is one intimation of sublimated plant-sensing. I trust that you will find many others as well.

Plant-Time

PG: You have said 'To live out of season in a way that is characteristic of humanity in modernity is to ignore the alterations and alternations of planetary time and to exist out of tune with the milestones of vegetal temporality.' This question of plant-time is important for humans in order to reassess the way we relate to the environment, both natural and unnatural. The role of art has historically been to disrupt, to reveal, and to politicise. Is there some way artists can learn from plant-time, to adjust and change our relationship with other species and one another? Can artists bring attention to these temporal issues and contribute to the 'long now' where we need to politically and socially plan for the future, free from short-term gratifications?

MM: I actually think that only very recently has the role of art been 'to disrupt, to reveal, and to politicize.' Throughout its history, art has been rather inseparable from religion and, later on, from the wealthy or powerful patrons who commissioned specific works, usually for their own aggrandizement. There is nothing wrong with nurturing the political dimension of art; the aesthetic endeavor simply cannot begin with and be motivated purely by politics. If it does, it becomes propaganda, rather than art, regardless of how progressive the message. How is all this related to the time of plants? Through the experience of patience. Vegetal temporalities are quite distinct from our lived time because they are much slower, proceeding at paces or rhythms that remain largely imperceptible to us due to the inevitable time lag separating us from plants. Thus, we can either gas fruit into ripeness or patient-

ly await its own temporality to do its work. Patience is, therefore, an attitude most respectful toward the time of plants. When you wish to intervene, ethically or politically, by means of art in a particularly problematic reality, patience is lacking. This is especially the case today when rage and indignation are the political sentiments du jour. I am afraid that such fast interventions often make for bad art, while good art is often not 'on time' to create any meaningful difference. I am not saying that we, whether artists or non-artists, should not intervene into the horrible and deepening injustices we witness all around us. It is, actually, indispensable to intervene, albeit with patient hopelessness. This is a paradox that is theoretically irresolvable, an antimony of political aesthetics, if you will. Note that I say it is theoretically irresolvable; practically, however, a resolution is possible and in fact necessary in every concrete instance of artistic engagement. Patience is never infinite; it is bound to run out sooner or later, and the important thing is to let it run out at the right (ripe) moment when hopelessness itself becomes creative calmly and almost vegetally, not with the animality of Nietzsche's ressentiment. Just as an almond tree monitors the increase of daylight, warmth, etc., before initiating the decision to blossom, so an artist should let expression grow and develop until the process is interrupted by an act it has been preparing all along.

Hiddenness

PG: In *Plant-Thinking* you discuss the hiddenness of plants. This is a reference to their vitality and complexity. Do you ever wonder if Plant Studies, emerging from Animal Studies, might bring *too much* attention to the relevance of plants? Are those of us interested in raising the status of plants ready for the fallout? Should they remain hidden from us?

MM: Let us not conflate two types of hiddenness: the provisional and the permanent. I take it that your questions refer to provisional hiddenness, which can be dispelled so long as you put that which is hidden in the spotlight or under a magnifying glass. So, we can shed more and more light on the capacities of plants, learn incredible things about them, and that will inevitably give rise to sensationalist media articles and tons of academic research. As a result, plants will gradually stand out from the blurry backgrounds of our existence, coming into the open. Admittedly, I have this kind of hiddenness in mind as well in my work on vegetal philosophy. But the other kind is more important for me. What do I mean by 'permanent hiddenness'? Certainly not the noumenal reality of the thing-in-itself, forever inaccessible to us, even if the experience of the world from the standpoint of a plant is, in part, that. What I mean, instead, is the constant allegiance of phutoi *to* phusis, *of plants to nature, the nature that, as Heraclitus put it, loves to hide—to encrypt itself in its very appearances. Permanent hiddenness is not the same as absence or lack; it is the shadow that makes light what it is and enables vision. It is not the same as inaccessible depth, for example, of the source, whence the 'ex-' of excrescence stems; on the contrary, it is the very superficiality of the surface, or, as we say in phenomenological jargon, the appearing itself that does not appear in any of the appearances. Whenever one invokes plants, at best, one arrives at frozen snapshots of a metamorphosis alluding to, yet also concealing, the time and being of plants. To sum up: permanent hiddenness is of a temporal and ontological nature—it will be unaffected by any degree of attention we pay to plants.*

Writing

PG: Should we adapt the way we write about plants to accord with the thoughtfulness and regenerative qualities of plant life?

MM: Absolutely! I have tried to do so, without any methodological planning really, together with Luce Irigaray in our co-authored book Through Vegetal Being *(Columbia University Press, 2016). It was but a beginning of plant writing, briefly outlined in the book's epilogue. Patience plays an important role here, as does absolute openness to the other. Connected to this, I always wonder how to give my writing back to plants. My dream for* Plant-Thinking *was to embed seeds into its covers and to urge readers to bury the book after it has been read, letting it decompose and germinate. Publishing conventions did not permit me to realize it. In* The Chernobyl Herbarium: Fragments of an Exploded Consciousness, *which is a beautiful collaboration with French artist*

Anaïs Tondeur, writing and thinking constantly revert back to plants and to art in the shadow of a disaster. My blog, The Philosopher's Plant, *is an offshoot of the book with which it shares its title. The development of both—at the level of form and of content—is quite vegetal. But, no doubt, more needs to be done, boldly and experimentally, to invent a way of writing that would respond and correspond to plant life, which means grow, decay, and metamorphose like plants, without freezing into a method.*

Anthropocentrism

PG: In my own research and writing, I have used your framework of 'plant-thinking' to actively investigate the interaction between plant philosophy, plant science, and plant art as a field of reciprocal understanding, possibility, and creative urgency. Plant Studies emerges from Animal Studies and draws attention to conventions of human exceptionalism. Can we ever escape this human-centred point of view or merely obscure its centrality by focusing on another species?

MM: People often do not understand that I do not 'use' plants as a foil for some extraneous issues such as human exceptionalism. And I do not 'do' Plant Studies, unless that means (tongue-in-cheek) studying like a plant or letting plants study you. I am interested in the ontology of vegetal life, in which I have discovered—I believe—a singular universal, a unique mode of existence that informs existence as such. And I am motivated to refashion thinking and acting on the basis of this singular universality, which has nothing to do with the abstract universal position arrogated by humans to themselves. For me, plants are not just another biological kingdom, and specific plants — not mere representatives of a given species. They are, as I have written on a few occasions, the synecdoche of what we automatically call 'nature' without realizing what we are talking about. Synecdoche is a rhetorical device, whereby a part stands in for the whole, in which it is ensconced. Plants are a part of nature that stands in for all of it. That is singular universality! I do not know what remains of anthropocentrism once you thoroughly contemplate the implications of this move. I hope not much, but that, in any event, is not my main preoccupation.

Fig. 1. Gadgur (phonetically [gadguːɹ]) tree 'Long-fruited Blood-wood', or *Eucalyptus polycarpa*, opposite The Oaks motel in Broome. Photo by the author.

2

Mixed Up with Trees:
The Gadgur and the Dreaming

Stephen Muecke

After talking to the Goolarabooloo people for a few years now, and thinking a bit about what they might mean by 'living country' in the West Kimberley region of Australia, I want to venture the idea that they understand life as networked and sustained among humans and non-humans. This idea, which is hardly surprising among students of ecology today — who are pushing back against the ancient Judeo-Christian concept of man's dominion over nature — turns out it may be more than just *an idea* in Indigenous Australian cosmologies. It may well be *structural*; built into what we used to call 'cultural' practices like ceremonies, but now search for a new name for, because they are more-than-cultural precisely because they mix up 'cultural' and 'natural' things. While each animal, tree and water source strives to persist in its own way, engendering its filiations, it is also a necessary mutually sustaining part of the heterogeneous network. Humans are not exceptional in this, because, like the others, they are 'reproductive beings.'[1] Living country is a whole network re-

1 According to Bruno Latour, humans, along with animals, plants and things have a reproductive mode of existence, or ontology. They are all essentially embarked on a trajectory of reproduction, making the risky leap from one generation to the next, in the case of humans, or growing or decaying, an irreversible progression. See Bruno Latour, 'Learning to Make Room,' in *An Inquiry into Modes of Existence: An Anthropology of the Moderns,* trans. Catherine Porter (Cambridge: Harvard Univer-

producing itself, and when the human communities organise to sing the country, to vitalise it and make it 'stand up,' they are performing what anthropologists call 'increase ceremonies' for animals or plants. And why not think of initiations of boys also as kinds of 'increase'?

Let's imagine an anthropologist approaching this scene, sitting down in the shade of *that gadgur* tree — 'whoops, wrong place' — just another annoying *gardiya* [whitefella]. She is sitting there with a notebook and a voice-recorder and clearing her mind of all assumptions: OK, so I'm supposed to determine *the facts* about these people's *land tenure.* How do facts get made? I'll ask them. No, they don't *believe* in facts. Sorry, I mean they are getting on quite well without the concept of 'fact.' So I'm the *subject* producing their knowledge as *objective,* across some kind of *divide.* Who put that divide there? But aren't they subjects of their own knowledge? Shouldn't they be authors of this report I'm writing as well? No, they don't understand why they need to determine the facts of their own land tenure. No wonder! This 'tenure' is asserting itself all the time, and in this very ceremony being conducted before my eyes. Did I write 'They don't understand'? *Shit,* erase that disrespectful line.

Facts, the anthropologist finally comes to understand after due meditation, are not established because they are sitting out there waiting to be picked up like pebbles on the beach; they are there because her discipline has a theory and a method for bringing them into existence, greeting them as they come, then sustaining them through reinforcement. And this world of facts that is built up is conceptually aligned with what her tradition is in the habit of calling the material world. It's 'out there', somehow independent of the experience of it.[2] This is why, says Bruno

sity Press, 2013), 97–122.

2   In Australia, Native Title Law often seeks to establish land tenure through descent, so Anthropologists have an apparatus called a genealogy, constructed with large fold-out sheets of paper, and/or with custom-made software (e.g., GEDCOM). They build it up by interviewing family members, and consulting State and parish records, until they construct the genealogy that exceeds the knowledge of any individual within it. After many expensive hours of hard work the genealogical facts are *pro-*

Latour, 'anthropology has never been able to encounter the others except precisely as "cultures,"' as he urges us to 'get back to the thread of experience, to become capable of learning from those who have worked out their relations with existents quite differently.'[3] And yes, those others, before they became 'cultures,' were 'natives' classified with the 'objective material world' that was invented in the European tradition, along with and parallel with the invention of Nature[4] over which man might have dominion. 'Material' is the half of the European world into which beings like trees are classified, along with stones, planets, atoms, etc.; the other half is the subjective world in which humans inhabit along with their diverse cultures.

But the Goolarabooloo don't have such a division, they sustain a cosmos composed of a network of connections among humans, plants, animals, and features in the country. The most fundamental and cherished aspects of this 'culture,' the ones associated with the deep-time ancestors, are in the Bugarrigarra, the dreaming law. It is up to humans to play their part of enlivening the Bugarrigarra through ceremonies that transform boys into men. In these ceremonies the *gadgur* tree plays a key role;

duced through long and complicated networking, but the anthropologist likes to think they were *always there.* But it is an imported apparatus, initially totally foreign to the families it is applied to; the 'concept' of it is not vernacular. What people experience with kinship is not a tree-like structure. They experience all sorts of kinship relationships on an everyday basis that could sustain another much more ethnographic report. So while the genealogical facts might seem solid ('Yes, X is my mother's mother'), or in doubt ('I'm not sure if Y was my grandfather, really, or if he was just living with granny'), no-one ever lives with the genealogical abstraction that is the descent diagram. Whether individuals are passionately attached to a piece of country, or indifferent to it, is immaterial to the extent that the proof (for Native Title purposes) is seen as lying in the genealogy, not in the person's experience. The experience of country is indeed something that can be followed up, but with whose tools? What other kinds of observational methods will determine that kind of factuality?

3   Latour, *An Inquiry into Modes of Existence,* 99.
4   Philippe Descola, *Beyond Nature and Culture,* trans. Janet Lloyd (Chicago: University of Chicago Press, 2013), chap. 3.

there is no law ground without a *gadgur* tree standing near, and its wood is cut for a part of the ceremony. In 1981, an anthropologist resident in Broome spoke to a Goolarabooloo elder, Paddy Roe, about the initiation ceremony, and he elicited some remarkable information about the tree:

> [Ancestor ████████] came from the north in his travels with kalatu (boys who had undergone circumcision [*angkui*]). The initiates were thirsty, so using a leaf he pierced ████████from the left side of his chest.
> ████████████████████and that side of the body.
> Katkur = name of leaf used.[5]

The *gadgur* tree thus asserts its belonging in this Goolarabooloo cosmos. I would say that it is not its ontology, or mode of existence, that is important, but its *mode of belonging* that surges forth with these special attachments that its wood and its leaves have to the making of men. Thus is the vitality of the tree forever connected to human life, and the tree must be protected, not because it is a 'form of life' like any other, not because it is *sacred,* but simply because it has a necessary role to play. About the same time he was talking to Kim Akerman, Paddy got wind of the plan to chop down a particular *gadgur* on Robinson St in Broome. He intervened, and to this day, the street is bizarrely diverted around the tree. At the end of that intervention, the white locals probably concluded it must be sacred or something.

The locals thought initially it was just a tree in the way of progress, an everyday dispensable bit of matter. But having been saved, it would be wrong to see this one tree, or this species, as *sacred,* existing in a state of exception, while all the others remain able to be chopped down. It belongs there, and other forms of plant life belong elsewhere in different ways. It belongs to that place because it is not an instance of a general material substance. The *gadgur* has its own participatory force, and I wonder if Pad-

---

5   Kim Akerman, 'Horde areas and mythological sites between James Price Point and Coconut Wells on the west coast of Dampierland, WA.' Retyped from photocopy of the original handwritten record of 1981 on December 23, 2010. Possibly restricted knowledge is redacted here.

dy Roe managed to convey that idea to the inheritors of Christian philosophies without using the word 'sacred,' or if he had to use that concept as a kind of short-hand translation. Michael Marder has shown that for the Jewish philosopher Maimonides, the Judeo-Christian metaphysical hierarchy 'prioritizes God's sovereign will over human intention (*kavanah*) — and human intention over the rest of the world,' such that plants in many cases are not really 'alive': 'Life-stunting values,' according to Nietzsche.[6]

In other cases, the Goolarabooloo designate special trees as *mamara.* Our Western botanical apparatuses that *make trees belong* to *kosmoi* of different sorts, tend to by-pass any connection of this kind. But today, the literature on Indigenous nature-cultures, like Matthew Hall, in *Plants as Persons,* is grappling with other modes of belonging, for instance Bill Neidjie on the communicative possibilities of trees:

Feeling make you,
Out there in open space.
He coming through your body.
Look while he blow and feel with your body....
because tree just about your brother or father....
and tree is watching you.[7]

Likewise, in the Broome area, people evoke the concept of *liyan,* a feeling for country, as a general concept for multispecies (cosmic) interaction linked to vitality and growth, which feeds into the multiple modes of belonging that need to be in place for ceremony to be successful. This concept of mutual sustainability linked to increase and transformation is a long way from how the *gadgur* is classified botanically, where its 'being' is positioned and identified in the process of translating it into *Eucalyptus polycarpa.* Were one to continue that Linnaean-type reality-building, another strand, its role in ceremony, might slip by unnoticed.

---

6 Michael Marder, *Plant-Thinking: A Philosophy of Vegetal Life* (New York: Columbia University Press, 2013), 100.

7 Matthew Hall, *Plants as Persons: A Philosophical Botany* (Albany: State University of New York Press, 2011), 79.

For me, Bruno Latour is the philosophically-minded anthropologist who can imagine the agency of trees, while demonstrating the provincialism of the materialist reduction that made them exploitable:

Its strength and its opinions extend only as far as it does itself. It fills its world with gods of bark and demons of sap. If it is lacking anything, then it is most unlikely to be you. You who cut down woods are not the god of trees. The tree shows what it can do, and as it does so, it discovers what all the forces it welcomed can do. You laugh because I attribute too much cunning to it? Because you can fell it in five minutes with a chain saw? But don't laugh too soon. It is older than you. Your fathers made it speak long before you silenced it. Soon you may have no more fuel for your saw. Then the tree with its carboniferous allies may be able to sap your strength. So far it has neither lost nor won, for each defines the game and time span in which its gain or loss is to be measured. We cannot deny that it is a force because we are mixed up with trees however far back we look. We have allied ourselves with them in endless ways. We cannot disentangle our bodies, our houses, our memories, our tools, and our myths from their knots, their bark, and their growth rings. You hesitate because I allow this tree to speak? But our language is leafy and we all move from the opera to the grave on planks and in boxes. If you don't want to take account of this, you should not have gotten involved with trees in the first place. You claim that you define the alliance? But this illusion is common to all those who dominate and who colonize. It is shared by idealists of every color and shape. You wave your contract about you and claim that the tree is joined to you in a 'pure relationship of exploitation,' that it is 'mere stock.' Pure object, pure slave, pure creature, the tree, you say, did not enter into a contract. But if you are mixed up with trees, how do you know they are not using you to achieve their dark designs?[8]

---

8 Bruno Latour, *The Pasteurization of France,* trans. Alan Sheridan and John Law (Cambridge: Harvard University Press, 1988), 194–95.

That gadgur tree is still there, in Broome, standing on its own specially constructed traffic island. And because Paddy Roe's descendants remember the story of how (and why) he saved it, they are likely to do so again should the occasion arise, *as if* it were using its human friends to continue its reproductive existence. Those of us imbued with Western philosophies might hesitate before saying that that tree is an active agent in that way. But if you were brought up in Goolarabooloo nature-cultures you might easily accept that there is a structure in place, reinforced by ceremony, in which trees and humans are not only mixed up with each other, but are destined and designed to care for each other.

3

Lover Nature

Paul Dawson

Do I dare love you, here, amongst the vines
that climb along the limbs of trees

that twine about your thighs, alive
with twisting desire in my fingers

travelling down your skin, legs exposed
like stripped saplings in the sun

until your feet are bared, planted in the earth
amongst the roots whose path I trace

through the loam, to erupt from the grass
the gnarled arch I have yearned to touch

mother no longer – lover nature, body
without organs, lay me down

inside you now and open me up, fuck me
the way a swallow plunges in the air

the way fronds caress a branch, and slip
your shoots between my lips: tell me now

how you have responded to your plundering
with a hot screaming in the sky, your violations

denied by those who want to raze you
yet keep a patch of you to escape to

tell me how to love you beyond morality
give me consent to fuck you

without a human witness
cell deep and shorn of metaphor.

4

An Ear to the Ground

Andrew Belletty

In late 2015, I was given the opportunity to be part of a song journey of sorts, led by a group of song custodians who were active in passing on the tradition to young people from the community. The location of this particular song site is a secret, the area is not marked on any map and the entrance to the site itself is kept under lock and key. The topographical features of the site are unique in the area — a profusion of white sand surrounded by sharp rocky outcrops that gives the space a cathedral like appearance, and remarkably vibrant acoustics. Due to mining activities, trespass, and clandestine land sales in and around the site, it is extremely vulnerable to intrusion, which is why I take great pains to protect the location of the site and the identity of the people. It was here, a thousand kilometers from the nearest city, that I encountered a particularly vibrant tree, a tree that made me want to understand if and how a tree may listen and respond to situated bodies.

I have participated in similar song journeys in the past, but this site was of particular interest as its topographical features produce the acoustic effects of an amphitheater, making it a unique and highly prized site for ceremonial song practices. As such the site is a unique place for cultural maintenance and is closely guarded by the small community who are the custodians of the site. The 20-strong community have ties to this song site which stretch back into millennia, and the performances are vital to maintain the health of the culture, the people and the country. The location of the song site is not marked on any map not because of its cultural significance, but because the site now lies within the boundary of a mining lease. The custodians fought the mining company to gain access to the site, which was granted but limited to cultural purposes only.

Sites such as these are important places for cultural production because of their acoustic characteristics, which means that the site has served as a venue for a wide variety of cultural performances for thousands of years. To the Western eye the site looks wild and untouched, but in fact the site is managed and maintained as a performance venue, the vegetation, sand and ochres are carefully prepared for this express purpose. The particularly vibrant tree plays its role of nurturing the local birds and insects with its sweet nectar, in turn, the birds and cicadas provide a pleasant background ambience during the interlude before falling silent during the performance. It appears as if the strong vibrations produced by the footfalls of the dancers resonate through the soil and up into the tree.

It is this perceived ability of the tree to respond to the vibrations of the performance which prompted me to perform some experiments at the site with the vibrational energy produced through the performance. I had already done some studio-based research into the ways that these vibrations travel through substrates, but never had the chance to apply these techniques in the field. Vibrational energies are produced in abundance by human and non-human bodies within the world but is largely ignored as it falls at the intersection between different human sensory systems.[1] Aboriginal song custodians are tacitly cognizant of different sensory modes and perceptual models and would appear to have different sensitivities to these vibrational energies both within a specific range of country, particularly at places of confluence within the topography, such as rocky outcrops, which gives them unique acoustic and vibrational characteristics. Sounds which travel through sand, water, and air change when the to-

---

1   'The perception of vibration is not a simple matter of 'feeling vibration in the bones.' The way in which different types of whole-body movement make their presence known is not entirely clear, but it is obvious that movement may be perceived by several different sensory systems.' M.J. Griffin, *Handbook of Human Vibration* (Amsterdam: Elsevier, 2004), 226.

pography changes dramatically, making rock-walls, caves, and outcrops ideal places for staging performative song and dance practices as the form natural amphitheaters. These changes in the topography cause changes in the acoustic and vibrational response of the place, and as such become attractive sites for song custodians to make and stage songs and dances that can foster cultural production.

The powerful footfalls produced by the dancers at the site were revealed more fully when I sat on the sand and could feel the thudding footfalls travelling up through my body. Listening to the microphones and vibration sensors I had placed near the tree and within the sand I could also hear the movement of the *Desert Grevillea,* I hear not only the tree in itself, but I hear the tree as part of an Indigenous connection to country; living and non-living, human and non-human, present, past, and future. The tree and its ancestors have lived in this same place for tens of thousands of years as have the song custodians and their ancestors, in a never-ending cycle of coming out of and going back into country. This being-in-place over such extended periods of time is unimaginable to my Western body, which has hundreds of itineraries imprinted on it, and whose ancestors moved freely across continents and oceans. It is this being-in-place that attracts me to the tree and to the Indigenous ways of embodied listening and knowing that might help me to understand the conversation that is going on in this country.

This particularly vibrant tree — a *Desert Grevillea* — sat in the distance, a flurry of small birds, honey eaters, drinking from the tree's nectar rich blossoms. But when the dancers changed paths, the birds suddenly disappeared. In order to use them in my artworks, I needed to inscribe this interaction between the tree, the sand, the birds, and the wind. I set up apparatus that could detect and inscribe low frequency vibrations, placing ultra-sensitive microphones, hydrophones, and transducers at the base of the tree, near its branches, and under the soil. Using these non-traditional techniques and technologies I was able to inscribe data that suggested a *tree*'s point of audition rather than a human's.

I experimented with my own footsteps fifty meters away from the tree, and again the particularly vibrant tree fell silent. When I listened back to the recordings made from the tree's point of audition, I observed that the tree was acting as an antenna, transmitting and receiving energy between the loose white sand, the birds, and the air. I could *feel* the subtle vibrations made by the bird's activity on the branches, the creaking of the trunk in the breeze, and the straining of the roots in the loose sand. My attempt to embody what the tree was hearing, feeling, and expressing in this sacred country enabled me to get a sense that the tree was vibrant in ways that I was only just beginning to understand.

My practice explores the energetic, temporal and ecological aspects of Aboriginal song and its complex systems of connections with what can be considered to be a sentient and responsive country. My research is based upon a model of listening that extends beyond audibility, to sub-audible energies and Vibrotactile phenomena and, thus, suggests a more complex and grounded notion of sound, perception and a connection to the environment. It challenges the compartmentalization of the dominant euro-centric sensorium where sound has become something that can be easily quantified, recorded, reproduced, stored, and disseminated through technological means and attenuated by digital media practices. Sound and listening is instead situated energetically, perceptually, corporeally, and environmentally, enmeshed with place and culture through practices connecting human to non-human bodies and entities. My creative practice is derived from my experiences and collaborative work with Aboriginal communities in song practices evincing a very deep, connection to 'Country' developed through highly trans-sensory attention and activation of place, and iterative through time unimaginable in Western cultures.

My thirty years of practice as a cinematic sound designer and artist means that my default mode of perceiving a place is anthropomorphic and Western, and as such it is primarily audiovisual. This becomes problematic when attempting to understand the ways in which other cultures perceive a place, and even more so when one attempts to account for the ways in which animal, mineral, and vegetable bodies perceive the same space. I will use this particularly vibrant tree as an example of how this mode of audiovisual perception can make it difficult to apprehend different ways of sensing place. The visual and aural acuity of humans is poor when compared to what we know about the audiovisual acuity of most animals. We are even able to make these types of comparisons because we use human scale techniques and technologies to measure the acuity of individual aural and visual sensors, but this tells us little about the ways in which non-animals perceive place.

In his 1902 publication, *Response in the Living and Non-living,* Jagadish Chandra Bose, a Bengali, polymath physicist, biologist, botanist, and archaeologist tapped into this vegetal vibration, suggesting that plants have a nervous system, a form of intelligence, and are capable of remembering and learning. He came to these conclusions by conducting a series of scientific experiments which relied upon the development of new methods and new apparatus which he devised for recording plant responses. The devices: the Phytograph, Kunchangraph, Morograph, Shoshungraph, and the Crescograph were only some of the many devices developed with great confidence by Bose. The colorful names and lavish claims behind some of these devices led to much skepticism within the scientific community at the time, but his confidence had its roots in Indian literature and mythology. As far back as the 4th century, the 'Mahabharata' described plant philosophy, physiology, and sentience, explicitly mentioning the senses of touch, hearing, vision, smell, and irritability. Bose's experiments were his attempt to scientifically *prove* the vegetal sentience and intelligence that he knew existed.

Bose's experiments were radical for their time and produced equally radical results that showed in graphical form that plants had a nervous system, a form of intelligence and are capable of remembering and learning, as well as understanding pleasure and pain. Bose's experiments studied the flows of energies within a plant, measuring electrical response, sap flow, and minute movements of leaves, branches, and roots. The graphs produced by his various machines provided a highly detailed account of the inner workings of a plant throughout its lifecycle, including death, where Bose's *Morograph* reveals that a sharp electrical spike occurs to signal the exact moment where life ceases.

My interest in this research area comes from my film and music work within urban and remote Aboriginal communities, but my Western body and its particular corporeal schema makes it difficult for me to fully understand my experiences of listening

to country. I know that the embodied experience of song performances *on country* always makes an indelible mark on me, but I
still struggle with my ability to attenuate my Western corporeally
located body and technology to Aboriginal bodies and schemes,
to expand one corporeal schema as it were to another. This has
meant a process of tuning and adjusting sensitivity thresholds for
my senses as well as similarly tuning my technologies to adapt to
the Aboriginal mode of listening to country. Listening as a professional and aesthetic practice is one of inscribing and reproduc-
ing sound as audio-media, which involves particular apparatus;
the microphone and headphone, and it also involves the entire
Western corporeal schema. My *ears* are finely tuned to the thresholds of sensitivity to acoustic energy inherent in the apparatus,
but this mediated, single sense focus, prevents me from connecting with the inaudible, subtle vibrations of country which for
me characterized Aboriginal listening to country. It is this pressure that drives my research and pushes me to experiment with
new ways of listening, inscribing, and experiencing the songs and
sounds of country.

The directions were simple enough. Head south from Darwin and drive for about twelve hours. Driving in a straight line
from sunrise to sunset causes enormous fatigue,[2] which is ex-
acerbated by the continuous vibrations inherent in any type of
road journey. Throughout the journey my guides told stories
about places and people along the way. The road we followed
was built by settlers, a bitumen road recently improved by mining companies and the military, whose massive vehicles ply the
roads twenty-four hours a day. Journeys like this are increasingly
common in the Northern Territory, where a Toyota 4WD and a
bitumen road make new song-lines through country, lines drawn
with a ruler and built by economic necessity. These new ways of

2   Whole-body vibration studies in humans are quite rare, but experi-
    ments have been carried out on motor vehicle seats, which consider the
    types of vibrations transmitted to the body through a combination of
    road and drive train. Experiments by Azizan and Fard at RMIT Univer-
    sity (Melbourne, Australia) in 2014 show a clear connection between
    driver fatigue and low frequency vibration as experienced by a motor
    vehicle driver. These results were noted after only twenty minutes.

traversing the land bring new ways of knowing, remembering, and listening to country.

As we neared her home, one of the women told of making the same journey on foot as a fourteen-year-old child, when she and her best friend escaped an Aboriginal girls home in Darwin, a place she was taken to when she was stolen from her family. Their journey back to their home took three weeks by foot, they could not follow the road or hitch rides, in case they would be caught by the authorities and taken back to Darwin. The fast pace of our journey connected places within country in quick succession, which triggered the memories of her escape to stream out in vivid detail. These memories drive her to teach young people the stories and the songs from her country and is also why I have driven twelve hours to get to this particular place.

My work within Aboriginal communities spans a period of more than thirty years, but as an artist whose medium is sound, my perceptual experience has always been guided by my ears, which invariably becomes guided by technologies of media inscription and reproduction. This time, however, I am being guided by vibration. My cinematic training in sound design has given me a framework that has become a default mode of perception, which, as Randy Thom suggests, is to 'starve the eye and feed the ear.'[3] This framework makes me feel that by using my ears, I am using a faculty that has been rendered invisible by audiovisual culture, which by default gives me a superior perception of the world. But this perception is shaped by media technology — that is, the tools of my trade (the microphone and the headphone, e.g.), which allow me to focus my attention on specific sonorous objects within space, and to ignore others. The aesthetic pleasure gained by this intense aural focus is not tacit, but it is learned through this mediated process. The sound of a bird flapping its wings, the wind singing through casuarina trees, or the creaking of a tree in a gentle breeze become fetishized sound objects for those with the tools to perceive these sounds, and for those with the cultural knowledge to aestheticize them.

---

3   Randy Thom, 'Designing A Movie for Sound,' *FilmSound.org,* 1999, http://filmsound.org/articles/designing_for_sound.htm.

This journey is different. This time I do not have the tools of my trade, but tools of a different trade, one that seeks the vibrations that fall into the hole between the heard and the felt, the audible and the inaudible, the sonorous and the somatic. For this I need to follow my guides and do what they do. In this secret, sacred place, they must first sing out to their ancestors, then they must burn the spear grass before getting down to business. The spear grass burns fast and hot, and the burning gives the place a different look, a different smell, and a different sound — even a gentle breeze causes the dried spear grass to hiss. After the ground has been prepared for the ceremony, my guides sit down and talk a little, but mostly they listen. The ground here is loose white sand atop which sits hard-faced rocks that rise to about ten meters in height. The rocky outcrop surrounds us on all sides, forming a cavernous roofless room of sorts. It is this geographical feature that makes this a secret, sacred place, as during the rainy season all the families from the low-lying surrounding area would take shelter here until the rain eased off. With the spear grass burnt away, the view of the shelter becomes much clearer, as does the sound of the shelter. It is now easy to hear frantic chirping from a small group of birds hidden from view by a rock face on the opposite side of the shelter. It is also much easier to hear and feel the footsteps of the young dancers, as they learn the steps from their elders, their feet impacting the loose white sand with sharp percussive stabs.

I sit on the sand with my guides, who are the song custodians, while the other elders concern themselves with teaching the dance. My training in acoustics kicks in as I begin to listen not to the sound object, but to the way the place responds to the sound. People who work with sound as a medium spend their lives perfecting this practice of listening to the sound of a place rather than the sound itself. The theory behind this is that the sounding object makes the same sound in itself, but our perception of that sound changes as the object moves within space, with each space having its own signature way of responding to the object. In the space between the object and the listener, the space itself responds to the sound object with resistance or pressure that changes the sound.

The response of the space varies with the pitch, energy, and timbre of the sound that is put into the space. Interior spaces such as rooms are typically closed at the top, bottom, and on all sides with flat, non-porous surfaces arranged in a rectangular fashion. In this space, the sound from an object reaches the listeners' ears directly, but also indirectly from the multitude of reflections created by the sound bouncing back from the surfaces. In this situation, the room is responding to the sound by changing the way that the sound is perceived by the listener. With basic acoustic science, this response can be quantified and modelled in a way that the sound of any room can be reproduced in a studio environment. For example: a typical tiled bathroom has a fast and dynamic response to sound but will respond to high and low frequencies quite differently. A church or concert hall typically has a slow, sustained response that amplifies even the quietest sound, to the extent that it fills the space. Although the signature is fairly constant, variations in the signature can be dramatic, as in the case of a concert hall which has two quite different signatures based on whether it is full or empty. The signature of the room changes when bodies fill the seats and stage, with each body absorbing a small amount of sound pressure, which adds up to a significantly different room response. The nature of audible low-frequency sounds mean that they contain significant energy, which can produce an excess of pressure in a room unless it is absorbed by the room or by bodies within the room.

Exterior and naturally occurring interior spaces are difficult to quantify and model in this way due to the sheer number of variables and the subtlety of the response. Exterior spaces have complex ground coverings and rely on the presence of trees and rocks to reflect sound from the sides and above. As such the sound tends to dissipate quite quickly, as the space absorbs rather than reflects sound.

In this sacred, secret space, I do not listen to the room as Alvin Lucier did, as in this shelter there is no room as such. The sound dissipates as quickly as it is produced. I do not listen to the silence as John Cage did, as the shelter is abuzz with noise, but I try to listen to the country in the way that my guides do, using an ear that is not located specifically inside the body, and which embodies knowledge that is specific to this country. Sitting directly on the sand, I can feel the percussive foot stamping from the dancers who are fifty-plus meters away, the vibrations carried easily by the loose white sand. As the sound dancers gain confidence, the percussive strikes become harder as their heels pound into the sand, which make strong vibrations travel through the sand into my body. From this position, the acoustic sound of the dancers is very faint, but the felt sound is very strong. I have felt this same energy coming through the earth in many other ceremony grounds, but here the loose white sand amplifies the vibration of the foot percussion in a way that I have not felt before.

Now my guides, the song custodians, start to sing, and the dancers join in, gaining strength and confidence with every repetition. The energy created by the performance of the song cycles is immediate, and the faces of the children literally light up as the cycles progress. I keep moving my attention between listening to the sound objects and feeling the vibrations produced by the whole performance. In the second part of the song, the dancers first beat the ground with small leafy branches, then beat the earth itself with the flattened palm of their hands, the latter producing a loud sound and strong percussive vibrations. The song ends as abruptly as it started, and I notice that the entire shelter has become quiet and still. In terms of room response, it is as if the space, the country itself, responds by absorbing the sound from the song performance, and for a moment has changed.

The following day I was taken back to the shelter and left on my own to make my own observations. The previous day I sat and listened to the song performance within country, now I wanted to listen to the country itself. I brought some of this equipment with me to the shelter and made a series of experimental recordings within this unique, situated space. The aim of these experiments was to gain an understanding of how vibrations produced by Indigenous song could be re-produced, inscribed, and transmitted using experimental methods. Aboriginal song performances often create vibrations that impact country directly and are traditionally performed standing, sitting, or moving through country. This would suggest a two-way communication between performer and country as the song comes out of, and goes back into, country — directly through vibrational flows between sentient bodies, which in this case is the sand, the tree and the birds. I experimented by attenuating traditional cinematic sound techniques and technologies to make, transmit, and inscribe these vibrations, as well as attenuating my Western corporeal body in order to *listen* to these vibrations in a way that embodies Aboriginal ways of *listening to country*.

Applying these experimental techniques at the site, provided an opportunity for me to sit and listen to country as the song custodians did the previous day, with my hips, feet, and hands in direct contact with the loose white sand, while inscribing the acoustic and vibrational energies with the apparatus that I had set up at the base of the bird-filled tree that I heard the previous day. The tree was still buzzing with activity, the birds obviously too busy drinking the nectar from the profusely flowering Desert Grevillea to notice my activity. It was only when I started stamping my foot into the loose white sand quite some distance from the tree, that I noticed the birds had suddenly disappeared. In the silence, I could hear the tree creaking loudly as its branches moved imperceptibly in the gentle breeze. Gradually the birds reappeared, and through my headphones I could hear and feel the slightest vibrations their feet made as they landed on a branch. The entire tree had turned into a communication hub linking human and non-human bodies with the earth and the air.

The Western body embodies a default audio-visual mode for communicating with and making sense of the world, making much electromagnetic and acoustic energy redundant. For plants and animals, the infrasonic and inaudible low frequencies of the acoustic spectrum have provided a clear channel of communication, which is increasingly being filled with anthropogenic noise — energies that threaten to disrupt the intricate web of connections between human and non-human bodies within country. The Aboriginal mode of *listening to country* suggest a worldview where bodies are sensitized to these inaudible low-frequency energies, through the tactile vibrations of song performance that come out of and go back into country, a worldview where the health of all bodies within country relies on this capacity to listen.

5

Gardening / Grasshopper in a Field

Luke Fischer

Gardening

I press my blue thumb into silence —
shoots quickly spread to the left and right.
A melody unfurls its fronds and
I understand why the violin's neck is curled.

Chord clusters in the Chopin nocturne
blossom into purple umbels then
vanish into night. An arpeggio climbs
the living room walls while a trill showers
wisteria petals as if I'd just been wed.

Intervals in a Beethoven sonata inch their way
up the bass clef like a cat stalking a birdbath.
A sudden shriek as feathers are scattered
among fallen petals and the rest of the flock, in panic, flee.

The second movement ushers in a quiet morning,
descending arpeggios lightly rain, a major third and fifth
call forth the sun and chirping birds crescendo.
A vine scaling the neighbour's trellis
winds through our open windows...

Grasshopper in a Field

Who took the young thin stems
and bent them to be your legs,
folded leaves like origami
to make a pair of wings?
I found you:
a green ear of wheat
mounting a stalk,
a walking plant,
self-enclosed, unbound from the soil,
early sentience
at home in your hall of mirrors.

6

Spores from Space:
Becoming the Alien

Tessa Laird

The masterpiece of pseudo-science, *The Secret Life of Plants* (1973), tells you everything you ever needed to know about plants, but were afraid to ask. Writers Christopher Bird and Peter Tompkins might have had former lives as a science journalist and a war correspondent, respectively, but by the time they publish *The Secret Life* (or *SLOP*, as I shall affectionately refer to it), it is clear they have partaken in some serious communion with the vegetal mind. *SLOP* is filled with telepathy and telekinesis, electric vegetables and flashing flowers, hypersensitive mimosas and undemonstrative radishes. Houseplants can sense their owners' pleasures and pains and, with the right gadgetry, can testify against murderers, or open garage doors. Bird and Tompkins's agenda is clear: to convince humanity it is really plants that are the earth's superbeings. Plants can grow as tall as pyramids, predict cyclones, and, most spectacularly, engage in intergalactic conversation.[1]

---

1   Over a decade ago, the American artist and writer Frances Stark penned a love letter to *The Secret Life of Plants* in *artext,* but she drew the line at intergalactic communication. While Stark's enthusiastic embrace of the rest of the book leads her to Bach flowers, aura photographs, and biographies of Nicola Tesla and Wilhelm Reich, she says, 'It became too incredible in Chapter 4, "Visitors from Space," so I just skipped that part.' I guess we all have our boundaries. Frances Stark, 'The Secret Life', *artext* 70 (2000): 22–23.

In connecting plants, those most earthbound of life forms, to space, *SLOP* and other contemporaneous instances of popular culture collapse two divergent tendencies of the late 1960s and early 1970s — the 'back to the land' hippie movement with the state controlled Space Race. These dialectically opposed but equally utopian trajectories come together in the trippy philosophies of *SLOP*, not to mention drug gurus such as Timothy Leary (and later Terence McKenna), proposing that certain plants are extra-terrestrial in origin, and thus can provide us with the key to interstellar communication.

One of the key figures in *SLOP* is L. George Lawrence, an electrical engineer who, in the early 1970s, sets up equipment in the Mojave Desert to receive audio signals from space. Lawrence suggests that the seemingly intelligent signals he picks up are not directed at humans, but are 'transmissions between peer groups,' and because we don't know anything about biological communications we are excluded from these conversations.[2] Apparently, these transmissions sound 'unpleasant' to human ears, but if played several times over a period of weeks, can lead to a 'fascinating degree of enchantment.'[3]

Enchanting emissions from space lead Lawrence to speculate that perhaps plants are extraterrestrials and have terraformed planet earth to support life, not least our own.[4] While conven-

---

2   Christopher Bird and Peter Tompkins, *The Secret Life of Plants* (New York: Harper & Row, 1973), 54. Lawrence speculates that these may be intergalactic calls for help. In a deadpan manner typical of *SLOP*, we are told a copy of Lawrence's tape and a seven-page report are being held at the Smithsonian Institution in Washington, DC, 'preserved as a potentially historical scientific document.'

3   Ibid., 55.

4   Ibid., 63. It is worth noting here, however, that it is fungi that are the true 'world makers,' and that plants would not have been able to migrate from the oceans to land if fungi had not first made soil by 'digesting rocks.' While fungi are not plants, they inhabit a deliciously slippery space that is both between, and completely outside of, flora and fauna. In this chapter I elide flora and fungi, both for anthropocentric convenience, and disanthropocentric solidarity, representing utterly entwined, inhuman worlds. Anna Lowenhaupt Tsing, *The Mushroom at the End of the World: On the Possibility of Life in Capitalist Ruins*

tional evolutionary science holds that a peculiar and accidental set of conditions led to the emergence of life on earth, proponents of panspermia argue that everything on earth originated elsewhere, and so we are all, already, aliens. Lawrence suggests that the plant intelligences that incubated Earth are in instant communication across vast distances, and what we need are not spaceships but 'the proper "telephone numbers."'[5] As emissaries from space, plants surely still have intergalactic family ties, and thus the need, and ability, to 'phone home.' Come to think of it, wasn't ET a botanist?[6]

While we can only speculate that plants communicate with space, it is certainly clear we humans often communicate ideas *about* space and all its concomitant strangeness via vegetal motifs. Our imaginings regarding weird worlds and beings are often mediated by what we hold dear and familiar about earth's flora, and what we can hypothesise about their extra-terrestrial counterparts. In dystopian sci-fi, we figure the loss of plants as the end of all hope, and the miraculous growth of plants in hostile environs as hope's beginning.[7] There are many ways in which we think with plants (and, to be fair, plants think with us). In science fiction, fabulated vegetal worlds feature radically inverted colours and scales, signaling the alien; hybrid creatures embody and flout

(Princeton: Princeton University Press, 2015), 22.

5   Bird and Tompkins, *Secret Life of Plants,* 64.

6   As was Mark Watney (Matt Damon) in *The Martian* (2015), who survives abandonment on Mars by growing potatoes, and Freeman Lowell (Bruce Dern) in *Silent Running* (1972), who takes care of a biodome spaceship carrying earth's flora, maintaining the diversity the planet can no longer support. Dern is magnificent as the wild-eyed Lowell who speaks for the trees as his indifferent crewmates laugh, including an impassioned monologue over a cantaloupe he has lovingly grown himself. Lowell's passionate connection to the vegetal world over humans (he even prefers the company of droids to his crew) speaks to a generational disenchantment with earthly politics and a suspicion that true empathy is more likely to be found in Walden-like woods or the wilderness of space, or both.

7   Witness some classic, comedic tales of 'endlings' and new beginnings, from *WALL-E* (2008) to *Idiocracy* (2006), featuring the unbeatable phrase: 'Electrolytes: It's what plants crave!'

anxieties about racial and species boundaries; contagious plants infect their human hosts with alchemical arsenals, leading to death or ecstasy, or both.

Science fictions of plant sentience and human-plant hybridity imagine worlds divested of anthropocentric control, where senses are heightened and interconnectivities flourish, for better or worse. Plants, fungi, and science fiction are mutually compatible vehicles for altered consciousness, and this chapter propounds *vegetalismo* (curing with psychoactive plants) in order to 'become the alien.'[8] As Félix Guattari puts it, the chaosmic Universe can be constellated with all kinds of becomings: vegetal, animal, cosmic, or machinic.[9] When chemically induced molecular revolutions are unavailable, however, the neuronal reorderings of minor literature can be just as revelatory. In this case, I intend to magnify the spores found in an episode of the Original Series *Star Trek,* alongside the multiple incarnations of sci-fi B movie *Invasion of the Body Snatchers,* with some help from spore-loving anthropologist Anna Tsing, thanks to her work on the matsutake mushroom.

In the 1967 episode of *Star Trek* 'This Side of Paradise,' the Enterprise heads to Omnicron Ceti III after contact has been lost with the 150 men, women, and children who have attempted to colonise the planet. Fearing that the colonists will be dead due to the lethal Berthold rays that are bathing the planet, the crew are startled to find on beaming down that not only are these hardy earthlings still alive, but in *perfect* health. Their leader, Elias Sandoval, avoids the issue of their literal 'radiance,' focusing instead on his philosophy 'that men should return to a less complicated

---

8 Terence McKenna, *The Archaic Revival: Speculations on Psychedelic Mushrooms, the Amazon, Virtual Reality, UFOs, Evolution, Shamanism, the Rebirth of the Goddess, and the End of History* (San Francisco: HarperCollins, 1991), 98.

9 Felix Guattari, *Chaosmosis: An Ethico-Aesthetic Paradigm,* trans. Paul Bains and Julian Pefanis (Sydney: Power Publications, 1995), 68. We might add to this list fungal becomings, since fungi are neither vegetal nor animal, but more than the sum of both 'Queendoms.' (I'm using 'Queendom' as opposed to 'Kingdom' following the example of Peter McCoy, founder of 'Radical Mycology,' although of course there are far more than two genders operating in the world of fungi).

life.'[10] The colonists possess no vehicles or weapons, and live in complete peace and harmony. When asked what happened to their animals, Elias replies simply 'We're vegetarians.'[11]

The rigorously logical Mr. Spock tries to get answers to the riddle of the planet from Leila, a botanist (naturally) who also happens to be a soft-focus blonde *and* Spock's ex-flame (it's a small galaxy). Leading him to a patch of rubbery, leggy looking shrubs with pink flowers, Leila tells Spock, 'I was one of the first to find them. The spores.' 'Spores?' Spock asks quizzically, just as one of the plants ejaculates in his face.[12] Clutching his head and falling to the ground in pain, Spock attempts to resist the vegetal realignment of his senses. Luckily for Leila and the viewers, his intense struggle is futile, and shortly, completely against character, Spock says 'I love you' to Leila. The couple kiss, and love, drugs, flower power, peace, harmony, and vegetarianism reign. All suspicions that Omnicron Ceti III is a 1967 middle-American sci-fi caricature of a hippie commune are confirmed when Spock willfully ignores the commands of his superior, Captain Kirk, while

10 True to many 1960s communes, the leader bears a biblical name, and appropriately to a planet in which the colonists 'should be dead,' Elias is a prophet who raises the dead.

11 Ralph Senensky, dir., *Star Trek,* 'This Side of Paradise,' writ. D.C. Fontana, Jerry Sohl, and Gene Roddenberry (Desilu Productions and Paramount Television), March 2, 1967).

12 Ejaculating vegetation seems an appropriate motif in 1967: a sexual revolution enabled in part by psychoactive plants, particularly marijuana and magic mushrooms, although LSD, of course, was synthesised in a laboratory and taken orally. Psychoactive dust is actually more reminiscent of cocaine (what Father Yod of the Los Angeles-based commune The Source Family christened 'sacred snow') as well as the psychoactive snuff powders of the Amazon, such as the powder of the *yākōanahi* tree inhaled by Yanomami shamans. *Xapiripë* spirits, which are themselves 'as tiny as specks of sparkling dust,' can only be seen if the powder of this tree is inhaled 'many, many times.' In fact, it is a process that takes as long to unfold as it does for a white person to learn to read and write properly. 'The *yākōanahi* powder is the food of the spirits. Those who don't 'drink' it remain with the eyes of ghosts and see nothing.' David Kopenawa, quoted in Eduardo Viveiros de Castro, 'The Crystal Forest: Notes on the Ontology of Amazonian Spirits,' *Inner Asia* 9, no. 2 (2007), 153–72.

lolling with Leila, watching clouds and rainbows, and swinging upside down from a tree with a broad grin on his face.[13] Spock suggests it is the increasingly apoplectic Kirk who needs to be 'straightened out.' He and Leila lead Kirk and two of his crew to a clump of flowers, where they are instantly sprayed with spores, yet Kirk remains unaffected, even as his crew fall under the plants' spell. It is as if, in the style of Bill Clinton, Kirk witnesses a utopian psychedelia unfolding before him, but 'doesn't inhale.'[14]

Spock's elven ears already associate him with mushroom people, so it is appropriate that he is the first to be 'infected' by love spores. In this intergalactic Eden, Spock is Pan, who has been reanimated after the enforced slumber that started on December 25, in the year 0 AD. Although the stardate is 3417.3, it is in 1967 that Pan awakens (and see what party-pooper extraordinaire Ayn Rand had to say two years later about muddy horizontal Dionysian revelries at Woodstock versus the upright, Kirk-like phallicism of the Apollo Mission).[15]

Kirk heads back to the Enterprise to find that the plants and spores have already beamed aboard (the ship's botanist saw to it), and now the entire crew is in summer-of-love mutiny against the Captain, the sole remaining proponent of order. Kirk rails against the planet's 'private paradise' (said with Shatner's famously plosive enunciation), while Spock tries to explain to him the miracle of spores drifting through space, then inhabiting plants while

13 The 'Acidemic' who writes 'Psychedelic Film Criticism for the Already Deranged' agrees with my prognostication that this episode is a parable for hippie culture's refusal of participation in the military industrial complex, while hinting at the War on Drugs to come. Erich Kuersten, 'Sex, Drugs and Quantum Existentialism: The Acidemic STAR TREK Short Guide,' *Acidemic Film Blog,* June 5, 2012, https://acidemic. blogspot.com.au/2012/06/60s-sex-space-drugs-existential.html.

14 For anthropologist and mushroom enthusiast Anna Tsing, there needn't be particulate matter in the inhalation, but smell itself is a transformative encounter with 'an other,' a response which 'takes us somewhere new; we are not quite ourselves anymore' (*The Mushroom at the End of the World,* 46). Indeed, 'spores model open-ended communication and excess: the pleasures of speculation' (ibid., 227).

15 Ayn Rand, 'Apollo and Dionysus,' in *The New Left: The Anti-Industrial Revolution* (New York: New American Library, 1971), 57–81.

waiting for human bodies to colonise. Thriving on Berthold rays, the spores live in symbiosis with their host body, promising complete health and peace of mind. But Kirk is disgusted by a planet with 'no wants' and 'no needs,' because human beings 'weren't meant for that.' According to Kirk, man 'stagnates if he has no ambition' or challenge. Eventually, though, even Kirk's resistance wears thin. He is the last man left on the bridge of the Enterprise, and a lurking flower sprays him. Finally, he understands, and prepares to evacuate the ship. But as he places a very mid-20th-century suitcase on the transporter pad (packed with his Star Fleet medals), the enormity of the situation overcomes him, and Kirk summons all his willpower to liberate himself from the tyranny of peace and love. Personal torment suddenly turns into relief as he realises the potential of violent emotion to break the spell of the flower's power. He hatches a plan to make Spock 'see reason' by goading him with insults until the Vulcan is driven to violence, which will allow him to break through the spore-induced haze.

'All right, you mutinous, disloyal, computerised, half-breed, we'll see about you deserting my ship,' Kirk begins. Spock answers him even-handedly, but Kirk persists: 'You're an overgrown jackrabbit, an elf with a hyperactive thyroid'; a 'simpering, devil-eared freak whose father was a computer and his mother an encyclopedia'...'rotten like the rest of your subhuman race'; a 'carcass full of memory banks who should be squatting in a mushroom, instead of passing himself off as a man'; 'you belong in a circus...right next to the dog-faced boy.' Mistrust of miscegenation, of human-animal-plant-machine hybridity, of machine elves and machinic assemblages, is writ large in Kirk's desperate attempt, as the ultimate in colonial power, to subdue via insult.[16]

16 The similarities between Captain James Kirk of the Enterprise, and Captain James Cook of the Endeavour, have been commented upon in numerous fan sites, while the quotation that begins each episode of STAR TREK, 'To boldly go where no man has gone before,' is said to be based on one of Cook's journal entries. Is Spock, then, an intergalactic Tupaia, the Tahitian navigator and priest who acted as Cook's translator throughout the Pacific? Spock is racially ambiguous, as Kirk's outburst proves, and as a result he is almost always Kirk's interface with and inter-

Kirk breaks Spock's spirit, thus breaking the spell of the spores, and Spock is 'himself' again — a patsy, Uncle Tom, strike breaker. Together, he and Kirk beam a sonic frequency to the planet's surface — perhaps something like the 'unpleasant' space signals Lawrence intercepts in the Mojave — just enough to make everyone irritable and pick fights with each other. Cue scenes of formerly peaceful colonists hitting each other with spades. Victory! Even founder Elias comes to his senses, realising there has been 'no progress' and the last three years have been wasted — never mind that intoxication with the plants has actually saved them from the certain death of the Berthold rays.

When the Enterprise leaves the planet with the colonists on board bound for a new home, the bridge crew gaze upon Omnicron Ceti III as it disappears from view. Dr. McCoy comments that this was the second time man was thrown out of paradise, but Kirk disagrees, stating, 'we walked out on our own.' Man, according to that most manly of men, Captain Kirk, was not meant for paradise, rather 'we' (humanity) were meant to 'struggle, claw our way up, scratch for every inch of the way.' Tellingly for a period in which politics were being played out musically, while the Vietnam war raged, Kirk opines: 'Maybe we can't stroll to the music of the lute. We must march to the sound of drums.' But this victory speech, and the restoration of order, is surely just a ruse, for viewers in 1967 wanted to be sprayed by cosmic spores, to run from swaggering authority figures with barrel chests and overly tight pants, to see Spock smile and swing from the trees. Kirk's martial rhetoric is immediately undone by an unusually pensive Spock, who, with as much sadness as a Vulcan can muster, muses: 'For the first time in my life I was happy.'

Eleven years after 'This Side of Paradise' put contagious spores from space and the vegetal mind on mainstream TV, Philip Kaufman's magisterial 1978 remake of *The Invasion of the Body Snatchers* signaled the final disintegration of the flower power decade. The opening credits feature gelatinous forms copulating in some anonymous location in space. The eerie sound effects — galactic pulsations, cellular chittering, ghostly screams — are 'unpleasant to human ears', like Lawrence's signals

preter of the 'alien other.'

from space. The opening sequence is a 'spore's eye view,' which is also the favoured perspective of writers as diverse as Terence McKenna, for whom magic mushrooms are aliens living in our midst, and anthropologist Anna Tsing, who writes 'under the influence' of the matsutake mushroom, such that she even takes on the perspective of a spore when writing an academic essay.[17] Kaufman's eerie spores sight our blue planet, Earth, then plunge through the atmosphere, through cloud cover, and into the gardens of San Francisco.[18] Thanks to the rain, the spores soak thoroughly into the vegetal fabric of the city, and soon strange pink flowers are popping up on host plants. The pinkness of the sensorially-penetrative flowers in both *Star Trek* and *Invasion 78* is remarkable: to 'pink' means to pierce or prick, appropriate to airborne insemination which is more akin to divine impregnation — asexual reproduction aided by a mere breath of wind (or an angel).[19]

Jack Bellicec (Jeff Goldblum) and his wife Nancy (Veronica Cartwright) own a bathhouse in which corpulent men bathe in mud, like spuds or pods.[20] Nancy fills the bathhouse with plants, insisting that classical music be piped throughout the establishment because the plants 'just love it.' She assures her customers that plants have feelings 'just like people,' and is fascinated by the idea that classical music stimulates plant growth, noting, 'They've done tons of experiments on them.' Clearly, Nancy has read *SLOP*, where an experiment on summer squashes demonstrates how those exposed to classical music grew towards the speakers, while those exposed to rock'n'roll literally climbed the walls to escape. Plants' enjoyment of Western classical music,

17 Anna Lowenhaupt Tsing, 'Strathern beyond the Human: Testimony of a Spore,' *Theory, Culture and Society* 31, nos. 2-3 (2014).

18 Blue echiums seem to be the first port of call, then a New Zealand flax bush, both of which I have in my garden (should I be worried?).

19 See more about pink and bodily invasion in: Tessa Laird, 'Pink Data: Tiamaterialism and the Female Gnosis of Desire,' in *Aesthetics After Finitude,* eds. Baylee Brits, Prudence Gibson, and Amy Ireland (Melbourne: re.press, 2016), 191–200.

20 The original 1956 version of the film popularised the term 'pod people,' meaning humans with no distinguishing features, signifying the undifferentiated and therefore sinister masses.

however, is far exceeded by their love for Hindustani classical music, as plants listening to Ravi Shankar actually embraced the speakers.[21] Interestingly, Tsing uses the concept of polyphonies as found in pre-modern musical forms such as fugues, to illustrate a way of listening to a world of multiple entanglements. Musical unity via a unified coordination of time is considered 'progress,' and in rock'n'roll, the strong beat resonates with the listener's heart, suggestive of individualism and a 'single perspective.'[22] Nancy Bellicec gets all of this, but nothing can prepare her, or the rest of the cast, for their conversion into alien spore-infected 'pod people.' In fact, for all her understanding of the vegetal mind, Nancy is the only one who manages to hold out and not be taken over by intergalactic plant consciousness. The film's classic denouement comes when she sees her friend Matthew Bennell (Donald Sutherland), and whispers to him conspiratorially, only to find that he has become one of 'them.' He points at her in psychotic fury, emitting an ear-splitting, non-human shriek, like a mandrake being pulled out of the ground.

It's a given that sci-fi reflects the world in which it is produced. The original 1956 *Invasion of the Body Snatchers* is primarily a McCarthyist red scare — communists, or at least communal thinking, have invaded middle America — although it can also read as a subversive *critique* of McCarthyist hysteria. 'This Side of Paradise' parodises flower children and the 'enemy within' of a drug-savvy youth culture, yet it too has some anti-communist paranoia: Spock dons rather Soviet-style overalls when he decides to ignore the orders of all-American Captain Kirk.

There is another common denominator between the 1967 TV episode and the 1978 feature — Leonard Nimoy. In *Star Trek,* his Vulcan armour is pierced by a pink flower, making him more emotional, while in *Invasion of the Body Snatchers,* he is Dr.

---

21 Bird and Tompkins, *Secret Life of Plants,* 141. It is also worth noting here that musician Stevie Wonder was so enamoured by the book that he composed a double album with the same name, and produced a documentary featuring some of the book's key findings, interspersed with his own songs (1979). The breathtaking finale features a fly-over as Stevie, in pseudo-Egyptian garb, sings in a field of sunflowers.

22 Tsing, *The Mushroom at the End of the World,* 23.

David Kibner, a psychiatrist and charismatic self-help guru who puts people in touch with their emotions. In both cases, Nimoy's playing against the expectations of his most famous character heightens the sense of emotional intensity. And while there are still hints of a mistrust of collectivity over individualism in *Invasion of the Body Snatchers,* what stands out more than political subtext is the breakdown of monogamous relationships. In the 1970s, the sexual revolution has mainstreamed, promiscuity is the norm, and divorce rates are surging. The 1978 version of *Invasion of the Body Snatchers* gives ordinary spousal dissatisfaction the sci-fi treatment: partners act indifferently with each other not because they are bored but because they are actually aliens! Kibner counsels countless individuals for whom the 'person I married' becomes someone, *something,* else![23]

Karen Barad refers to slime moulds, or 'social amoebas,' as exemplary beings because they 'queer' identity, resisting classification as either group or individual, and existing somewhere between animal, plant, and fungal kingdoms. Barad notes the unease with which such social amoebas are portrayed in the media, given their self-sacrificing behaviours (individuals 'committing suicide' for the betterment of the group). Depending on your interpretation, the 'sticky contingencies' of slime moulds either paint Nature as 'an exemplary moral actor or a commie activist (or, heaven forfend, both)!'[24] Barad compares the xenophobia lurking in popular science literature to another 1950s horror sci-fi film, *The Blob,* and notes that systemic incitement of fear did not die off with McCarthyism, and does not only take the form of rabid anti-communism. According to Barad, the smeary fingerprints of *The Blob* can be seen in the hysterical responses

23 This dis-ease with the institution of marriage is brilliantly lampooned at the end of *Invasion* (1956), where Dr. Miles Bennell narrates as he runs from a crowd of pod people, 'I didn't know the real meaning of fear until I kissed Becky. A moment's sleep and the girl I loved was an inhuman enemy bent on my destruction.' *Invasion of the Body Snatchers,* dir. Don Seigel (Walter Wanger Productions, 1956).

24 Karen Barad, 'Nature's Queer Performativity,' in *Toward an Aesthetics of Living Beings,* eds. Cord Riechelmann and Brigitte Oetker (Berlin: Sternberg Press, 2015), 250–61.

to the AIDS epidemic, mad cow disease, and avian flu, each of which have demanded mass sacrifices of human and non-human scapegoats. Racism and Islamophobia are today's incarnation of *The Blob,* which 'is very much alive on the contemporary political scene.'[25] But what if, Barad asks, 'Nature herself is a commie, a pervert, or a queer?'[26]

In the 2007 remake *The Invasion,* we have come full circle to 1967, and there are hints (as with 'This Side of Eden') that 'becoming the alien' is really the best way to go, since peace on earth finally prevails. While the primary plot centres on Nicole Kidman's and Daniel Craig's attempts at escaping alien contagion (here Barad's 'blob' has become avian flu paranoia about sneezing and body fluids), we see secondary glimpses of a changing world. Peace treaties are being signed. Violent crime is nonexistent. While plants themselves are not a feature of the 2007 film, when Craig has 'become alien' his attempts to placate the hysterical Kidman involve vegetal metaphor. 'Remember our trip to Colorado?' he asks her. 'Remember the Aspen grove? Recall how peaceful it was. Remember what you said to me? You wondered how it would be if people could live like these trees... completely connected with each other, in harmony, as one.'[27]

The vegetal is the trope of ultimate interconnectivity (or the fungal, as Tsing would have it). Craig promotes a world without suffering, where 'no one can hurt each other' because 'there is no other,' which can be read as either edenic utopianism or totalitarianism, be it communist, fascist, or Borg. When Kidman,

25 Ibid., 252. Jeffrey Jerome Cohen invokes two more 1950s sci-fi horror flicks, *The Astounding She-Monster* (1957) and *Them!* (1954), featuring a horde of giant ants, which Cohen is quick to point out are really communists. He notes that feminine and cultural others are monstrous by themselves but 'when they threaten to mingle' as with Barad's queering of nature, 'the entire economy of desire comes under attack.' Jeffrey Jerome Cohen, 'Monster Culture (Seven Theses),' in *Monster Theory: Reading Culture* (Minneapolis: University of Minnesota Press, 1996), 3–25. For Cohen, the monster's destructiveness is really 'a deconstructiveness' that undermines notions of fixed identity (14).

26 Barad, 'Nature's Queer Performativity,' 254.

27 *The Invasion,* dirs. Oliver Hirschbiegel and James McTeigue (Warner Bros., 2007).

unconvinced, cries 'You're not Ben!' Craig replies, 'I'm not Ben, I'm *more than* Ben,' unconsciously echoing terminology coined by ecophilosopher David Abram. Abram's 'more-than-human' speaks to a world in which inhuman others are not less-than, or in-opposition-to, humanity, but affirmative co-producers of a collective landscape. As an acknowledgement of intersubjectivity, the term has been enthusiastically embraced by a range of ecotheorists eager to move beyond the constructs and constraints of humanism.

McKenna had no problem with 'becoming the alien' — he saw it as the only means to thwart alienation. He said, 'The next great step toward a planetary holism is the partial merging of the technologically transformed human world with the Archaic matrix of vegetable intelligence that is the Transcendent Other.'[28] Of course, the best way to achieve this was by ingesting magic mushrooms, which he had done with such frequency and intensity he was able to open a communications channel with the mushroom as easily as if he was Lieutenant Uhura sitting at her console on the deck of the Enterprise. 'The mushroom speaks to you when you speak to it,' letting you in on such secrets such as: 'I am old, fifty times older than thought in your species, and I came from the stars.' McKenna says he argues with the mushroom about how much information it will reveal. As the propagator, he feels he has certain rights, but the mushroom does not want to reveal the secrets of intergalactic space travel — yet. When McKenna asks what this alien entity is doing on earth, it replies: 'Listen, if you're a mushroom, you live cheap; besides, I'm telling you, this was a very nice neighborhood until the monkeys got out of control.'[29]

McKenna's conversations with the mushroom support a theory of panspermia — that life on earth originated from cosmic microorganisms drifting through space — space dust, or maybe even 'space spunk.' In keeping with the Hermetic teaching 'As above, so below', comets certainly look like macro-scale sperm, with planets as incubatory eggs.[30] While Tsing inhabits a spore's

---

28 Terence McKenna, *Food of the Gods: the Search for the Original Tree of Knowledge* (New York: Bantam Books, 1993), 93.

29 McKenna, *Archaic Revival,* 99.

30 Mette Bryld and Nina Lykke make a feminist critique of panspermia as

eye view in order to 'infect' anthropology and transform it into a (paradoxically) *more than human* discipline,[31] McKenna is infected with the mushroom itself, such that it speaks through him:

> By means impossible to explain because of certain misconceptions in your model of reality all my mycelial networks in the galaxy are in hyperlight communication across space and time. The mycelial body is as fragile as a spider's web but the collective hypermind and memory is a vast historical archive of the career of evolving intelligence on many worlds in our spiral star swarm.[32]

McKenna's mushroom mediumism is an example of what Tsing calls 'Contamination as Collaboration.'[33] McKenna, or rather the mushroom, says this goes beyond mere 'collectivism' and into far 'richer and even more baroque evolutionary possibilities,' including symbiotic mutualism, 'a relation of mutual dependence and positive benefits for both of the species involved.'[34] For Tsing, contamination describes a transformative encounter, and it is 'contaminating relationality' which makes diversity, and cre-

---

phallogocentrism writ large, in which cosmic life is made to follow the pattern of the stable yet ceaselessly colonizing, patrimonial family, while earth is figured as a virgin, waiting planet (Bryld and Lykke suggest the Earth in this narrative is in fact 'raped'). For these authors, the only real 'seeding' taking place is phallogocentrism itself, which resows itself in susceptible minds. Mette Bryld and Nina Lykke, *Cosmodolphins: Feminist Cultural Studies of Technology, Animals and the Sacred* (New York: Zed Books, 2000), 100–16.

31 'The radical potential of anthropology has always been this: other worlds are possible' (Tsing, 'Strathern beyond the Human,' 225).

32 O.T. Oss and O.N. Oeric [Terence and Dennis McKenna], *Psilocybin, Magic Mushroom Grower's Guide: A Handbook for Psilocybin Enthusiasts* (Oakland: Quick American Publishing/Lux Natura, 1991), 14.

33 Tsing, *The Mushroom at the End of the World,* 26. Another brilliant sci-fi example of a plant's-eye, rather than a fungus-eye view, is Mark von Schlegell's *Venusia* (2005), which features, among many other tales, strange rituals with psychoactive plants on Venus, and ends with the reader's realisation that the entire novel has been narrated by a potplant.

34 Oss and Oeric, *Psilocybin,* 15.

ates a 'happening,' that is, an event that is greater than the sum of its parts.[35] Even without non-fungal participants, the lives of fungi are already made up of many players — in particular, they have famously non-binary sex lives, which Tsing describes as akin to 'having a child together with your own arm,' resulting in a 'mosaic body, stuffed with heterogeneous genetic material...you, and you, and you, and me, all in one.'[36]

The networked intelligence or 'mosaic body' is often figured in sci-fi as pertaining to plants rather than fungi. Ursula K. Le Guin's ecological parable *The Word for World is Forest* (1972) features furry green forest people, surely an inspiration for the Na'vi of *Avatar* (2009), who worship a sacred 'Tree of Souls' which connects directly to the Na'vi nervous system via a bio-machinic neural linkage system that looks unnervingly like the universal signifier for unwashed hippiedom: a dreadlock. I cannot help but superimpose *Avatar*'s hippie fluoro rave aesthetics on Tsing's description of subterranean fungal interconnectivities, where 'thread-like filaments, called hyphae, spread into fans and tangle into cords through the dirt.' Tsing asks us to imagine that the soil is liquid and transparent, and that we have sunk into the ground, only to find ourselves surrounded by nets of fungal hyphae. 'Follow fungi into that underground city, and you will

---

35 Tsing, *The Mushroom at the End of the World,* 27–29; 40. Interestingly, her use of the word 'happening' chimes with 1960s counter-cultural language: the activation of the masses into culturally-productive play, rather than passive spectatorship — but see how this term is negatively detourned by M. Night Shyamalan's ecological horror film, *The Happening* (2008).

36 Tsing, 'Strathern beyond the Human,' 225–26. This has all kinds of precedents in anthropological lore (e.g., among the Yanomami, women were said to be born from the calf of an ancestral male). This also chimes well with Eduardo Viveiros de Castro's description of a singular shaman as always already multiple: 'The concept of spirit essentially designates a population of molecular affects, an intensive multiplicity...the same applies to the concept of shaman: "the shaman is a multiple being, a micro-population of shamanic agencies sheltered in one body"': Viveiros de Castro, 'The Crystal Forest,' 156, quoting Peter Roe, *The Cosmic Zygote: Cosmology in the Amazon Basin* (New Brunswick: Rutgers University Press, 1982).

find the strange and varied pleasures of interspecies life.'[37] My-chorrhizal networks can be compared to the Internet, a veritable 'woodwide web' carrying information across the forest, and allowing ecosystems to respond to threats.[38] Taking this concept to a darker place, M. Night Shyamalan's *The Happening* figures a world in which trees kill humanity en masse with poisonous spores, although it can be argued this is Gaian self-defense, a kind of militant disanthropocentrism (enacted by guerillas who are already wearing camouflage).[39] *The Happening* is a dystopian take on the epiphany Michael Pollan has in his garden, when he realises that it is the plants, and not the gardener, who is in control: not objects of human desire, but agential subjects, 'acting on me, getting me to do things for them they couldn't do for themselves.'[40]

As the hysterical hero of the original *Invasion of the Body Snatchers* tries to warn oncoming traffic, 'They're here already... you're next!' And, throughout the 60s and 70s, plants really did invade the popular imagination, from little old ladies talking to their begonias, to Ozzie Osbourne singing 'You introduced me to my mind,' in the song 'Sweet Leaf' (an ode to marijuana, not

37 Tsing, *The Mushroom at the End of the World*, 137.
38 Ibid., 139. Tsing refers to the 'intellectual woodland' (286) and 'the spore-filled airy stratosphere of the mind' (228).
39 Shyamalan's lacklustre movie nevertheless possesses a (literally) killer premise, in which plants can work cooperatively in networks that far exceed anything humanity has achieved to date. This idea, in concert with another of Shyamalan's missed opportunities, *Signs* (2002), a film about crop circles, proposes an answer (via *SLOP*) to the question of who makes these strange geometric symbols? Instead of looking for an extra-terrestrial intelligence, or a series of human tricksters, why not look for a more intrinsically terrestrial culprit — the plants themselves? Though, if we truly believe in panspermia, the plants are the extra-terrestrials. Or, continuing with panspermia, crop circles are akin to inter-galactic cum stains, what is left over when inter-dimensional heavenly bodies collide.
40 Michael Pollan, *The Botany of Desire: A Plant's Eye View of the World* (New York: Random House, 2001). It is this shift in point of view, this perspectivism, that Viveiros de Castro, Tsing, and many others see as being the only true decolonial and dis-anthropocentric methodology, and one which shamans, via *vegetalismo*, are adept at practicing.

stevia). But plants could be villains too, as the 1978 *Invasion of the Body Snatchers* and a host of other sci-fi plots made apparent (let us not forget the chilling British 1980s *Day of the Triffids* TV series, or the campy family film *Little Shop of Horrors*). And while *The Secret Life of Plants* is generally regarded as a period piece of dubious scientific and literary worth, successive generations of writers and artists unearth it to again ponder plant consciousness, and the possibility that, via electrodes, or ingestion, or maybe just conversation, we could tune in, not only to plants' ancient, inhuman wisdom, but to the stars from whence they came.

II

Thinking Plants

7

Brain Trees: Neuroscientific Metaphor and Botanical Thought

Baylee Brits

Our understanding of the brain is bound up with our images of plants. One of the dominant metaphors for the way the brain works is the tree. If we reduce a tree to its most basic caricature — the sphere on the top of the trunk — we have an echo not only of the brain and the brain stem, but of the neuron and its branching dendrites and extensive axon as well. In addition to this broad structure of stem and efflorescence, this visual metaphor capitalises on the bloom of synaptic connections, redolent of the thinning and multiplying of twigs from branches. These metaphors of the brain become all the more significant given recent developments in the inverse field, as new work in plant science is changing the way we think about vegetation and thought. Studies of plant behaviour now suggest that plants engage in processes of what we might call thinking and learning, even if this thought does not exactly resemble the sort of conscious rationality that vastly overdetermines our ideas about what the human brain primarily does. While the brain is often envisaged as a tree, this metaphoric exchange has only ever gone one way: it remains anathema to associate plants with brains in anything more than an illustrative sense. Although the neurological armoury of images seems to be phytological — and phytology is now deploying the concepts once unique to brain science — any exchange between the two is often rendered trivial, as if images and names existed in the realm of conceptual small change. Here I consider the way that current key popular texts in neurology deploy the metaphor of the plant, in particular the tree, and explore the ways that this metaphor works to both stabilise and 'extinguish' its object. I consider the way that the 'tree' is simultaneously a material and immaterial metaphor, an embodiment of both neural object and function. This curious mode of metaphor, which I will associate with Paul de Man's definition of 'formal allegory,' actually models the cognitive processes that it seeks to describe.

A formal allegory occurs where the text allegorises its own formal processes, its own processes of composition. If the 'tree' allegorises the very processes of thought that it is meant only to refer to, it does not so much *represent* the brain, but present the very neural processes at issue. This demands a reconsideration of the significance of the neural metaphor and also suggests a rhetorical mode by which we might approach new work on vegetal thought. My argument will be mediated through the idea of the 'garden of bifurcating paths,' the title of one of the best-known stories by the great Argentine writer, Jorge Luis Borges. My contention here is that these neural and phytological image gardens are best understood, and best brought into dialogue, by literary criticism and a critical approach to the triadic relationship between concept, image and thing. By braiding three different allegories — the brain as tree, the thinking plant and the allegory of a garden of forking paths in Borges' short story — I will demonstrate that this tropology is far more substantial than illustration or ornamentation, and is essential to the mediation between neural object and event.

Brain Trees: Anatomy and Physiology, Analogy and Allegory

There are many accounts of the metaphors of the brain used in medical or scientific literature. One of the most prominent metaphors likens the brain to a computer. This metaphor arose in the twentieth century out of the nineteenth-century precedents that imagined the brain as machinic. The brain has long been viewed as a machine, whether as a hydraulic pump or as a telegraph machine. In the 1850s, 'the arrival of the telegraph network provided Helmholtz with his basic neural metaphor, as did reverberating relay circuits and solenoids for Hebb's theory of memory' almost a century later.[1] These machinic metaphors served the ends of nineteenth-century determinism and, in the twentieth century, have abetted a sort of behaviourism appropriate to networked society, revolving around inputs, outputs, and attention spans.[2] The brain is also frequently compared to writing utensils, be it a blackboard and chalk, a pen and paper, or Freud's famous mystic writing pad.[3] However, both the metaphor of the computer and the metaphor of the writing pad are essentially metaphors of the mind, rather than the brain itself. What makes the metaphor of the tree significant is that it is deployed to describe how the brain, or the neuron, might look as well as how it might function. Whereas the telegraph network, the computer, and the blackboard only evoke the way the brain might work, the metaphor of the tree is multifaceted, refracting an array of different aspects of the brain that are often considered in mutually exclusive terms. The tree is powerful because the metaphor is a material one as well as an immaterial one, it is structural as well as functional.

The comparison between the brain and the tree exists primarily in the armoury of metaphor attached to popular neuroscientific discourse. The explanation of neural anatomy from the Queensland Brain Institute is exemplary of this and bears quoting at length:

> A neuron has three main parts: dendrites, an axon, and a cell body or soma, which can be represented as the branches, roots and trunk of a tree, respectively. A dendrite (tree branch) is where a neuron receives input from other cells. Dendrites branch as they move towards their tips, just like tree branch-

1 John G. Daugman, 'Brain Metaphor and Brain Theory,' in *Computational Neuroscience,* ed. Eric L. Schwartz (Cambridge: MIT Press, 1990), 24.
2 This is argued by Hunter Crowther-Heyck in 'George A. Miller, Language, and the Computer Metaphor of Mind,' *History of Psychology* 2, no. 1 (March 1999), 37–64; https://doi.org/10.1037/1093–4510.2.1.37.
3 See Douwe Draaisma, *Metaphors of Memory: A History of Ideas about the Mind,* trans. Paul Vincent (Cambridge: Cambridge University Press, 2000), for an account of this, in particular Freud's vision of the mystic writing pad.

es do, and they even have leaf-like structures on them called spines. The axon (tree roots) is the output structure of the neuron; when a neuron wants to talk to another neuron, it sends an electrical message called an action potential throughout the entire axon.[4]

Already, in this simple botanical tropology of the brain, the parts of the tree express both anatomy and physiology. The 'branch' of the dendrite is used in the above description to indicate material extension as well as action. The 'branch' doubles, here, as a noun and verb; the dendrite is a branch and, although this functionality is not detailed explicitly here, it also *branches*, an oblique reference to the role the dendrite plays in the propagation of neural electrochemical current. The word dendrite is the Latin for tree, and the term 'cortex,' which is used for the outer layer of neural tissue, is Latin for 'bark.'[5] These Latin terms, and their afterlives in metaphors of the brain, leads Giorgio Ascoli to coin the word 'neurobotanical.'[6] Ascoli views the 'entire brain...as a whole neurobotanical world completely filled with trees.'[7] For Ascoli, the notion of a 'neurobotanical garden' allows for an expression of the diversity of neuronal shape, size and function.

It is just as common to compare the links that exist between neurons with trees in a forest. For Ascoli, 'much of the brain complexity is due to the massive web of connections and communication formed by its tens of billions of nerve cells through tiny tree-like structures.'[8] Ascoli's epigraph, by Stanford neuroscientist Stephen J. Smith, gives substance to this vision of brain complexity; Smith speculates that 'our most beautiful landscape is the one within.'[9] Smith's similic gesture is significant, because it renders complexity aesthetic: the mind is like a beautiful land-

---

4   'What is a Neuron?,' *Queensland Brain Institute,* http://www.qbi. uq.edu.au/the-brain/physiology/what-is-a-neuron.

5   Giorgio A. Ascoli, *Trees of the Brain, Roots of the Mind* (Cambridge: MIT Press, 2015), 6.

6   Ibid., vii.

7   Ibid.

8   Ibid.

9   Ibid.

scape, full of trees, mirroring the outside world. This 'outside world' here is, of course, not the world of blocks of flats or streetscapes or parking lots, but a forested world. In this sense, the trope of the tree works to produce an aesthetics of the brain, a landscape that is rich with foliage and vegetal life. So these metaphors do more than just serve as a tool for anatomic explication: the illustrations also render the brain scenic. The word 'scene,' of course, comes from the Greek word for the stage, and the 'scenic' implies the capacity of something to be performed.

This scenic capacity of the trope also indicates the mode in which the metaphor goes beyond simple description. The metaphor of the computer, for instance, hardly lends itself to a broader neural aesthetics that approaches both the awe and fascination that surround the brain. More specifically, the computer does not lend itself to the notion of either the organic object or the object that might grow or expand. The tree, on the other hand, is a useful metaphor because it entails an idea of organic growth, both individually and in terms of the forest of neurons. The tree is a material and even finite object, but it also does not have fixed boundaries. The tree is an emblem of complexity, growth and proliferation as much as a model for an object composed of a centre and branches in the case of the neuron, and an object with a 'stem' and 'bark' as in the case of the brain as a whole. In this sense, the tree is a complex symbolic object. It is both analogic and allegorical: a tree looks like a neuron and a brain, and it illustrates physiology, significance, and affect.

The combination of analogy and allegory means that the tree allows us to grasp not just the matter of the brain but that matter electrified. This combination offers us a rendering of the brain in language as it exists in both space and time. This is exemplified in the recent work of Stanislas Dehaene, in particular his work on neurology and reading. Dehaene's use of the tree to describe the organisation and 'location' of words in the brain adds another intriguing dimension to this tropological coupling of green and grey matter. According to Dehaene, we are able to read by virtue of the unique physiology of the human brain. What is important here, in Dehaene's account, is that humans did not evolve to read and, as such, reading is a relatively recent phenomenon in the long history of the species: we have only been reading for five thousand to ten thousand years.[10] It is also significant that other primates, closely related to the human species, are unable to read. One of the things that makes humans unique is their ability to read, and for Dehaene this comes from a unique physiology of the brain, in particular the functional resemblance between neural pathways and trees.

For Dehaene, 'every word is a tree.'[11] Physiologically, 'every written word is probably encoded by a hierarchical tree in which letters are grouped into larger-sized units, which are themselves grouped into syllables and words.'[12] Dehaene's work boldly suggests that the neural encoding of language happens through a spatial organisation in the brain, which, remarkably, resembles the aural and visual organisation of language. The matter of our brain spatially resembles the relations between the things we see and hear:

> Shapes that appear very similar, such as 'eight' and 'sight,' are sifted through a series of increasingly refined filters that progressively separate them and attach them to distinct entries in a mental lexicon, a virtual dictionary of all the words we have ever encountered.[13]

Our brain is structured so that, moving down this 'hierarchical tree', we decompose morphemes to understand the composition of words, even those that we may not initially recognise. In similar ways, the brain processes the graphemes that constitute the morphemes. As such, we move down or through a branching organisation that leads us to an increasingly specific understanding of the word, which captures its graphic and morphological singularity. For Dehaene, the 'final point in visual processing leaves the word parsed out into a hierarchical structure, a tree made up of branches of increasing sizes whose leaves are the letters.'[14]

10 Stanislas Dehaene, *Reading in the Brain: The New Science of How We Read* (New York: Penguin, 2009), 2.
11 Ibid., 21.
12 Ibid.
13 Ibid.
14 Ibid., 24.

Structure and logic come together seamlessly in Dehaene's unusual account of the reading process. Indeed, for Dehaene, it is the resemblance of human neural organisation to plants that allows for the recursive processing necessary for textual comprehension: 'Tree structures require a specific recursive neural code, as yet unidentified by electrophysiology, possibly unique to humans, and which may explain the singularity of human language and cognition.'[15] It is, moreover, the fact that human neurons are more 'tree-like' that enables the level of neural connectivity that facilitates reading comprehension:

> Some long distance connections, such as those that link the inferior prefrontal cortex to the occipital pole, may exist only in humans... Their dendritic trees, which receive incoming inputs, are bushier, and synaptic contacts are massively more numerous than those of other primates.[16]

So reading occurs, here, *like a tree.* This fascinating contention mixes the spatial and the temporal use of the metaphor. A physiological process is rendered material here and vice versa. These descriptions of the relation between biology and physiology, between matter and language, recursive code and dendritic branching, mirror the rhetorical dexterity of the metaphor of the tree, encompassing both analogy and allegory, structure and function, space and time. In other words, what is extraordinary about the longstanding metaphor of the brain as a tree, which is realised most fully in the recent work by Dehaene, is the fact that the trope is redoubled: the brain is, metaphorically, like a tree, but the form of this metaphor itself—specifically the bridging that occurs in this metaphor across matter and time, form and function—resembles the content.

To put this in the simplest terms, the metaphor of the brain as a tree is what we might call a 'formal allegory.' What is impor-

---

15 S. Dehaene, F. Meyniel, C. Wacogne, L. Wang, and C. Pallier, 'The Neural Representation of Sequences: From Transition Probabilities to Algebraic Patterns and Linguistic Trees,'*Neuron* 88, no. 1 (2015): 2–19, at 2, http://dx.doi.org/10.1016/j.neuron.2015.09.019.

16 Dehaene, *Reading in the Brain,* 24.

tant in Dehaene's use of the tree metaphor is not only the fact that function is mixed with structure, as in all good neurology, but that the use of the metaphor itself enacts the very process to which it refers. My understanding of formal allegory draws on Paul de Man's classic theorisation of tropes as the essential features of language. For de Man, interpretation is always an act of reading another meaning into the text, and 'any narrative is primarily the allegory of its own reading.'[17] This seemingly convoluted circuitry of textual allegory happens via what de Man calls the 'rhetorical model of the trope.'[18] In its structure of deferred or displaced reference, the model of trope mirrors the model of reading and interpretation. In de Man's theory of literature and meaning all language involves a displacement between referent and significance. A symbol of an olive branch, for instance, refers to 'reconciliation', but this meaning is entirely independent of the olive branch itself. The referent — the olive branch — is independent of its significance, which occurs by virtue of interpretation. This displacement is essential to all language: it always circumvents what it purports to capture in representation. In de Man's powerful rereading of this essential feature of language, all figural form in fact allegorises its own reading: the very construction of the trope, which involves a divergence rather than a bridge between referent and significance, is the same as the process that occurs between text and reader, between the words on a page and the instability of their interpretation. This 'rhetorical model' is also a 'formal allegory': an instance where the text allegorises its own formal processes. The metaphor of the brain as tree is a formal allegory insofar as it not only describes the brain, but also models it. It performs this latter function through the branching in language — from brain to tree — that occurs in the form of the metaphor itself and mirrors the neural and neuronal differentiation that it purports to describe.

Reading happens 'like a tree' twice here. For Dehaene, reading visually and logically resembles the structure of the tree and the functions implied in that structure. As this neural process is

17 Paul de Man, *Allegories of Reading: Figural Language in Rousseau, Nietzsche, Rilke, and Proust* (New Haven: Yale University Press, 1979), 76.
18 Ibid., 15.

rendered in the linguistic art of the trope, this structure is rep-
licated in the rhetorical form that bridges, differentiates, and
specialises, branching out from the initial referent. The 'jump'
that the trope enacts between the neural and the botanical does
not *represent* reading so much as *present* it: the material signature of the neuron indicates the abstract function, biological divergence indicates logical branching, and in order to represent
this in language we must, inevitably, inscribe the very process of
reading into the attempt to describe the branching of the brain
by branching our language, from brain to tree. The object — the
brain, here, and specifically the uniquely human ability to
read — is utterly implicated in its own representation. This is the
moment in which neurology comes to resemble the quantum
physics of the early twentieth century, which had to abandon the
notion of objectivity in scientific representation because the object changed depending on how it was observed. Reading, here,
is entailed in the very attempt to describe or understand reading.

In this botanical metaphor of the brain we have two versions
of the bifurcating path. The content of the description contains
a fork, a branching, and the form of the description equally contains a fork, a branching. This fork refuses the totality inherent in
less subtle comparisons such as the computer, by mimicking that
which it is meant to rhetorically subsume. As the trope attains its
symbolic power it also divests itself of the capacity to represent its
object, becoming implicated in it. In Walter Benjamin's words, an
allegory 'signifies precisely the non-being of what it represents'
and this observation is key to de Man's work as well.[19] In this sense,
allegory does not affix a meaning to something, or delimit meaning, but both extends and nullifies it simultaneously. The metaphor of the brain does this quite perfectly for neurology: just as
it renders the morphology and function of the brain in language,
making it communicable and recognizable, all recognizability is
lost as the trope refuses its own status as metaphor and becomes
its object. The formal allegory — the metaphor, here — is significant because it does something scientifically invalid: the mode of

19 Walter Benjamin, quoted in Paul De Man, *Blindness and Insight: Essays
    in the Rhetoric of Contemporary Criticism* (Minneapolis: University of
    Minnesota Press, 1983), 35.

representation mirrors the object of representation. In this sense, language threatens to dislodge from its status as representation and occupy a strange presentational position. The very formal qualities of the trope start to threaten the idea of formalism itself: the idea that something can be represented, outside of its context and presence, in a stable notation system. This allegory, then, complicates the simple representational structure of language at issue here and implicates it in its object.

Allegory as Bifurcating Path

Allegory, here, is the road not to the scientific object, but instead is much more akin to a 'garden of bifurcating paths', whose metaphysics departs from the critical regime that still governs scientific description. The metaphysics of neurobotanical allegory is, instead, the kind that belongs to what de Man calls the 'temporal labyrinth of interpretation.'[20] Jorge Luis Borges' short story 'The Garden of Forking Paths' is a classic example of formal allegory, and as a third bifurcating line in this essay, it provides us with a theory of narrative with which to understand this strange implication of 'neurobotanical' language in its object. 'The Garden of Forking Paths' (otherwise known as 'The Garden of Bifurcating Paths') is a story about the relation between language and time, and it echoes many of Borges' other stories in that it deals with questions of the infinite, in particular the possibility of a sort of infinite book. The story opens with a reference to a battle against the Serre-Montaubaun line in Liddell Hart's *History of World War I*. This battle, we are told, is illuminated by a statement written by a certain Dr. Yu Tsun, and the rest of the story presents Tsun's account for our consideration. Dr Tsun, we find out, was a German spy in World War I, who was captured in Britain after he discovered the location of an important British artillery park. He was arrested, however, not for locating this information but for killing an eminent sinologist by the name of Stephen Albert. Tsun had realised that he was being pursued by an intelligence agent, an 'Irishman at the orders of the English,' Richard Madden, and that his time was up, and he needed to communicate

20 Benjamin, quoted in ibid., 35.

to German intelligence the name of the town where the artillery park was located.[21] The town's name was Albert, and by making front-page news for killing Stephen Albert, Tsun successfully alerted German intelligence to the name of the secret location. However, the meeting between Stephen Albert and Yu Tsun is not an entirely random one. Tsun tells us that he grew up in the 'symmetrical gardens of Hai Feng' and that his great grandfather was Ts'ui Pen, 'who was governor of Yunan province and who renounced all temporal power in order to write a novel containing more characters than the *Hung Lu Meng* and construct a labyrinth in which all men would lose their way.'[22] Stephen Albert is an expert in Ts'ui Pen's work, and the brief meeting between the two men reveals, for Yu Tsun, the way that his mysterious ancestor managed to construct an infinite book.

Albert, who is excited to meet an ancestor of Ts'ui Pen, explains that '"The Garden of Forking Paths" is an incomplete, but not false, image of the universe as conceived by Ts'ui Pen.... He believed in an infinite series of times, a growing, dizzying net of divergent, convergent and parallel times.'[23] Although Pen's so-called 'novel' appears only as 'chaotic manuscripts,' Albert tells Tsun that he has solved the mystery of this profoundly important yet seemingly disordered work:

'The Garden of Forking Paths' is a huge riddle, or parable, whose subject is time; that secret purpose forbids Ts'ui Pen the merest mention of its name. To *always* omit a word, to employ awkward metaphors and obvious circumlocutions, is perhaps the most emphatic way of calling attention to that word. It is, at any rate, the tortuous path chosen by the devious Ts'ui Pen at each and every one of the turnings of his inexhaustible novel.[24]

21 Jorge Luis Borges, 'The Garden of Forking Paths,' in *Collected Fictions,* trans. Andrew Hurley (New York: Penguin Books, 1999), 119.

22 Ibid., 122.

23 Ibid., 127.

24 Ibid., 126–27.

In their brief time together, before Tsun shoots the eminent sinologist, Albert explains that Ts'ui Pen's work is a giant riddle. And, like all riddles, it omits the key to unravelling the conundrum. In this case, it omits the word 'time.' In Pen's garden of forking paths, characters do not choose one fate or future, but many, with each future in turn consisting of many forking paths. Yu Tsun is given a sudden impression of Ts'ui Pen's 'labyrinth' — not a vision of it, as such, but some more ephemeral sense of the infinity that the labyrinth opened: 'I sensed that the dew-drenched garden that surrounded the house was saturated, infinitely, with invisible persons. Those persons were Albert and myself- secret, busily at work, multiform — in other dimensions of time.'[25]

Ts'ui Pen's bifurcating paths are temporal; they are divergent futures. Stephen Albert discovers the 'secret' to the garden because he reads the text allegorically, even if his is an unusual type of allegorical reading, far more speculative than traditional allegorical interpretation. Ts'ui Pen's novel is, in Stephen Albert's understanding, an allegory of time. Here lies one of the more interesting aspects of 'The Garden of Forking Paths': there is a split between the narrative that is described in the story (Ts'ui Pen's novel) and the form of the story itself (Yu Tsun's account, in Borges' short story), a common Borgesian construction. In 'The Garden of Forking Paths', we are dealing with three layers of narrative: the framing narrative, which introduces Yu Tsun's 'statement,' rendering it an artefact within the story itself; Yu Tsun's linear account of his murder of Stephen Albert; and, of course the 'novel' by Ts'ui Pen, which is described in the story, although we never actually see the text. There is a fourth narrative dimension here that is also relevant: the presence of a kind of hermeneutic endeavour that we see in Albert's interpretation of Ts'ui Pen's work as well as in the German recognition of Yu Tsun's message. Albert reads a double meaning into the absence of a word, and the Germans recognise a double meaning in the Yu Tsun's crime. Recognition, here, involves being able to register the polysemy of a certain word in the context of intention: Albert's name is recognised as exceeding its immediate signifi-

25 Ibid., 127.

cation and meaning something entirely different. It is the very act of reading, rather than writing, which facilitates this 'bifurcation' in meaning, suggestive of the temporal rather than the spatial infinity that Ts'ui Pen creates. Here we encounter — to paraphrase de Man again — the 'temporal labyrinth of interpretation,' another layer of 'bifurcation' that forks away from the literal meaning of words.

The allegory for time is embedded in a narrative that revolves around textual interpretation. In each example of textual interpretation in this story, what we see is the displacement of either a voice or a word from where it should be. At the most basic level, the word 'Albert' means something entirely different to the reader from its intended or referential or contextually based meaning. As such, the story is itself composed of bifurcating paths in language: action occurs because of acts of interpretation and the ability to recognise concealed or hermetic meanings in words. Kyoo Lee has referred to de Man's concept of allegory as 'a calligraphy of time,' which is, equally, a perfect description of Ts'ui Pen's labyrinth. So, inasmuch as the labyrinth in this story is time, it is also language as a temporal medium. It is not for nothing that Ts'ui Pen's route to discovering time as the ultimate labyrinth happens through his writing a novel. What is important, here and in many of Borges' stories, is that this particular 'novel,' this 'garden of forking paths,' is not presented for direct consumption. In other words, the path to Ts'ui Pen's extraordinary work is forked away from a direct representation of this work. And although we read of the bifurcating futures in Ts'ui Pen's novel, the text enacts it by virtue of the multiple levels of narrative, bifurcating between frame, quotation, narrative, and interpretation. In this sense, Yu Tsun's story is also an allegory of its composition.

David Baulch has argued that Borges' short story offers a challenge to literary criticism in the form of a 'multiverse' that contests the dominant configuration between narrative and time. He writes that 'foremost among the concepts of classical/empirical science that structure literary realism in particular, and narrative in general, is the assumption that time is a more or less endless linear progression and that events within time refer to a single-valued, objectively verifiable world.'[26] Insofar as Borges' 'The Garden of Bifurcating Paths' is a formal allegory, it refuses both the linear progression and the single world that is recognisable for literary criticism. Baulch claims that the problem with literary criticism is that it remains thoroughly 'Newtonian': 'Despite roughly a century of study of the various paradoxes quantum phenomena present for science's understanding of the behavior of the material world at its most minute, literary criticism continues to regard its object in predominantly Newtonian terms.'[27] In addition to Baulch's reading of the 'multiverse' in Borges' fiction, formal allegory is an important way of approaching this textual inventiveness, not least because this type of allegory, as de Man notes, extinguishes its object as it defines it. It is stories like 'The Garden of Forking Paths' that challenge modes of reading that privilege distinctions between subject and object, cause and effect, and put under pressure our ideas about narrative time.

In order to access the full satisfaction of Borges' story, we cannot take the story at face value, reading it as a strange and singularly unsatisfying account of a seemingly impossible infinite book. We need, instead, to be able to read the story with full attention to the bifurcations in the narrative and, above all, to the way that these bifurcations facilitate an elaborate formal allegory of the relation between time and language. In order to understand allegory as a bifurcating path, we need to be able to read the story in non-linear, or even non-Newtonian, terms, reading across the different levels of narrative and understanding that the allegory, here, serves precisely to bifurcate the lines of the narrative rather than, as in traditional allegorical interpretation, to fix and stabilise meaning. This modality of reading, taught to us by an exquisite formal allegory, must be applied to the 'neurobotanical world,' to use Ascoli's term again, to grasp the implication of the strange formal allegory deployed by the sciences. The tree undoes our ability to represent the brain as much as it provides a

26 David M. Baulch, 'Time, Narrative, and the Multiverse: Post-Newtonian Narrative in Borges's "The Garden of the Forking Paths" and Blake's Vala or The Four Zoas,' *The Comparatist* 27 (May 2003): 56–78, at 56, https://muse.jhu.edu/article/414766/pdf.

27 Ibid., 56–57.

vital key to understanding it. It differentiates the scientific object, rather than containing it. In other words, the branches of the neuro-botanical tree are temporal as well as spatial — the word trees that Dehaene writes of offer routes to both literal and allegorical interpretation.

Future (Neural) Forests: Plant Sapience as Allegory

The tree is a powerful metaphor in neurology because it allows simultaneously for a temporal and a spatial metaphor. As a formal allegory, the tree models the object that it is meant to describe, implicating metaphor in that which language is only supposed to represent. Borges' 'The Garden of Bifurcating Paths' offers a key to imagining this neurobotanical world, not as a stable case of symbolic illustration but as a three-dimensional set of intersecting and bifurcating narratives, whose interaction brings into being a clear scientific object and extinguishes it simultaneously.

This knotting together of tree and brain through formal allegory also presents a modality by which to address one of the new challenges emerging out of evolutionary biology. One of the key challenges in plant science today relates to our ability to understand the inverse of what this essay has been preoccupied with: plant thought. New studies of plant 'learning' and memory suggest that plants are capable of what we might call 'thought'. Part of the difficulty in approaching current work on plant learning relates to our inability to see plants as temporal objects. What is unique about our relation to plants is that we do not perceive them temporally, or when we do, it is only through crude schemes of growth rather than change, behaviour, or learning. Monica Gagliano's recent work on plant learning provides experimental grounds with which to begin to conceive of plants differently. Although we have long understood plants' capacities for habituation, whether plants could 'learn through forming associations [has] remained unclear.'[28] Gagliano and her colleagues embarked on a series of 'Pavlovian' experiments to test whether plants were able to learn through forming associations. They dis-

28 Monica Gagliano et al., 'Learning by Association in Plants,' *Scientific Reports* 6 (2016): 1–9, at 1, doi:10.1038/srep38427.

covered that if plants were exposed to a fan that accompanied their light source, they would respond by growing in the direction of the fan even when it was no longer accompanied by the light source. These experiments revealed:

> Learned behaviour prevails over innate positive tropism to light, which is thought to be the major determinant of growth direction in plants. In both experiments, the ability of seedlings to anticipate both the imminent arrival of light ('when') and its direction ('where') based on the presence and position of the fan indicates that plants are able to encode both temporal and spatial information and modify their behaviour under the control of environmental cues.[29]

Prudence Gibson, in her report on Gagliano's experiments, notes that one of the key problems presented by this work is that 'there is no vocabulary that can be used to talk about brain-like plant structures beyond mere vascular and survival processes, nor about decision-making, sentience, intelligence, learning, and memory in the plant world.'[30]

This is evident in Gagliano et al's work. Key to their findings is the fact that plants can think, although the presence of 'traces' of this thought differs from anything one might find in neurology:

> In multicellular organisms with a nervous system, changes in the synaptic strength between neurons, for example, can be stored as a memory trace that sustain associative learning. In plants and other organisms that do not have a nervous system, modifications of the patterns of interactions between molecules and communication between cells can be stored in a way rather similar to neural networks.[31]

29 Gagliano et al., 'Learning by Association in Plants,' 3.
30 Prudence Gibson, 'Pavlov's Plants: New Study Shows that Plants can Learn from Experience,' *The Conversation,* December 6, 2016, http://theconversation.com/pavlovs-plants-new-study-shows-plants-can-learn-from-experience-69794.
31 Gagliano et al., 'Learning by Association in Plants,' 4–5.

The authors acknowledge the difficulty involved in conceptualising plant sentience without the presence of a measurable, observable brain, and circumvent the radical acephaly of this vegetal thought by positing a comparison between the information networks of the brain — ironically, in the work of Dehaene and others, the 'brain trees' — and plant epigenetics: 'Presumably, then, the mechanisms maintaining associative learning operate in plants as in other organisms on the basis of fundamental 'rules' that alter the flow of information by modifying the shape and connections within a network via epigenetic changes.'[32] Although Gagliano et al. do not pursue the issue of these material traces of thought, if we read their conclusions in terms of the neurological preoccupation with botanical metaphor, this bifurcation from phytological behaviour to the logic of brain processes presents a fascinating reciprocal gesture that mirrors and complicates the question of the 'neurobotanical.'

Understanding plant sentience requires a prior conception of the tree as no longer an object; it requires a supplementation of the visual and spatial relation of the tree with temporality, both in terms of the temporal nature of learning and epigenetics. It also seems to require a similar allegorical structure to the neurobotanical metaphor, in that the object of thought is extinguished as it is rendered in language. Although the mechanisms that facilitate learning follow the same networked, bifurcating structures as the nervous system in multicellular organisms, there is no nervous system to speak of here. Obviously no plant has a brain, and we cannot measure neural currents that suggest thought or consciousness. This is a kind of acephalous thinking, which happens without some material centre devoted to the orchestration of cognisance. The comparison to neurological structures in other organisms functions to reveal the absence of a brain just as it posits an analogy to physiological organisation of thought. This presents yet another fork in the neurobotanical garden of bifurcating paths: vegetal thought that, to use Lee's term again, can be traced as a 'calligraphy of time'.

Plant sapience may then require the sort of language that Ts'ui Pen achieves in his 'The Garden of Forking Paths': descrip-

32 Ibid., 5.

tion and representation that is not Newtonian. Allegories that fork are valuable not for some stable parallel 'deciphering' of meaning but instead for a kind of linguistic differentiation that enacts the 'branching' of thought common to both brains and trees both figuratively and formally. Plant science that attempts to represent plants as capable of thought without necessarily being subjects in the traditional sense would benefit precisely from the non-Newtonian and non-objective modalities of language that are already implied in neuroscientific metaphor. Biology is now presenting us with an inverse form of 'neurobotany' to the one I considered in this essay, which involves a restitution of the capacity of thought to the form of the plant. These future 'forests' of sentience will also need to be 'gardens of forking paths' in the sense that the powerful image of a neurobotanical world now describes that which was meant to be supplementary to it. Where the tree had always been the illustration that describes the brain, the two may mutually illustrate each other now, in a double allegorical bifurcation. Attending to the types of allegories used in science, and their implications in scientific objects, allows us to account for the dissolution of the scientific object that is subject to allegorical reading. It is precisely this textual dissolution that also opens up the allegory to other meanings and other connections, including this image of plant thought.

8

Metaphoric Plants: Goethe's *Metamorphosis of Plants* and the Metaphors of Reason

Dalia Nassar

Philosophers have long appealed to various metaphors or images to describe, elucidate, or explicate reason and its place in the universe. These metaphors usually came from the natural world, and more often than not, they involved trees. Porphyry's tree might be the most well-known example of a philosopher invoking the metaphor of the plant in order to elucidate the structure of the world and the place of reason within it, but it was by no means the only. In his *Principles of Philosophy* (1644), René Descartes uses the metaphor of a tree to explicate his understanding of the various sciences and of the place of philosophy (as metaphysics) within his system: 'The roots are metaphysics, the trunk is physics, and the branches emerging from the trunk are all the other sciences, which may be reduced to three principal ones, namely medicine, mechanics and morals.'[1] These metaphors provided (and continue to provide) significant means by which to articulate fundamental philosophical ideas. Porphyry's and Descartes' images express unity, on the one hand, and hierarchy, on the other. While Descartes' metaphor implies that reason furnishes the foundation of reality, Porphyry's regards reason (the highest

---

1 René Descartes, "Principles of Philosophy," in *The Philosophical Writings of Descartes,* Vol. 1, eds. John Cunningham, Robert Stoothoff, and Dugald Murdoch (Cambridge: Cambridge University Press, 1985), 186.

branch of the tree) as the most complex manifestation of what is already present in other parts of the natural world (in other branches of the tree). By contrast, Leibniz's image of reason as a seed 'implanted' in the mind by God — an image invoked to explicate the notion of innate ideas — carries a different implication: human reason is eternal, independent from the ephemeral world of the senses.

Despite the prevalence of plant-based metaphors in the history of philosophy (from ancient to early modern[2]), in the *Critique of Pure Reason* (1781), Immanuel Kant appeals to the image of the animal body in order to describe reason and elucidate the structure of his system. Significantly, Kant did not identify reason with only one aspect or element of the animal body, but with the whole of the body. By 1807, however, reason is once again identified with the plant. In the preface to the *Phenomenology of Spirit* (1807), G.W.F. Hegel writes that his method involves the 'progressive unfolding of the truth,' and goes on to explicate this unfolding in terms of plant development: 'the bud disappears in the bursting-forth of the blossom, and one might say that the former is refuted by the latter; similarly, when the fruit appears, the blossom is shown up in its turn as a false manifestation of the plant, and the fruit now emerges as the truth of it instead....'[3] Hegel, however, was not the first to recast reason in terms of the metaphor of the plant. Almost a decade before the publication of the *Phenomenology,* Friedrich Schlegel and Novalis had appealed to the image of the seed and its development in the soil to describe the character of thought and they modeled their systematic ambitions on the developmental structure of the plant.

What inspired these transitions in metaphor and how did these metaphors influence our understanding of rationality? What effects did these varying conceptions of reason — modeled

---

2   As Maryanne Cline Horowitz argues, the image of the seed that grows to become a tree was widespread in ancient, medieval, and Renaissance theories of knowledge and virtue: the seed of virtue and knowledge becomes the tree of wisdom. See Maryanne Cline Horowitz, *Seeds of Virtue and Knowledge* (Princeton: Princeton University Press, 1998).

3   G.W.F. Hegel, *Phenomenology of Spirit,* trans. A.V. Miller (Oxford: Oxford University Press, 1977), 2.

on the animal body and on plant development—have on our understanding of our place in the universe? These are the questions I'd like to consider here. To answer them, I will argue, we must trace the development from Kant to Romanticism (and Hegel) via Goethe, and more specifically, Goethe's distinctive focus on form and transformation, as opposed to mere structure. It is this emphasis on the 'transforming form,' that, I believe, inspired Goethe's admiring contemporaries and led them to invoke the symbol of the plant to describe and illuminate the historical, grounded, and transforming character of reason that became the hallmark of modern philosophy.

Kant's Metaphor

Although plant metaphors were traditionally important sources for elucidating the structure of the universe, plants themselves were not at the centre of philosophical discussions of nature. By contrast, animals and animal souls pervade discussions from Aristotle through medieval and early modern philosophy. Thus it was animals, and the 'problem' of animal generation, that posed the greatest difficulty for mechanical philosophers in the 17th century, as they sought to reduce all material phenomena to the laws of motion.[4] It was also animals that were at the centre of the 18th-century debate between epigenesist and preformationist models of generation. Chick embryos were placed under a microscope in order to demonstrate the existence of pre-formed germs from the beginning of development—as the preformationists argued—or its opposite—i.e., the epigenesist view that the embryo is originally inchoate, and its form develops over time.[5] Plants were excluded from the debate.

---

4 See, for instance, Justin Smith, ed., *The Problem of Animal Generation in Early Modern Philosophy* (Cambridge: Cambridge University Press, 2012).

5 Shirley Roe's book, *Matter, Life and Generation: Eighteenth-Century Embryology and the Haller-Wolff Debate* (Cambridge: Cambridge University Press, 1981), remains the key scholarly contribution on this area of research. Roe examines the debate between Albrecht von Haller (who espouses preformation) and Caspar Wolff (who espouses epigen-

Kant differed from his contemporaries in that, from early on, he placed plants and animals side by side, and argued that both were inexplicable from mechanical principles. Thus, in his 1755 essay *Universal Natural History and Theory of the Heavens,* he contends that it is vastly more difficult to explain the origin of a 'plant or insect' than it is to explain the origin of the solar systems (AA 1: 230).[6] His claim seems to assert that a plant or an insect cannot be (at least not easily) explicated through the mechanical laws of motion. He does not, however, clarify why this is the case. After all, it might simply be the case that the caterpillar's body is an infinitely more complex mechanism, one that is beyond the grasp of our finite mind. In his 1763 essay *The Only Possible Proof for the Existence of God,* Kant is more explicit: plants and animals exhibit a structure or a unity, which cannot be explicated through the mechanical laws of motion (AA 2: 107). What distinguishes animals and plants, in other words, is not a matter of degree (they are not simply more complex and thus more difficult to explicate), but of kind: the unity between the parts of a plant or an animal body fundamentally differs from the mechanical unities achieved through the laws of motion.

Kant's remarks strongly contrast with those of his contemporaries, especially with regard to plants. The German metaphysician Christian Wolff (1679–1754), who coined the term 'teleol-

esis), which was focused on the chick embryo. Plants were so far outside of the debate on generation that when Abraham Trembley presented his discovery of the fresh water polyp to the Academie des Sciences in 1741, the scientific community came to a halt. The fact that the polyp could be divided into two parts, and out of these parts, two new polyps emerged, not only challenged the preformationist model (where, one must ask, are the pre-existing germs from which the new polyp emerged?), but it also undermined the hard and fast distinction — a scientific orthodoxy — between plants and animals. The polyp, after all, evinced both plant-like and animal-like characteristics, such that it was impossible to categorize it. For more on the consequences of Trembley's discovery, see Stephen Gaukroger, *The Collapse of Mechanism and the Rise of Sensibility* (Oxford: Oxford University Press, 2010), 357ff.

6   References to Kant will follow the Akademie Ausgabe edition pagination (AA), with the exception of the *Critique of Pure Reason,* which follows the A/B pagination.

ogy' and argued that it must play a role in our understanding of physical beings, regarded plants as a mere means for the service of humans and animals, writing in 1737 that plants are the 'means [*Mittel*] through which humans and animals could be preserved.'[7] This view is echoed by other Enlightenment thinkers, such as Hermann Samuel Reimarus (1694–1768), who in 1755 argued that plants must be understood as 'machines which are produced for the benefit of living beings,'[8] and five years later added that a plant is 'a composite machine, created out of many smaller machines' — a description that coheres with the general view of the time.[9] Carl Linnaeus, the most important botanist of the 18th-century, described plants as 'hydraulic machines,' whose growth and nutrition is explicable through mechanical principles.[10]

Though Kant's statements signal disagreement with his contemporaries, in light of the widespread view of plants as mere machines, it is not surprising that in 1781, he chose to describe reason not in terms of the plant but rather in terms of the animal body. In the section titled 'Architectonic of Pure Reason,' in the *Critique of Pure Reason,* Kant exclaims to his readers that reason

7   Christian Friedrich Wolff, *Vernünftige Gedancken von den Absichten der natürlichen Dinge* (Frankfurt and Leipzig: Rengerische Buchhandlung, 1713), 464. I want to thank Ryan Feigenbaum for this and the references to Reimarus below. See Ryan Feigenbaum, *The Epistemic Foundations of German Biology 1790–1802* (PhD diss., Villanova University, 2016), chap. 3.

8   Hermann Samuel Reimarus, *Abhandlungen von den vornehmsten Wahrheiten der natürlichen Religion* (Hamburg: Johann Carl Bohn, 1766), 172.

9   Hermann Samuel Reimarus, *Allgemeine Betrachtungen über die Triebe der Thiere, hauptsächlich über ihre Kunsttriebe* (Hamburg: Johann Carl Bohn, 1773), 321.

10 See Werner Ingensiep, "Organismus und Leben bei Kant," in *Kant Reader,* eds. W. Ingensiep et al. (Würzburg: Königshausen and Neumann, 2004), 125. As Ingensiep elsewhere puts it, in the 18th-century "a plant was viewed either as a physical vessel with canals and valves in which liquids are flowing or as an organic machine or as a chemical laboratory." See W. Ingensiep, "Organism, Epigenesis, and Life in Kant's Thinking," *Annals of the History and Philosophy of Biology* 11 (2006): 59–84, at 64.

is like an 'animal organism,' insofar as in reason 'the whole is...articulated and not heaped together; it can, to be sure, grow internally but not externally, like an animal body, whose growth does not add a limb but rather makes each limb stronger and fitter for its end without any alteration of proportion' (A833/B861). Reason, in other words, is not governed by external laws (such as the laws of motion) and reason's parts (the forms of thought, i.e., the categories of the understanding) are not simply 'heaped' together. Rather, like the animal body, Kant contends, reason grows according to an internal principle, and its parts are manifestations of this principle — they are coordinated elements of a unified whole.

Kant's metaphor has two significant outcomes. In the first instance, it implies that reason can only be understood (explicated) through its own principles or laws, or more specifically, through an *internal* critique of pure reason. It also implies that the various expressions of reason (the forms of thought or the categories of the understanding) are inherently connected to one another and to the whole (to reason). These two points are the essence of the metaphor; however, given that in 1781 Kant did not provide a clear explication of the structure of animal (and plant) bodies, its meaning and implications may have been lost on some of his readers. In fact, his readers had to wait nine years, for the publication of the *Critique of Judgment* (1790), in order to fully comprehend Kant's metaphor and its significance for his understanding of the character of reason and his system of philosophy.

Kant on (the Mechanical Inexplicability of) Plants and Animals

It is a remarkable coincidence that Kant's *Critique of Judgment* and Goethe's *Metamorphosis of Plants* were published in the same year. It is equally remarkable that neither was aware of the other's publication, and yet both placed significant emphasis on plants. The *Critique of Judgment* does not, however, concern plants specifically (nor does it specifically concern nature — the first part of the work is on aesthetic judgment). Nonetheless, by claiming that plants are — like animals — organized beings, it initiates an important shift in the way in which plants were regarded.

Kant disagrees with Wolff, Reimarus, and Linneaus in one key respect: he regards plants as organized beings that fundamentally differ from machines. For this reason, he argues, in order to grasp plants and animals we must invoke a non-mechanical principle, which he designates as 'teleological,' but which should not be confused with Wolff's conception of teleology.[11] For Kant, the teleological principle in organized beings must be distinguished from what he calls 'external teleology,' i.e., the view that natural entities serve some *external* end, such as human needs and desires (i.e., Wolff's view). In contrast, Kant contends, organized beings exhibit 'internal teleology.' This is because the end (telos) is *internal* to organized beings — i.e., organisms are their *own* end, such that means and end are fundamentally indistinguishable. In an organism, the means are the material components and the form that these components take. The means serve to generate and maintain the end (the organism). The organism is, however, not separable from its material and structural make-up (what, after all, is an organism if it is divorced from its material-structural make-up?). This is one respect in which organisms differ from machines: in a machine, the end is external to the machine in two ways — it is imposed by something external (i.e., the maker of the machine) and the machine is a means to a goal that is external to itself (the delivery of a product, for instance). Thus, while the machine is certainly organized — its parts act *for the sake of an end* and are brought together in order to achieve this end — it is not *self*-organizing.[12] Though Kant remains agnostic as to whether plants (and animals) are *in fact* internally organized (he maintains that we must regard them *as if* they were organized),

11 On the difference between Kant and Wolff's conceptions of teleology, see Hein van den Berg, "The Wolffian roots of Kant's teleology," *Studies in History and Philosophy of Science Part C: Studies in History and Philosophy of Biological and Biomedical Science* 44, no. 44 (2013): 724–34, https://doi.org/10.1016/j.shpsc.2013.07.003.

12 On the difference between the two kinds of mechanical inexplicability (in machines and in organisms), see Hannah Ginsborg, "Two Kinds of Mechanical Inexplicability in Kant and Aristotle," *Journal of the History of Philosophy* 42, no. 1 (2004): 33–65.

his claim is relevant in this context: plants (just like animals), are from our perspective mechanically inexplicable.[13]

According to Kant, an entity can be explicated through the mechanical laws of motion if the activity or behaviour of its parts can be explicated through these laws. Thus, any composite (as opposed to simple) entity would be mechanically explicable if a) it is explicable through its parts, and b) these parts behave according to the laws of motion. Thus a complex entity is mechanically explicable if it fulfills two conditions: the whole is explicable through the parts, and the relations between the parts are purely mechanical. But what does it mean for the parts to relate purely mechanically toward one another?

In the *Critique of Judgment* Kant describes mechanism as 'the capacity for movement' (AA 5: 374), 'in accordance with the mere laws of motion' (AA 5: 390). In his 1786 *Metaphysical Foundations of Natural Science,* Kant had explained that the laws of motion are purely spatial. Thus, in a mechanical unity, the parts' coming together or moving apart has nothing to do with a principle that inheres in the parts or in their qualitative (as opposed to quantitative-spatial) relations; rather, the behaviour and action of the parts are dependent entirely on their spatial location and determination, i.e., the laws of motion, such that any change in their activity is explicable through their place in space and the laws governing motion in space. As Kant puts it in the *Metaphysical Foundations,* 'matter, as mere object of outer senses, has no other determinations except those of external relations in space, and therefore undergoes no change except by motion' (AA 4: 543). Kant contrasts a mechanical unity with a 'determinate unity,' which is not simply the outcome of its parts and their extrinsic relations (spatial forces), but exhibits an internal principle according to which the parts come together (AA 5: 421).

This means that while the relation between parts in a mechanical unity is governed by efficient causality — two parts in-

---

13 For an account of why Kant remains agnostic on this issue, see my "Analogical Reflection as a Source for the Science of Life: Kant on the Possibility of the Biological Sciences," *Studies in History and Philosophy of Science* 58 (Aug. 2016): 57–66, https://doi.org/10.1016/j.shpsa.2016.03.008.

teract with one another in accordance with the external laws of motion — the relations between parts in 'determinate unity' are not governed by efficient causality.[14] For the relation is not purely external, but internal: it forms the parts, such that they could not exist outside of this relation.

Kant's first explication of this view invokes trees (AA 5: 371). His claim is that trees — plants, in general — are mechanically inexplicable because of three key characteristics which they share with animals and which reveal plants as both ends and means of themselves, or, as he puts it, 'cause and effect of themselves' (AA 5: 370). The first concerns the plant as a species: a particular tree species maintains its genetic line through individuals (thus, every individual is both cause and effect of its species). The second concerns the individual plant's ability to maintain itself through nutrition and healing (its growth and its ability to overcome injury are effects of its own activities). And, finally, the third characteristic considers the tree as a complex rather than simple being, which is nonetheless *not* the result or outcome of independently existing parts. In a plant, the parts cannot exist independently of the whole (unlike cogs in machines, branches or leaves cannot exist *prior* to the plant). If the parts do not pre-exist the whole, then their movement and behaviour may not be reducible to the movement and behaviour of simple parts in space (i.e., the laws of motion). In fact, if the parts exist only in the whole and in relation to one another, it follows that their movement and behaviour are inextricably linked to the whole, and, in turn, their relations are not purely external, based on their place in space. After all, if they did not pre-exist the whole, but only emerged *with one another,* i.e., through the whole, then their relation cannot

14 Efficient causality is the only causality that makes sense from the perspective of the mechanical laws of motion. Efficient causality is a relation that occurs through the movement of independent parts in space, and is thus entirely spatial or external. The kind of change that efficient causality effects is, in turn, entirely external — explicable by the laws of motion. This goes hand in hand with Kant's position in the *Metaphysical Foundations,* where he argues that all change in matter must be entirely external (thus causality as the source of change must be external) (AA 4: 543).

be based on their spatial location — it must be based on another principle: the whole of which they are part.[15]

What this means is that in an organized unity, as Kant calls it, the relation between the parts is *intrinsic* to each of the parts. The unity is inscribed onto the individual part, such that the individual part exists only because it is a part within *this* whole. Thus Kant writes that the parts 'reciprocally produce each other' (AA 5: 373) — no part is independent of the other parts. For this reason, he goes on, an organized entity is 'both an *organized* and *self-organizing* being' (AA 5: 374).

What Kant recognized in the structures of plants and animals, and what led him to identify reason with the animal body, is the fact that the whole (reason) is not an outcome or product of its parts (i.e., the various faculties of cognition and their products: sensations, images, and concepts). Rather, in both organized beings and reason we witness a unity that underlies and makes the variety possible: the parts (the forms of thought, the categories of the understanding) are inextricably tied to this unity, such that they only exist within this unity. What they are, and how they function is, in turn, not dependent on some external law — the law of motion in the case of organisms, and in the case of forms of thought, either contingent empirical sensations or innate ideas, implanted in the human mind through a divine act without reference to the nature of the mind (the whole).[16] As Kant explains in the *Critique of Pure Reason,* if we conceived of the forms of

15 It is here, in the relations between the parts, and the role that the whole plays in determining their relations, that the fundamental difference between organisms and machines emerges. For while the parts of a machine are useless independently of the whole (and thus function only in the whole), they can and do exist prior to the whole, such that their relations — the relations between the parts — are independent of the whole. The relations are purely external, based on efficient causality and the laws of motion. See also Ginsborg, "Two Kinds of Mechanical Inexplicability."

16 For a detailed account of how Kant uses this metaphor to explicate the relation between reason and the forms of thought, see Daniela Helbig and Dalia Nassar, "The Metaphor of Epigenesis: Kant, Blumenbach and Herder," *Studies in History and Philosophy of Science* 58 (2016): 98–107, https://doi.org/10.1016/j.shpsa.2016.05.003.

thought (the categories) as 'implanted' by God, then we must conclude that they are highly arbitrary — God could have, after all, implanted a different set of categories. By contrast, the notion that the forms of thought can only exist within this unity, that this unity inheres in each of the forms, implies that these forms are not the outcome of contingent circumstances (specific sensations or a divine act), but are necessary. For just as in an animal body it is impossible for a heart to exist or function without a kidney, and vice versa, so it is impossible for any form of thought (any category) to exist or function without the other forms of thought. They are inherently dependent on one another, and this demonstrates that these forms (and only these forms) are the necessary forms of thought.

Ultimately Kant's insight is that in an organized being, difference and unity are absolutely simultaneous, such that the different parts *exist only insofar as they are part of a unity*. Kant does not, however, consider the specific character of the different parts of this unity — the members of an animal or plant body, the forms of thought — or their distinctive relations. By focusing solely on the part-whole relation, Kant neglects the relations between the parts, and in so doing, fails to recognize an important difference between plants and animals — a difference that guides Goethe's interest in plants and leads him to the view that plants exemplify, in outward or visible form, what takes place internally in animals.

Goethe's *Metamorphosis of Plants*[17]

It was during his Italian journey (1786–1788) that Goethe undertook serious study of plants and formulated his idea of an archetypal plant or *Urpflanze*. In April 1787, at the Botanical Garden in Palermo, he was struck by both the diversity and unity

17 Aspects of this section are based on two previously published articles: "Romantic Empiricism after the 'End of Nature'," in *The Relevance of Romanticism: Essays on German Romantic Philosophy,* ed. Dalia Nassar (New York: Oxford University Press, 2014), and "Sensibility and Organic Unity: Kant, Goethe and the Plasticity of Cognition," *Intellectual History Review* 25, no. 3 (2015): 311–26.

of what he observed. As he puts it in his *Italian Journey*: 'I was confronted with so many kinds of fresh, new forms, I was taken again by my old fanciful idea: might I not discover the *Urpflanze* amid this multitude? Such a thing must exist after all! How else would I recognize this or that form as being a plant, if they were not all constructed according to one model' (MA 15, 327).[18] What is it, Goethe asks himself, which enables him to recognize the manifold varieties of plants as plant? Or, what is the unifying principle of plants?

It is not until a few months later, however, that Goethe furnishes an answer. In a report from July 1787 in which he includes the passage quoted above, he adds the important conclusion: 'it has become apparent to me that in the plant organ we ordinarily call the leaf a true Proteus is concealed, who can hide and reveal himself in all formations. From top to bottom, a plant is all leaf, united so inseparably with the future bud that one cannot be imagined without the other' (MA 15, 456). By this Goethe does not mean that the plant is reducible to the physical leaf, but that the parts of the plant are various manifestations of what he saw as a single organ. The process through which this archetypal organ manifests itself in the various parts of the plant, achieving various functions and undergoing changes of form, is what Goethe in 1790 called 'metamorphosis.'

His 1790 *Essay on the Metamorphosis of Plants* is dedicated to presenting this insight in detail. An observation of the plant, Goethe begins, reveals 'that certain of their external parts sometimes undergo a change and assume, either entirely or in greater or lesser degree, the form of the parts adjacent to them' (MA 12, 29, no. 1). This is most evident in what might be called intermediate parts, cases where stem leaves have taken on attributes of the calyx, or where the calyx is tinted with the colour of the blos-

18 All references to Goethe's works will be made in the body of the text and are as follows: MA = Johann Wolfgang Goethe, *Sämtliche Werke nach Epochen seines Schaffens (Münchner Ausgabe),* ed. Karl Richter (Munich: Hanser, 1985–98); and LA = Johann Wolfgang Goethe, *Die Schriften zur Naturwissenschaft,* eds. D. Kuhn et al. (Weimar: Hermann Bölhaus Nachfolger, 1947). "No." refers to paragraph numbers in the *Essay on the Metamorphosis of Plants.*

som, or where petals show resemblances to stamens and so on. Goethe's claim is that if the plant's parts are perceived alongside one another, one begins to recognize continuity between the *forms* of the parts, and it becomes clear that each part assumes a form that is either a progression on or an anticipation of the other parts. The various parts of the plant are thus moments in a continuum of formation — which the plant undergoes from seed to fruit (or seed). Thus, Goethe continues, 'this makes us all the more aware of nature's regular course; we will familiarize ourselves with the laws of metamorphosis by which nature produces one part through another, creating a great variety of forms through the modification of a single organ' (MA 12, 29, no. 3).

Goethe is not saying that one and the same part physically transforms and becomes a different part; rather, his point is that close observation of the plant's parts reveals a distinctive kind of unity — a unity that is literally inscribed on the varying parts, such that each manifests the *form* of the part that preceded it, and anticipates the *form* of what comes after it. Close observation further reveals that this unity of form — this metamorphosis — occurs through two different operations: contraction and expansion, on the one hand, and intensification, on the other hand. Every part of the plant (from seed to fruit) exhibits an intensification of the preceding stage, by manifesting what preceded it in a new — more developed, more complex — light. This intensification proceeds through moments of contraction and expansion. Thus, the seed (the moment of 'maximum contraction') is intensified in the bud (also a moment of contraction), while the leaf (a moment of expansion) is intensified in the flower (a moment of expansion), and the fruit (the moment of 'maximum expansion').

By taking note of the forms of the various parts of the plant and their relations, two things become immediately clear: first, the plant's parts are in dialogue with one another, and second, this dialogue proceeds according to a specific sequence. Every stage presupposes what came before it *and* prepares the way for what is to follow. The parts are not completed parts that come together to produce a whole (an end), which is external to each of the parts (as in a machine), nor are they parts that emerge *simultaneously* with one another (as in animal). Rather, the parts of a plant proceed *sequentially,* step-by-step, and each part represents a moment of development.

Goethe's claim, then, is that the essence of the plant — what makes it a plant — lies in the fact that its development follows a necessary sequence (from seed to fruit, or back to seed). Those exceptional plants that do not follow this sequence (such as the proliferous rose which Goethe references[19]) demonstrate the regularity of this sequence (i.e., the exception demonstrates the rule). There is, furthermore, nothing arbitrary about this sequence, as is evident in the fact that the sequence is inscribed on the plant's parts — that is, on its forms. Consider the fact that each part is either a contraction that follows a moment of expansion, or an expansion following a moment of contraction. The two parts (the contracting and the expanding) are in dialogue with one another in the sense that the one emerges in light of the other. This dialogical emergence is also evident in the fact that the sequence exhibits greater intensification (complexity) as it approximates the plant's final goal (the fruit). Each of the parts — as a moment of intensification — is moving in a particular direction and its form exhibits this movement, exhibits its role within this sequential development. This connection between form and development is also evident in the fact that each part contains traces of what precedes it and, similarly, anticipates what comes after it.

By focusing on the forms of the plant's parts — their specific morphology — Goethe discerns an internal relation between form and development, between part and sequence. The parts are *parts of a sequence,* such that the sequence (the development) determines each of the parts (determines the part's form) and thus underlies the plant's unity and coherence. Thus, what it means to be a plant is inseparable from its sequential development: a plant *is* (in) its sequence. For this reason, plants cannot

---

19 Following a brief description of the proliferous rose, in which four new flowers develop out of the flower, Goethe remarks that this illustrates 'that nature usually stops the growth process at the flower and closes the account there, so to speak; nature precludes the possibility of growth in endless stages, for it wants to hasten toward its goal by forming seeds' (MA 12, 62, no. 106).

be regarded as static entities. They are in time and their temporal character (the sequence) is essential to their nature.

While Goethe's approach to the question of plant genera-tion shares some features with Kant's, Kant does not pay heed to the way in which plants emerge over time, and thus fails to consider how plant development differs from animal develop-ment. While mammals develop sequentially in their embryonic state, upon birth their development is largely non-sequential: the hand does not emerge out of the arm; rather, both hand and arm grow in size. In non-mammals such as birds or reptiles, sequential development might be more evident: the egg is the first stage while the born chick is the second. But that these two moments are part of one sequence is by no means self-evident; given that in the 18th-century discussions of generation focused on chick embryos with no consideration of the sequential char-acter of this emergence, it is clear that the two moments were not regarded as stages or sequences.

In insects, the sequential character of development is more evident: from egg, to worm, to adult. And in certain kinds of in-sects, we witness a fundamental transformation or metamorpho-sis. Still, Goethe notes, there is an important difference between plant development and insect metamorphosis: in the plant, all the stages of development *remain* such that the 'whole' contains all the stages. In an insect, each of the stages is shed, and the new stage implies an entirely new form — one can say that each stage is completely superseded by what follows such that there is no trace of the preceding stage (think of the relation between the butterfly and the caterpillar). In the plant, by contrast, the stages are present before us, and appear both as successively developed and simultaneously co-existing.

This difference is significant from a historical and a systematic perspective. Historically, and as previously noted, the focus on animals in the debates on generation made it difficult to discern successive (stage-based) development, leaving open the possibil-ity that development could be understood in purely mechani-cal terms (i.e., the mechanical increase in size of the pre-formed parts). Once plants enter the discussion on generation, the ques-tion regarding the origin of form (is it already there, or does it emerge over time?) takes on a different hue. Plants transform *be-*

fore us; we see the parts emerge, one after the other, or one out of the other. These parts could not have been pre-formed or present in the seed. After all, and as Goethe notes, several parts of a plant (the bud, the branch, the seed, the bean) could be cut off a tree and planted in soil and a whole new plant emerges — demonstrating, contra the notion of pre-formation, that these various parts possess the capacity to generate whole plants *anew* (MA 12, 15). This fact, coupled with the successive character of plant generation, makes explicit something that animals could not: generation involves the emergence of new forms over time.

From a systematic perspective, Goethe argues, plant generation is significant in two ways. In the first instance, it reveals the similarities and differences between various living beings and between living and non-living beings. The fact that successive development is most evident in plants and becomes increasingly less evident (in insects, in reptiles and birds, and then in mammals) reveals a continuum in the natural world, a continuum moving from more explicit to less explicit manifestations of the sequential character of generation (moving from a stage in which the sequential character is expressed *in* the structure itself, such that development and structure are one and the same, to one in which succession is only expressed in the embryo, and is thus largely out of sight). What is explicit in the plant kingdom becomes increasingly implicit — what is exterior becomes an increasingly interior process. This reveals a new way by which to understand the relations between different kingdoms, phyla, and classes: each exhibits either a lesser or a greater degree of exteriority or interiority and we can discern that increasing interiority is coupled with increasing complexity and increasing individuality.

This continuum of increasing interiority can, in turn, be used to compare living and non-living beings. In plants we see both successive and simultaneous development; in mammals, the development becomes largely simultaneous. In non-living nature, Goethe notes, development is solely successive — where we see gradual shifts over time, as evident in rock formations. Plants thus give us a clue by which to perceive the relation between organic and inorganic processes and function as a 'link' between the two (MA 12, 210–1).

Plants, furthermore, give us insight into the kind of cognitive tools we need in order to properly understand natural development. This is because plants reveal the role of transformation (and temporality) in development, and thus demand that we seek to grasp the plant whole, the *Urpflanze,* not as a static substance or blueprint, but as a being that is inherently in motion, or, more accurately, as a form that is inherently transforming.

Plant Metaphors

Kant invoked the metaphor of the animal body in order to elucidate the structure of reason as a self-directing, self-organizing entity. As such, however, reason is not regarded as changing or transforming; the significance of the metaphor, rather, has to do with the systematic unity of reason: like the animal body, reason's parts are inherently connected to one another. Reason is not the outcome of independently existing parts, an aggregate, but a unified whole, that precedes and makes the parts possible. While the metaphor achieves Kant's aim of depicting the unity of reason, it has one major shortcoming—a shortcoming that Kant's first critics and followers acutely noted.

The trouble with Kant's account is that it fails to provide a justification for the particular forms of thought which it invokes—the specific categories of the understanding which Kant lists in the Table of Categories. Why, Kant's critics repeatedly asked, do we possess *these* categories (these forms of thought) and not others?[20] By merely listing these forms of thought and

20 The skeptical attacks against Kant's critical philosophy came from a number of directions, but the Humean-empiricist ones were the most scathing in that they pressed Kant on precisely this point: on what ground can he justify the necessity of these specific categories? Did he not need a fundamental (indubitable) principle from which these categories could be *derived*? Lacking such an account of the relation between reason (as the unified ground of the categories) and the categories (as entities *derived* from this ground), Kant could not respond to these attacks. For this reason, Kant's followers sought to determine the fundamental principle of reason and offer an account of the relation between this principle and the categories of thought. For an account of the skeptical backlash against Kant, see Frederick Beiser, *The Fate of Reason*

declaring that they are the outcome of a unified rationality, Kant does not specify how each of the forms is itself a manifestation of this rational capacity (i.e., how each category exhibits or instantiates the structure and character of reason). What Kant needed, some philosophers came to agree, was a proper demonstration of the necessity of the categories, i.e., an account of how these specific categories belong to and manifest the fundamental principle of reason.[21]

It is precisely this relation of necessity between the various parts and the whole that Goethe sought to elucidate in his account of plant metamorphosis. By focusing on form, and demonstrating how the various forms of the plant are inherently related to one another and are manifestations of the whole, Goethe was able to arrive at the kind of insight into unity that Kant needed. Put differently, by emphasizing form, and noting the connection between each form and its place within and contribution to the whole, Goethe provided a concrete account of the unity between every *specific part* and the whole. His insight into the specific and necessary relation between part and whole goes hand in hand with the fact that he regarded each part as emerging in *relation to* the other parts — reiterating what preceded it, anticipating what comes after it, manifesting either contraction or expansion, and approaching greater intensification or complexity. In other words, Goethe's insight into the necessity of each of the parts is inseparable from his insight into the dynamic character of the parts and the whole — i.e., because he regarded the parts not as static elements but as developing members contributing

(Cambridge: Harvard University Press, 1987); for the skeptical attacks themselves, see Brigitte Sassen, ed. *Kant's Early Critics* (Cambridge: Cambridge University Press, 2000).

21 This was Reinhold's and Fichte's response, and also the early Schelling's. For an account of Reinhold and Fichte's attempt to save Kantian philosophy, see Daniel Brezeale, "Fichte's *Aenesidemus* Review and the Transformation of German Idealism," *Review of Metaphysics* 34, no. 3 (1981): 545–68. For Schelling's role in these discussions, see my *The Romantic Absolute: Being and Knowing in German Romantic Philosophy 1795–1804* (Chicago: University of Chicago Press, 2014), chap. 9.

to a transforming unity, he was able to see that each of the parts must be a part of the whole.

It is, I think, this perspective that led Goethe's contemporaries to reclaim the metaphor of the plant in order to describe reason.[22] What they saw in Goethe's emphasis on transforming forms was a significant response to skepticism, a response that may be able to salvage the Kantian project — albeit under a very different guise. Their task then was to show necessity in the specificity of forms and demonstrate how the distinctive forms are necessary members of a transforming whole.

While I cannot consider the many and various ways in which Goethe's understanding of plant metamorphosis influenced post-Kantian conceptions of reason, I can point to one significant and abiding effect of Goethe's influence. Goethe showed his contemporaries that the idea (the essence of the plant) could only be grasped through careful observation of the distinctive character of the forms or appearances in their context (both temporal and geographic or spatial), with an eye to discerning how the forms are in dialogue with one another and with the whole that emerges through this dialogue. In turn, the necessity of the underlying unity (the plant) — the fact that it is not merely an outcome of individual parts coming together at a particular (arbitrary) moment in time — can only be exhibited or portrayed, but not explained or derived from an a priori concept or an abstract principle. For the necessity emerges *through* the specific forms of the various parts, *in their appearances* in specific contexts, and in their *distinctive* contributions to the whole. The underlying unity, in other words, can never be grasped abstractly, or through a priori derivation; rather, it can only be grasped in its appearances, in its specific forms. (Otherwise, we once again lose sight of the forms, and end up with Kant's difficulty.) This means that we must trace its development (or its successive manifestations) from one stage to the next and find a way by which to behold this

22 Goethe's influence on his contemporaries has been recently highlighted. For an account of his influence on romanticism (including Schelling), see my *The Romantic Absolute*. For Goethe's influence on Hegel, see Eckaft Förster, *The Twenty-Five Years of Philosophy* (Cambridge: Harvard University Press, 2012).

unity in and through (rather than beyond or above) its varying forms and their relations.

Goethe's emphasis on this contextual, temporally-attuned perspective is clearly present in Hegel's account of reason and his attempt in the *Phenomenology of Spirit* to *exhibit* the *transformations* of reason, that is, to *portray* reason *in and through its transformations* (i.e., through the forms of thought that enable it to perceive, represent and conceive of the world).[23] The developmental character of Hegel's account of reason follows Fichte's and Schelling's similarly sequential depictions of reason which they described as 'pragmatic histories' of reason where history involves the depiction of the necessary stages of reason's development.[24] The aim is to trace the specific forms (stages or moments) through which reason must emerge in order to achieve self-consciousness, in order to grasp its unity.

Similarly, Novalis and Friedrich Schlegel invoked the metaphor of the plant to describe the fragment and Schlegel's so-called 'system of fragments' (KFSA 18, 100, no. 857; KFSA 18, 97, no. 815).[25] '*Systems*,' Schlegel writes, 'must grow,' and for this reason he goes on to distinguish a philosophical system from a mathematical one (KFSA 16, 165, no. 953). The latter is static; its forms are unchanging. By contrast, 'a philosophical system has

---

23 Eckart Förster regards Hegel's understanding of the concept and his emphasis on transitions between forms of thought as fundamentally influenced by Goethe. See Förster, *The Twenty-Five Years of Philosophy*. Though I agree with Förster about the influence, I think Hegel's interpretation of Goethe's notion of metamorphosis or development is slightly misguided, and approximates the metamorphosis of insects, where each stage is shed (as Hegel puts it 'refuted') by the preceding stage.

24 Johann Gottlieb Fichte, *Gesamtausgabe der Bayerischen Akademie der Wissenschaften*, Series 1, Vol. 2, eds. R. Lauth et al. (Stuttgart-Bad Cannstatt: Frommann, 1965), 364; F.W.J. Schelling, *Sämtliche Werke*, Series 1, Vol. 2, 39, ed. K.F.A. Schelling (Stuttgart: Cotta, 1856–61).

25 All references to Schlegel's works will be made in the body as follows: KFSA: Friedrich Schlegel, *Kritische Friedrich-Schlegel-Ausgabe*, eds. E. Behler, J.J. Anstett, and H. Eichner, 35 Vols. (Paderborn: Schöningh, 1958–). I will cite volume number, then the page number, and (when available) the paragraph number.

more similarities with a poetic and historical system' (KFSA 18, 84, no. 650). In fact, Schlegel continues, 'everything systematic is historical and vice versa' (KFSA 18, 86, no. 671).

The fragment is, as Novalis describes it, like a seed, which, if sown in good soil, becomes a blossom or fruit. Or, as Schlegel puts it, it is a 'living idea' that can grow if placed in the right context (KFSA 18, 139, no. 204).[26] Like the seed, a fragment is on its own incomplete and incapable of completion. It must be placed in the right context and properly nourished in order to grow and flourish. The fragment's inherent incompleteness — the fact that its meaning and its relation to other fragments are not immediately evident — demands active engagement from its reader: she is drawn to consider the intention of the fragment, which (given its inherently incomplete nature) requires that the reader herself contribute to its meaning — try to discern its significance through various prisms. Thus one significant sense in which the fragment, on its own, is incomplete has to do with the fact that it depends on the thinker (the soil) for its development.

The fragment's open-ended character also implies that its relation to other fragments is not immediately evident. A fragment, after all, is not a proposition deduced from preceding propositions such that its relation to other fragments is neither linear nor conclusive. For these reasons, Schlegel's ambition to develop a system of fragments means that his aim is to develop a system that is inherently, or in some significant way, non-systematic. It must be at once ordered and open-ended, open to transformation, depending on its context and the changing relations between its fragments.

It is for this reason that Schlegel likens the system of fragments to both a plant and a musical composition: both exemplify an inherently differentiated unity that emerges over time and through transformation. In the plant and the musical composition, each of the parts contributes to the development of the whole such that this development determines the different roles and relations of the parts. The kind of unity exhibited in a work of music

26 Schlegel also writes, 'the fragment is the actual form of the philosophy of nature' (KFSA 2, 100, no. 859) and 'the true form of universal philosophy are fragments' (KFSA 2, 114, no. 204).

or plant is thus neither a hegemonic, undifferentiated substance nor an overarching, abstract concept — both of which are cases of externally imposed unities. It is, rather, an immanent unity that cannot be separated from the parts, their developments, and their relations. Furthermore, no part is negated on account of the other parts; rather, each part offers a distinctive expression of the whole.

Moreover, in both the work of music and the plant, the unity emerges only through a successive unfolding in time. It is thus more apt to speak of musical unity as *movement,* like the unity of a plant, where each part evidences a moment in the *development* of the whole — each part is a member of an unfolding sequence. In turn, the temporality that is at work in music and plants is not merely futural — i.e., a work of music does not *simply move linearly toward the future.* Rather, it moves forward *and* looks backward. For it is only through anticipating what is to come and *reflecting* on what has already come that the unity of the work emerges.

Despite the differences between Hegel's system, where each stage is a refutation of the preceding one, and Schlegel's system of fragments, they agree on the most essential point: reason can only be grasped as it is presented, as it appears, in its various forms, in context and through time. This means that the forms of thought — like the parts of the plant — are not static and their necessity is not based on their unchanging character, but lies in the connections between them — connections discerned through their specific forms and the (temporal) relations between these forms. It is this temporally and contextually attuned perspective, this perspective that emphasizes transformation and appearances rather than downgrading them as merely empirical or contingent, that highlights observation and portrayal or depiction over derivation and a priori determination, which, I believe, the idealists and romantics learned from Goethe, and which led them back to the plant.

9

Icaro / Heyowicinayo

Tamryn Bennett

Fig. 1. Jacqueline Cavallaro, 'The Chanting Plants,' mixed media, 2016.

Icaro

caapi, cipó
yagé, yajé
natem, shori
aya spirit vine

       icaros
       in grandmother tongue
           cantos de medicina
           liana chanting

la selva, la serpiente
songs of feathered trees
         fractals of leaves
     chakapa, ritual begins

    – breathe –

       seeds in your mouth
       music in your hands
    thunder, fire, storm
    soil sparks

punga for protection
puma bone and smoke
mirrored nights
clear clouded eyes

       curandero cleansing
          floating, flaring
          bones and roots
          full of light

Heyowicinayo

a west away
mara'akame
call cactus god
Tatewari – grandfather flame

> along Wixáritari trail
> deep mountain mescaline
> Mitote dreaming
> Hikuri healing

where the sun was born
in silver valleys
sacred footprints of
Kauyumari

> tobacco gourd
> womb of water drum
temple of flowers
shrine of wind

ghost dust dances
peyote prayers
> to wake the rain
> return us crystalline

Notes

Caapi, cipó, yagé, yajé, natem, shori are alternative names for ayahuasca.

Chakapa is a ritual rattle made of leaves.

A *curandero* is a traditional healer or shaman in Latin America.

Icaros are healing songs or chants sung to evoke plant spirits during ayahuasca ceremonies.

Kauyumari is the scared blue deer figure whose footprints are said to be
peyote.

Mara'akame is a Wixáritari shaman.

Tatewari, also known as Hikuri, is the oldest peyote god of the Wixáritari.

Wixáritari or *Huichol* are native Mexicans living in the Sierra Madre Oc-
cidental.

10

Continuous Green Abstraction: Embodied Knowledge, Intuition, and Metaphor

Ben Woodard

Is there a relation between de-centralizing forms of thought in the various research programs of the cognitive sciences and the democratization of thought across species in philosophy? Or, put otherwise, do the forms of thought articulated in human cognition (reason, imagination, intuition, etc.) map in any adequate way onto embodiment across numerous species in terms of how such species cognitively function, as well as how they rely upon physical embodiment to think? And, lastly, do the various theories of 4E Cognition (embodied, enacted, embedded, and extended) clarify or needlessly complicate this?

While it critiques of classical cognitive models often go hand in hand with critiques of epistemology, or human-centered ways of knowing, such projects seem to over-rely on a *metaphorical disjunction,* which itself is not anti-epistemological but embedded within both the embodied modes of cognition and more disembodied transcendental accounts. This is particularly evident in recent works that have attempted to argue for the presence of thinking in so called 'lower lifeforms,' while at the same time invoking, and capitalizing on, highly abstract concepts taken from philosophers such as C.S. Peirce (a thinker who is anything but anti-epistemological).

To explore and question this tendency, I will examine the recent turn to plant thinking and how this relates to earlier attempts to transcendentally naturalize cognition in the work of F.W.J. von Schelling (of whose concepts Peirce saw himself as a more scientifically literate inheritor). Furthermore, the work of Gilles Châtelet, ever more sympathetic to Schelling, will serve to address the non-trivial function of metaphor in demonstrating that the continuity of thought does not imply the flattening of transcendentally naturalized capacities for, and of, cognition.

Epistemology or Intuition or…?

> Intuition is not clairvoyance. It's not guesswork either. Intuition is executive summary, that 90 percent of the higher brain that functions subconsciously — but no less rigorously — than the self-aware subroutine that thinks of itself as *the* person.[1]

What does it mean that in the course of investigating something like cognition, for instance, we not only spread out its material locus in the human body (as being not merely in the head, or in the brain only), but we also wish to philosophically grant cognition to traditionally unthinking beings such as plants? This problem often emerges in a strange paradox — the outside world is infinite but only to the extent we can think it, and thus, how do we know that a limit to thinking is a limit as such, a limit to thinking, or a limit to our thinking? In other words, if we reach a limit, once we know we have reached it, in what terms does it cease to be a limit, one of knowing or one in being? An emphasis on such questions is too quickly dismissed in contemporary debates as harking back to Kantian times, of an overemphasis on the human, or on human knowledge as the center of the philosophical cosmos.

The knot in which we find ourselves concerns whether our inability to know *how* we think means that many things *may* think, or, following various lines of research in embodied cognition, that thinking is not *primarily* neuronal. While it is readily admitted that thinking is more than *strictly* neuronal (or in the head) and that thinking is not merely information processing and concept forming *ex nihilo,* it seems all too easy to starkly oppose the

---

1   Peter Watts, *Maelstrom* (New York: Tor, 2001), 320.

brain as a centralized governor to the body as its subordinate. But is the correct response to spread thought throughout the body and neglect the particularity of the neuronal, to potentially erase, the difference between thinking and its relation to the body's actions? Many thinkers within the field of embodied mind (or 4E cognition, as it is generally known), such as Antonio Damasio, have attempted to dethrone the neuronal aspect of cognition through an appeal to the physiological role of emotions.

Damasio is well known for the somatic marker hypothesis, which makes the claim that purportedly rational decisions have, at their base, emotional content. In *Descartes' Error,* Damasio argues that the somatic dimension comes into play since a rational choice is affected by physiological sensations, thereby indirectly affecting one's decisions.[2] Thus, either consciously or unconsciously, how we feel about a decision affects which decision we make. This is easy to see in terms of bodily feedback mechanisms. Experiences which makes one's heart beat faster and pulse race are connected with high-risk activities. Other activities that trigger these same bodily responses are emotionally coded in similar ways, since the other risky activities, which quicken the pulse, are liked by the person doing them. Put otherwise, Damasio would say that things we think are exciting feel exciting *before* we think they are exciting. Actions and events that make our bodies react automatically become exciting events before we consciously think they are.

However, one could argue that the decisions that Damasio is generally talking about are already laden with certain value structures or emotional charges. While rationality in these situations can be said to be undergirded, and/or disrupted, by emotional content, this assumes that the thinking-feeling agent has some sense of the general picture — that they have some notion of the consequences of each choice.

This is not to claim that 'outer' knowledge, or more abstract knowledge, is divorced from the body, but should make us question exactly how much of that feedback process could be thought as emotional content. Thus, for instance, one simply may not

2   Antonio Damasio, *Descartes' Error: Emotion, Reason, and the Human Brain* (New York: Penguin, 2005).

know whether an experience which one has been told is risky will be exciting, boring, or simply frightening. How rational guessing or imaging functions here is not altogether clear.

In tracing the sensorimotor feedback structures of thought, and of how intuition functions in relation to different forms of thought, we will appear to be 'reducing' thought to its bare constituents in terms of being outside the mind (in terms of the emphasis on the body), as well as in terms of intra-conceptual capacities, like that of intuition, that seems the least accessible to intentional thought. That is, once we think about what we have intuited, it is no longer intuition at work but reflection, imagination, and the like.

Now we may ask if the relation between distributing thought beyond the neuronal relates to other kinds of thought — that is, whether the various forms of thought (intuition, imagination, reason, judgment, etc.) are more or less neuronal. Following this question, we can also ask whether the differences between these different forms can be mapped onto the difference between species, specifically onto the embodiment of thought in other species, in a way that is not merely metaphorical. That is, since we do not know what thought is, or what thought is *for us,* can applying thinking to other species be separated from how we perceive such species within our articulation of thinking (however complex)? In this regard we can take intuition as a test case.

Intuition, as Gilles Châtelet has it, sprouts from devices, such as measuring instruments, in which thought, and the demonstration of the thought, go hand in hand.[3] Put simply, intuition thinks and displays itself simultaneously. Once intuition becomes a form of knowing, however, it ceases to be intuition. It is dissolved by a certain degree of intentionality and becomes something else altogether. But does this mean that knowing, as a general category, should be generalized in terms of its relation to cognitive capacities, or species lines, more broadly? Before addressing this question, it is important to address intuition broadly, particularly as it appears in Châtelet and Merleau-Ponty. Both Châtelet and Merleau-Ponty utilize metaphors of continuity,

3   Gilles Châtelet, *Figuring Space: Philosophy, Mathematics, and Physics,* trans. Robert Shore and Muriel Zagha (Boston: Kluwer, 1999), 85.

metaphors that often cross into organic and especially botanical territory.[4]

As Châtelet writes on intuition:

> This 'overview' (the global overview of philosophy) is not the dilettante's distant contemplation; it takes part in the action: it is an intellectual intuition, in the sense intended in the philosophy of nature. It transports us to that privileged zone where intuition and discursivity become knotted into a living unity. It is neither a priori nor a posteriori: it is contemporaneous with what it grasps. It takes each being at its own level without decomposing it into elements or placing it in a vaster stock of reality.[5]

He then writes:

> Like intellectual intuition, the scientific method demanded by Grassmann introduces a knowledge that does not leave the subject/object dualism intact, but on the contrary, ventures to create the object itself to assert the fundamental identity of product and productivity. The more precise the mode of articulation that distinguishes between them, the better this identity is conceived. We will not be surprised that the notions of dimension and orientation play such a crucial role in the capture of the extension. They always surreptitiously threaten the neutrality of the observer faced with his object. They cannot be conceived in the same way that one can make certain of a thing. They suggest the existence of an unobjective knowledge of the being-in-the-world, which is not, however, nothing.[6]

Let us try and unpack these rather dense passages and discern why they might belong in a discussion of organic thinking and as

4   This occurs throughout Maurice Merleau-Ponty and Claude Lefort, *The Visible and the Invisible,* trans. Alphonso Lingis (Evanston: Northwestern University Press, 1968).

5   Châtelet, *Figuring Space,* 104.

6   Ibid., 105.

well as how thought might navigate inside an organic structure, a structure where one is uncertain as to the location of the divide between oneself, the act of thinking, the location of thought, and the possible locations of thought (across species). Châtelet's invocation of intellectual intuition, which we will address in full below, points to the injection of a critical distance between being an actor and observing oneself being an actor. The language that follows may strike us as decidedly Kantian, as it speaks to knowledge that creates its object as well as the impossibility of being a non-neutral observer. One could conclude that a contradiction arises between an apparent validation of intellectual intuition and an appeal to Kant, given that the latter dismissed the possibility of the former.

But what is key is that intuition, in the *Naturphilosophical* sense of the world (following Schelling, for instance), is not immediate knowledge in the way that Kant articulated and criticized it. Intellectual intuition, as Châtelet emphasizes, also following Schelling, is non-objective knowledge and not knowledge that instantly gets to the depths of things.

In this case, intellectual intuition is a form of knowledge that arises from our being-in-the-world, but this being is only ever obliquely observed — it cannot be directly perceived as it is the state of affairs from which, and of which, we perceive. The same nature that produces the world and everything in it produces our capacities to perceive and intervene in that world. But this should not amount to a naïve realism that we have some direct access to the world, nor should it necessarily mean that we are left in a neutral monism or panpsychism that would necessitate that all the components of the world, or the world itself, are always-already thinking. The fact that the world appears to be a generative continuum does not necessarily entail that all the objects of the world that derive from that continuity necessarily have the same capacities (mental or otherwise). Whether we could even make this claim is questionable, given how localized our own species genesis is, and how parochial our capacities seem to be in the grander scheme of things.

Châtelet's invocation of the continuum is simply the assumption that there is a unity both formally (perhaps following Peirce) and naturally (following Schelling) that accounts for the fact that the world interacts with itself, yet appears broken up into separate entities.[7] Nor does the continuum entail without a doubt that we can access that which is apparently outside of us. Such a feeling is not altogether alien from certain strands of the phenomenological condition, particularly prevalent in Merleau-Ponty's *The Visible and the Invisible,* where he goes to great lengths to try and articulate how it is we humans are a part of the world, yet our access to it remains twisted and indirect. How the issue of our limitations relate to a continuum that might undo those limitations, or suggest that our capacities may be more ubiquitous across the continuum, is apparent in Merleau-Ponty's metaphorical use of plant language — a language which, recently, could find a home in the emerging field of plant thinking. As Merleau-Ponty and Lefort write,

> Whether in discussion or in monologue, the essence in the living and active state is always a certain vanishing point indicated by the arrangement of the words, their 'other side,' inaccessible, save for him who accepts to live first and always in them. As the nervure bears the leaf from within, from the depths of its flesh, the ideas are the texture of experience, its style, first mute, then uttered. Like every style, they are elaborated within the thickness of being and, not only in fact but also by right, could not be detached from it, to be spread out on display under the gaze.[8]

Plant Thinking?

As mentioned above, there has recently been a further development in the 'non-human turn' that involves discussing vegetative life and, in particular, the role of thinking in plants and plant-like entities (such as fungus). These texts include Richard Doyle's *Darwin's Pharmacy* (which discusses evolution in tandem with a history of psychedelics), Matthew Hall's *Plants as Persons* (which addresses the moral standing of plants), Elaine Miller's *The Vegetative Soul* (which deals with the treatment of plants in Roman-

7   Ibid., 44.
8   Merleau-Ponty and Lefort, *The Visible and the Invisible,* 119.

ticism), Michael Marder's *Plant Thinking* (which takes a more general posthumanist approach to plants), and Eduardo Kohn's *How Forests Think* (which adapts Peirce's semiotics for the relations between numerous entities of the rainforest).

From fog-drinking trees in Chile to the networks of fungus that seem to pass messages between distant trees, there is a sense that plants are more communicative, or at least more agential, than was previously allowed. While plants have always been granted a dynamic or generative aspect (they grow, blossom, produce fruit, reproduce, etc.), they are seen as certainly brainless, as generally less intentional and less mobile, or otherwise as limited forms of life. Often because of a general sense of motionlessness, of being immobilized by their rooted being, the vegetative state of being is an unthinking state of being. The assertion here is that thought is possible because of constant mobile stimulus in conjunction with cerebral development. This of course poses the question: are there forms of thinking that are less dependent upon motion?

On the other hand, studies of plant thought combine nicely with notions of thought described as maximally distributed agency, whether networked thought or other forms of hive mind. Giving up on the location of thought as necessarily existing within neural matter is useful not only for studying plant life but also for various models of AGI (artificial general intelligence) and forms of cognitive science that are interested in embodiment — of thought not being in our heads (as Alva Noë put it famously) and being instead largely a result of exterior stimulus and the means by which mind attempts to map that extension.[9]

So a tension arises between extended mind and embodied mind. Or, in other words, a tension arises between the maximally distributed mind that has a low requirement for motion or movement (only one of growth over time, in terms of spatial expansion) and the embodied mind in which the senses carving up the world into knowledge go hand in hand with being a mov-

---

9 And of course it can assist studies of animal intelligence in order to understand how very different cognitive architectures can produce similar results.

ing, chasing, pursuing, fleeing entity. But certain communicative capacities may overcome their limited mobility.

Recent studies have discovered that certain species of plants can warn other plants of an impending insect invasion by releasing chemicals that stimulate the other plant to begin to prepare its defenses.[10] This is a more complex and two-species-networked version of the kinds of reactivity and recognition plants exhibit in terms of chemically altering their growth and various outputs in relation to stimulations of all kinds (physical, magnetic, radioactive, etc). It has long been documented that plants can also change strategies depending upon soil environment or exposure to light, chasing resources in both cases. Furthermore, plants can compute the risks of growing more or less depending upon resource availability.

Various controversies have erupted over whether this kind of 'signal integration' — basically, a plant's ability to combine various sets of sense data into an action — should count as a form of intelligence. The central reason why plants do not generally qualify as having intelligence is due to their lack of neuronal and synaptic structures. In a functional sense, plants can communicate to their own bodies, to other plants, and to animal species (luring wasps to attack caterpillars, e.g.) through what has been referred to as hormonal sentience. While generally slower than neuronal connectivity, high-speed reactions do take place, such as in carnivorous plants and in *Mimosa pudica* (or sensitive plant), which retracts and covers its seeds when touched. The sleepy plant collapses itself by rapidly releasing positively charged potassium ions that shrinks the leaves inward. Monica Gagliano has claimed that the 'sleepy plant' can learn and must have an active sense of memory in that it is capable of ignoring certain stimuli and privileging others (shrinking when shaken, but not dropped, e.g.), since it requires a good deal of energy to suddenly become 'humble.' [11]

10 Dan Cossins, 'Plant Talk,' *The Scientist,* January 1, 2014, http://www. the-scientist.com/?articles.view/articleNo/38727/title/Plant-Talk/.

11 M. Gagliano, M. Renton, M. Depczynski, and S. Mancuso. 'Experience teaches plants to learn faster and forget slower in environments where it matters,' *Oecologia* 175, no. 1 (May 2014): 63–72, https://doi.

But does this reactivity amount to intelligence? Is the processing of external stimuli that feeds into slight behavioral modification tantamount to intelligence? The point has been made elsewhere that complex discrimination of data may not be equitable to intelligence. Gagliano seems to suggest that sensitivity and reactivity would constitute intelligence, but this would grant inorganic objects, such as thermometers, intelligence (since they arguably have the capacity to discern and react to differences of environment).

Marder's *Plant Thinking* does not equate experience with intelligence, but Marder is interested in the ways plants are used to describe a low level or absence of intelligence, or more specifically, cognitive capacity (just think again of the term 'vegetative state'). Marder utilizes the usual suspects (Heidegger, Derrida, Levinas) in order to defend a generic sense of vegetative otherness. As Dominic Pettman argues in his review of *Plant Thinking,* this falls into the trap of romanticizing the plant world, of claiming plants as a generic source of harmonious generation.[12]

In another review, Jeffrey Nealon focuses on the ethical aspects of Marder's book. Nealon reads the book as an extension of the projects of thinkers such as Butler and Brown in troubling identity politics writ large via a critical form of post-humanism. Nealon argues that Marder attempts to ontologically romanticize the plant by claiming that it carries capacities for the generation of life that we mammals do not. In this sense, Marder's book avoids the potentially interesting topic of non-intentional intelligence (as Pettman puts it) — the question of how vegetative life (and fungal life) can find efficient paths without anything that looks like brains, as we understand them.

To attempt to ethically shore up plant life via an ontology of the other seems to completely elide the problem of intelligence and begs the question as to whether the discussion of the uniqueness of a set of entities' experiences has any bearing on whether we destroy them, eat them, and so on. For example, in the west-

org/10.1007/s00442–013–2873–7.
12 Dominic Pettman, 'The Noble Cabbage,' *Los Angeles Review of Books,* July 28, 2013, https://lareviewofbooks.org/article/the-noble-cabbage-michael-marders-plant-thinking.

ern world, people do not balk at the idea of eating dogs because of their intelligence (if this were the case, we could not, in good conscience, eat pigs). Instead, the issue is an anthropological and historical one: dogs have been a companion species for humans as long as we have had a history.

Marder attempts to shift companion status to one of communication. In an opinion piece for the *New York Times* entitled, 'If Peas Can Talk, Should We Eat Them?', Marder discusses recent research demonstrating that peas can communicate to their vegetable neighbors, sharing drought stress and other signals. But is communication co-creative or co-existent with experience?[13]

While the ranking of being as analogical to depth of experience is no doubt false and sloppy philosophy (for instance, Heidegger's discussion of things being poorer and richer in world), the question becomes less about the existence of different experiences (this appears hard to ignore), and is rather about how sensibility feeds into experience and how, and in what ways, experience can be communicated and recorded.[14] The question here is: what has to happen to information processing (whether somatic, hormonal, or neuronal) before it becomes intelligence?

To say that some forms of life possess intelligence and others do not is not particularly helpful. The question that is too often ignored in critical animal studies, and the posthumanities more broadly construed, is what happens to intelligence in human beings that makes us so much better at exporting and recording the results of our intelligence (or what the scientists Jack Cohen and Iain Stewart have referred to as 'extelligence').[15] The relation between sense and the recording of data itself has implications for continuous and organic notions of being already hinted at above.

---

13   Michael Marder, 'If Peas Can Talk, Should We Eat Them?' *The New York Times: Opinionator* (weblog), April 28, 2012, http://opinionator.blogs.nytimes.com/2012/04/28/if-peas-can-talk-should-we-eat-them/?_r=0.

14   Martin Heidegger, *What Is Called Thinking?*, trans. J. Glen Gray (New York: Harper and Row, 1968), 16

15   Jack Cohen and Ian Stewart, *The Collapse of Chaos: Discovering Simplicity in a Complex World* (New York: Viking, 1994).

Utilizing the work of C.S. Pierce, Eduardo Kohn's *How Forests Think* addresses the spatial and behavioral carving that species do to one another. Kohn is particularly interested in how life as a semiotic system relates to Peirce's categories of firstness, secondness, and thirdness. Secondness represents everyday occurrences and events that index thirdness and firstness, with thirdness being real patterns or laws of nature that exist outside the human mind, whereas firstness is the category of potentiality or maybes.[16] Peirce is quite an anomaly, because he focuses on semiotics and symbolism, while emphatically endorsing mind-independent nature in the form of thirdness. Peirce saw one of the greatest threats to the history of philosophy as that of nominalism — namely, that the world is made of individual entities and they are pasted together by experiencing minds into something like continuous experiences. The fact that Kohn downplays the notion of continuity in Peirce, which we encountered above, should surprise us given the focus on nature in Kohn's text. One possibility is that Kohn wishes to treat Peirce as a thinker of plurality as opposed to continuity.

In 1903 Peirce wrote: 'The heart of the dispute lies in this: The modern philosophers — one and all unless Schelling be an exception — recognize but one mode of being, the being of an individual thing or fact.'[17] Writing almost one hundred years earlier, Schelling would express a similar statement: 'The whole of modern European philosophy has this common deficiency — that nature does not exist for it.'[18] To return to Merleau-Ponty, this problem occupies him in the course notes on Nature as well as his notes on Husserl and finally, as we have already seen, in *The Visible and the Invisible*. What separates Kohn from Merleau-Ponty, at least at first glance, may be the role of nature providing

16 Eduardo Kohn, *How Forests Think: Toward an Anthropology Beyond the Human* (Berkeley: University of California Press, 2013), 58–59.

17 Charles S. Peirce, *The Collected Papers of Charles Sanders Peirce, Book 1,* eds. Charles Hartshorne and Paul Weiss (Cambridge: Harvard University Press, 1931), 21–22.

18 F.W.J. Schelling, *Philosophical Investigations into the Essence of Human Freedom,* trans. Jeff Love and Johannes Schmidt (Albany: State University of New York Press, 2006), 26.

fuel for sense, albeit in different ways, whereas in his latter days, Merleau-Ponty was more invested in trying to unveil the unseen side of the visible, that primordial or savage being.[19]

Kohn, in taking up Peirce, argues that life as a semiotic or signaling system cannot be reduced to information exchanges nor abstracted from the particular chemical and physical medium those information systems inhabit. The continuity, or more accurately, plurality of nature, for Kohn, suggests a naturalism, but one that appears to have no outer edge, and the difficult task becomes tracing the lines of communication between species and how those lines differ in kind or only in degree.

What remains difficult for Kohn, or anyone embracing such a notion of continuity, is that the actions of certain agents seem to have broader ramifications and more specific goals – essentially the problem seems to be that of intentionality (to return to the thermostat versus the sensitive plant).

Essentially, Kohn is interested in what intelligence consists of and how it is related to the mobility of animal, plant, and human life. Mobility, of course, differs greatly in terms of species but also relative to the medium of their respective biome (terrestrial or marine for instance). Since the great exodus from the sea, creatures had to become adept at consuming enough nutrients to maintain their land-locked fuel inefficiency (compared to that of aquatic creatures). In this sense, life on land can be viewed as upping the ante in the biological bet against entropy — biology becomes the medium for chaotic routes of movement that fail more quickly as life progresses, but also produce stranger and stranger results.

As the philosopher and scientist Giuseppe Longo has put it, 'Life goes wrong most of the time.'[20] Whereas inorganic patterns

19 Merleau-Ponty emphasizes the darker or more troubling side of a connectivity that is always behind our backs. In regards to the seedier side of plant thinking, one can look at T.S. Miller, 'Lives of the Monster Plants: The Revenge of the Vegetable in the Age of Animal Studies,' *Journal of the Fantastic in the Arts* 23, no. 3 (2012): 460–79.

20 Giuseppe Longo, Maël Montévil, and Stuart Kauffman, 'Not Entailing Laws, but Enablement in the Evolution of the Biosphere,' *GECCO '12: Proceedings of the 14th Annual Conference on Genetic and Evolution-*

are far more stable (in that they are more responsive to the structure of the earth, such as rivers following the most efficient path to the ocean), life follows far less predictable paths and whole species fail to survive in the long run.

Intelligence is a particularly odd biological implement in that it in no way ensures high reproductive numbers (if it is a numbers game, as Stephen Jay Gould was fond of pointing out, bacteria win) and it is a high risk gamble on top of the high risk gamble of life.[21] Brains are incredibly expensive physiologically and are not merely geared towards survival, but are only 'worth it' in a narrow biological niche. What seems to us to be 'high level' intelligence is a biological accident of adaptation, bringing unexpected results and nothing more.

The positive feedback loops of technology and human development are central to theories of cognition and mental development gathered under embodied mind, actionism, distributed cognition and the like. The theorists gathered under these various monikers of 4E Cognition assign larger and smaller roles to the brain as a processing center, either as still contributing a large degree of novelty to the construction of conscious acts or as a filter of the sensations coming from outside.

In broad strokes, embodied cognition, the most popular of the 4E variants, is the umbrella term for emphasizing body over brain, whereas embedded cognition focuses on brain and body in an environment, and extended cognition goes even further in stating that cognition is 'out there' and not at only 'in the head.'

The philosopher and cyberneticist Andy Clark is one of the more compensatory figures, arguing for a middle ground between neuronally and/or linguistically-centered models of consciousness and the embodied models that assign a far less central role to the brain. For Clark and others, technology functions largely as a physical and informational off-loading (and the boundary between the two of these is thin once we enter the

ary Computation, ed. Terence Soule (New York: ACM 2012): 1379–92, http://dx.doi.org/10.1145/2330784.2330946.

21 Stephen Jay Gould, *The Richness of Life: The Essential Stephen Jay Gould,* eds. Steven Rose and Paul McGarr (New York: W.W. Norton, 2007).

realm of physics). Technology is a way for us to export physical and mental labor, whether it functions as a lever and pulley system to move a heavy object, or as a writing system that can encode data that would otherwise have to be demonstrated through live speech or action. Proponents of embodied cognition pursue different arguments for why the body of a thinker cannot be set aside in order to investigate the cognitive structure of that thinker with that body. One example is that our learning is so dependent upon mimicry and mirroring, the role of gesture in speech, and, for Alva Noë, the role of vision.

Noë's emphasis on vision is particularly relevant to the notion of thought being rooted in motion. Noë argues that our vision functions as a direct contact with the world, not as a representation of a presentation that is in some sense given phenomenologically. The limits of vision are experienced when we guess at the full outlines of an object, simply because we cannot see all of its outlines. Noë argues that we can guess what the back of an object looks like because we guess what moving the object, or moving around the object, would do to our perception of it. Noë develops this argument in his striking text *The Varieties of Presence,* where Noë describes the everyday experience of looking at an object, such as a piece of fruit sitting on a table in front of you. The back of the piece of the fruit, or of any object, is that which is not immediately present but is 'amodally present,' and furthermore, the fact that 'nothing is given in perception, only an array of foci based on place.'[22] means that what is 'here' is not what I can see but is determined by degrees of access (equally mental and physical).

Or as he puts it elswhere: 'perceptual consciousness as a visual style, a style of access, I know how to move to see what is 'over there.'[23] Or, in other words, vision is primarily a modeling of potential movement where picturing is the capacity of the mind that makes up for greater and hard to think temporal and spatial distances.

22 Alva Noë, *Varieties of Presence* (Cambridge: Harvard University Press, 2012), 17–18.

23 Ibid., 20.

In a quite different but not unrelated sense, George Lakoff argues that metaphors in speech are primarily about mapping our navigational and spatially embodied life onto non-embodied activities, such as transferring talk about moving and traveling to that of relationships. Very common phrases, such as 'Life is journey' or 'I/we got hitched,' are examples of this. Furthermore, and in line with these turns of phrase, Lakoff sees the body more as a constraint than as a distributor or regulator.[24]

While embodied cognition emphasizes the particular body of a thinking entity, distributed cognition, of which enactivism is one form, expands the aforementioned off-loading model to natural, social, and cultural levels. Or, put otherwise, whereas Damasio's embodied cognition focuses on the brain-body circuit, enactivism focuses on the wider environment. To bring us back to our vegetative life above, what does it mean when we have distributed or extended cognition that is only physical and chemical, and does that increase or decrease its claims to being an intelligence among other intelligences?

Enactivism focuses more on body and environment relations and is based on the work of Maturana and Varlera, and is attentive, like the work of Clark, to the inanimate factors of cognitive functioning. Eleanor Rosch famously applied the insights of enactivism to color perception in studying the Dani people of Papua New Guinea. Rosch discovered that while the Dani's notion of color was one of brighter and darker only, they could distinguish and identify favorite colors that they did not have a word for. Rosch's conclusion was that colors could be linked to physiological responses. Even though those responses could not be linguistically coded in different colors, they could still be expressed using terms of intensity as well as physical gestures.[25]

Despite disagreements about how embodied, or non-neuronal, cognition is, and about how much work is done by the brain in relation to the signals sent by the brain, the central point is that

24 Mark Johnson and George Lakoff, *Metaphors We Live By* (Chicago: University of Chicago Press, 2003).

25 Francisco J. Varela, Evan Thompson, and Eleanor Rosch, *The Embodied Mind: Cognitive Science and Human Experience* (Cambridge: MIT Press, 1992).

cutting thought from its physical medium (chemical, hormonal, physio-electric, etc.) causes a series of problems for defining and measuring intelligence. This begs the question of whether movement is required in order to obtain higher orders of intelligence, or if a proper intelligence can be contained in a purely internalized, or mostly closed, system (the implications for research on AGI should be relatively obvious).[26]

The various theories of embodied cognition at times run the risk of remaining too close to their phenomenological precursors and fail to examine the ramifications of organisms existing in a greater natural and abstract continuity — as Peirce suggests above with his notion of thirdness, of real laws (or laws of nature). In other words, even though many strands of phenomenology would reject an overemphasis on language, or a logic-based model of cognition, their emphasis on the body (if it remains too steeped in phenomenological lore) remains tied to structures of the humanist subject, the ego, or other human-centered biases that ignore the effects of the outside material world just as much as analytic and mathematical theories of cognition ignore the body. That is, enactivism in particular, may become another form of ego-centric phenomenology if environment is always cultural, or representational, in a way that does not depend upon an outside — a generative nature. Peirce's intellectual lineage here can be traced to the German Idealist and naturalist F.W.J. von Schelling. Not only did Peirce respect Schelling's anti-nominalism, but he also, as he wrote in a letter to William James, saw himself 'as a Schellingian transformed in the light of modern physics.'[27]

---

26 Artificial General Intelligence is general because it involves a strong interpretation of intelligence as producing and performing intelligent acts rather than simply mimicking certain human behaviors deemed to be intelligent. While for some time work in artificial intelligence was done by programming software several thinkers (such as Thomas Metzinger) have argued that a programmed intelligence should have a mobile body if we hope it to be a general intelligence in the true meaning of the word.

27 Letter of C.S. Peirce to William James, 1894, quoted in Joseph Esposito, *Schelling's Idealism and Philosophy of Nature* (Lewisburg: Bucknell University Press, 1977), 203.

Hopefully we can now begin to see what is at stake in the various forms of continuity, whether continuity refers to the generic space of physics (Grassman and Schelling), of mathematics (Châtelet and Peirce), or in an ontological axiom (Merleau-Ponty). My wager here is that these thinkers each think there is a real structure to the world, but it is one that can only be accessed through oblique strategies. To say that all things think, or to pluralize the world into thinkable signs, avoids the problem of access, and does not give us any clue as to why thinking takes the different shapes it does, not only in our heads but in our bodies, and in the heads and bodies of other species. To be able to think the generic in natural, mathematical, or phenomenological terms, look at the problem from the bottom up. What structures might there be across the world that different kinds of intentionality, thinking-like processes, touch upon, and in what ways?

Schelling and Life as Augmentation

I had after this described the rational soul, and shown that it could by no means be derived from the power of matter — as the other things of which I had spoken — but that it must be expressly created. And that it is not sufficient that it be lodged in the human body exactly like a pilot in a ship, unless perhaps to move its members, but that it is necessary for it to be joined and united more closely to the body, in order to have sensations and appetites similar to ours, and thus constitute a real man.[28]

> Now, we would admittedly degrade animals to the status of machines if we asserted that they were set in motion directly by an external impulse (under which one can conceive everything that acts in a straight line, including attraction), for every merely mechanical impulse passes directly into motion. However, I assume that even where sensibility disappears directly into external movements (i.e., where the movements appear as completely involuntary) they are still not directly

28 Rene Descartes, *Discourse on Method,* trans. Donald Cress (Indianapolis: Hackett Publishing, 1998), 33.

produced through the external impulse, but are mediated by sensibility (as the universal, dynamic source of motion).[29]

The progenitors of embodied cognition, such as Varela and others, have attempted to connect embodied cognition more explicitly with the philosophical tradition — namely with the phenomenological tradition of Merleau-Ponty and Husserl. For both there is an emphasis on the inaccessible aspects of the body. But Schelling goes a bit further. Châtelet concludes the introduction of his remarkable text Figuring Space by celebrating Schelling's model of cognition as being outside of the head while also emphasizing a naturalistic, but expansively naturalistic account, of movement. Thought is a form of motion that clashes with, and is affected by, forces and motions often taken to be located in the physical world. Again, quoting Schelling: 'Mind sleeps in stone, dreams in the plant, awakes in the animal and becomes conscious in man.'[30] Or, as Peirce wrote in relation to the inanimate: 'Inanimate matter is mind whose habits have become fixed so as to lose the powers of forming and losing them.'[31]

Bemoaning both Aristotle's and Plato's obscure notions of matter, Schelling writes: 'The first natural motion of what sinks into proto-materiality is to re-emerge as principles, by which means dimensions, however, requires a mapping of direction.' It is the capacity to map and to place, via dimensionality and direction, that Schelling argues is the fundamental meaning of soul in Aristotle's work.[32] Rationality is consequent upon an augmented

---

29 F.W.J. Schelling, *First Outline of a System of the Philosophy of Nature,* trans. Keith Petersen (Albany: State University of New York Press, 2004), 137.

30 F.W.J. Schelling, attributed quotation in Horatio Dresser, *An Interpretation of Life in Its Relation to Health and Happiness* (1895). There has been speculation that this phrase is Sufi and was translated by Schelling and then misattributed to him.

31 Quoted in Kohn, *How Forests Think,* 62.

32 F.W.J. Schelling, *Philosophische Einleitung in die Philosophie der Mythologie oder Darstellung der Reinrationalen Philosophie* in F.W.J. Schelling, *Sämtliche Werke,* trans. Iain Hamilton Grant, ed. K.F.A. Schelling (Stuttgart: J.G. Cotta, unpublished manuscript, 1856), 9. Bd. XI, Lecture 19.

series of motions built upon a further series of motions — sentience (the ability to track motion and map dimensions) feeds into sapience (self-reflective thought), which pushes sentience behind it as a ground but does not fully escape it. Nonetheless, this structure of dependence will mean that exploring the consequences of sentience will have unexpected consequences for sapience (such as, as Longo argues, when the visual line of navigation and perception became the mathematical line of geometrical construction). While texts such as Steven Shaviro's *Discognition* are more cautious in maintaining some distinction between sapience and sentience, and also illustrate the importance of holding onto different degrees of intelligence, sentience is too often dismissed altogether in many posthuman texts, while sapience is rejected as only primitive in many texts of cognitive science.[33]

Naive idealism (if there really is such a thing) would have to deny actual consequences of human self-modeling (sapience). Schelling is repeating an old critique from his *Ideas for a Philosophy of Nature* in which he argues that mere reflection is a disease that 'fills the world with chimeras, against which, because they lie beyond all reason, it is not even possible to fight. It makes that separation between human being and the world permanent.'[34] Yet, at the same time, one cannot disregard the modeling power of reason merely due to its apparent artificiality. The modeling capacity of reason, and of reason to make judgments and draw conclusions, is one of containment in a world of extainment.[35]

To return to plant life, for Schelling, plants have a less complex faculty for sensation but make up for it through an abundance of creative power. The buds and shoots of plant life for Schelling

---

33 Steven Shaviro, *Discognition* (London: Repeater Books, 2016).

34 F.W.J. Schelling, *Ideas for a Philosophy of Nature,* trans. Errol Harris and Peter Heath (Cambridge: Cambridge University Press, 1988), 11.

35 This is Gilles Châtelet's term used throughout his book *Figuring Space.* Extainment is Grant's translation of Châtelet's use of *extimité* taken from Lacan's seventh seminar. While usually translated as extimacy in an attempt to override the psychical division of inside and outside, Grant follows the topological traces and opposes to it containment in the form of extainment. Simply put, extainment is an expansion outwards that simultaneously contains what is pushes out.

are potentially infinite.[36] On the relation of animal motion to the plant, Schelling writes: 'The animal destroys the atmosphere about itself, and preserves, increases and moves itself like the mobile, growing flame. The plant returns the power of combustion to the burnt, ubiquitous substance, and returns to the atmosphere that substance which makes combustion possible.'[37]

Schelling describes both animals and plants as more or less permanent chemical processes — essentially, clusters of chemical reactions that tend to last a bit longer. These reactions are different in terms of how they relate to sensibility, and how sensibility is transformed first into irritability (how the organism pushes back against its environment), then into reproduction, and finally into technical drive or the manipulation of the inorganic or other-organic beings in the world.[38]

Schelling is then careful to distinguish the difference between regular patterns in nature that seem like intentionality and reason (again pointing to Peirce's thirdness as natural law). Schelling points out the dilemma that if reason is absolute as it claims to be it must be in nature, or caused by nature or, if nature functions by degrees, if bodily perception and intuition shapes the kind of reason a creature can perform, than reason must be additive or augmentative from non-reason.

That is, just as human reason represents the world only according to a certain form, whose visible expression is the human organization, so every organism is the expression of a certain schematism of the intuition of the world. Just as we surely see that our intuition of the world is determined through our original limitation, without our being able to explain why we are precisely limited in this way, and why our intuition of the world is precisely this and no other, so too the life and the intelligence of animals can be just a peculiar (although inconceivable) kind of original limitation, and only their mode of limitation would distinguish them from us.[39] Here Kohn's statement that forests think in a sense because we can 'think them' takes on interesting valences.

---

36 Schelling, *First Outline,* 47.
37 Ibid., 59.
38 Ibid., 131.
39 Ibid., 132.

Schelling argues less in terms of human privilege, but more in terms of how reason has been historically defined. He claims that it does not make sense to grant reason to animals if the reason we wish to do this is because we see them performing orderly acts. Schelling's point is that certain creatures (and perhaps even us) appear to be doing things intentionally because nature has produced them to do those acts, and has granted them those capacities. A few years after the *First Outline,* however, Schelling waxes far more poetic. In his *Presentation of My System of Philosophy,* Schelling writes that the flower is the brain of the plant, whereas the human mind is the bloom of the entire Earth.[40] Schelling repeats this sentiment many years later:

> We must of course assume that the Earth is the point of emergence for humanity — why, we do not know, it refers to relations we cannot survey, but humanity is therefore not specifically a product of the Earth — it is a product of the entire process — not the Earth alone, the entire cosmos contributes to humanity, and if of the Earth, as, continuing from the earlier standpoint, he is, then humanity is not exclusively created for the Earth, but [390] for all the stars.[41]

Schelling's argument is that if humans arrived late on the evolutionary scene, then it may well be that their capacity for thought is one that required a colossal series of processes augmenting and ramifying one another. This is what he means by 'highest' — we are the latest consequence we know of, at least relative to the augmentations of the cosmos. This does not mean, of course, that there is something about the fact of the human that is the highest, as this would completely sever the connection between Peirce and Schelling, in that they both emphasize the synthetic continuity of creation.

In his earlier *Naturphilosophical* works, Schelling discusses and sympathizes somewhat with Goethe's attempt to find the primal germ (*Urpflanze*) — to find that actual entity that could

40 Ibid., 203–4.
41 F.W.J. Schelling, 'Exhibition of the Process of Nature,' trans. Iain Hamilton Grant (unpublished manuscript, 2013), 52.

serve to be the seed of the world. But Schelling soon doubts this search and abandons it. In his latter work, Schelling writes: 'No primal germ, scattered into chaos by ourselves as if fallen from the creator's hand, is required. Everything is primal germ or nothing is.'[42]

Here, once again, we see the connection to Peirce and Schelling and the limits of viewing the world only or even primarily in terms of its fact-hood or in terms of individuals. Both Peirce and Schelling assert the reality of habits as being the mediation or as reading and shaping ourselves in relation to real patterns, to laws of the world. Though, as Vaihinger claimed, Goethe's *Urpflanze* could also be taken as a regulative fiction meaning that Goethe did not really believe there was an original plant, only that thinking as if there was one allowed him to discover the most basic shapes and forms of plant life[43]

For Peirce, the world cannot solely be an amalgamation of facts or things, a belief shared by Schelling. Peirce argues this from the point of view that such a belief would deny the future and its potentiality since, if everything was an amalgamation of particulars, how would we claim there is any substantial future without falling back into a crude notion of teleology? Schelling, meanwhile, returns to the model of the plant, and through the impossibility of the perfect plant, he identifies the Peircean field of firstness — the raw potential and raw sensorial quality at the 'bottom of the world.'

This realm of firstness for Schelling, which the brute genericity of plant life illustrates, is the field of the *potenzen,* or potencies, or what Iain Grant calls 'can-beings.' A potency is, by nature, that which is on the cusp of being, which leaps ahead of itself: a genericity, but bound by its own limitations in not ever being *only* generation. Therefore, nature is not only creation, but a law of

---

42 F.W.J. Schelling, quoted in Iain Hamilton Grant, 'Everything is Primal Germ, or Nothing Is: The Deep Field Logic of Nature,' *Symposium: Canadian Journal of Continental Philosophy* 19, no. 1 (2015): 106–24, https://doi.org/10.5840/symposium20151919.

43 Hans Vaihinger, *The Philosophy of 'As if': A System of the Theoretical, Practical and Religious Fictions of Mankind,* trans. C.K. Ogden (New York: Harcourt Press, 1935), 27.

creation, a materialized habit writ large. This is also why life goes wrong most of the time. While we may know this potentiality as thought, this speaks to our configuration more than nature's.

The strange result of this, however, is not an open world of pure creation, but creation, Schelling argues, in a seemingly backwards sense, runs from the wide to the narrow. The world becomes crowded with actualities, yet at the same time, what *is* must always be less than what *could be* if what is, is the result of the halting creativity: the impure becoming which he takes to be the first principle. The continuity and apparently unbounded creativity of the plant then comes at the cost of complexity, and productivity interrupted becomes that productivity repeated at a more augmented or complex level. While it could be said that a certain notion of connectivity or continuum can be thought by examining vegetative life, saying that such forms of life therefore think would suggest that we understand our own cognitive capacities enough to make the comparison.

And even if we did understand our own cognition this does not guarantee we could understand non-human thought given the ways our species translates concepts between whether through metaphor or via other speculative tools.

Conclusion

> If we compare an animal's body with a house, then the anatomists have studied closely the way it is built and the physiologists have studied closely the mechanical appliances located in the house. Ecologists, too, have demarcated and investigated the garden in which the house is located. But the garden has always been depicted as it offers itself to our human eye, and it has therefore been neglected to take into account how the garden changes when looked at by the subject who lives in the house.[44]

> It's a question of seeking confrontation and of crying Down with grey! Down with the Neutral! Long live Anger! Long

44 Jakob von Uexküll, *A Foray into the Worlds of Animals and Humans* (Minneapolis: University of Minnesota Press, 2010), 200.

Live the Red! We should never forget that grey neutralises intensities by mixing together all the colours that are already given. Style is not a polite way of thinking: no style, no thinking! Style is a discipline of breaking language out of itself, a martial art of metaphor. The haranguing tone of the pamphlet is a working on language, and style is an entirely integral part of thought qua thought experiment. The effectiveness of the philosophical concept is fuelled by a work of torsion of material language on itself.[45]

The fact that nature pervades our forms of thinking does not obstruct, but in fact engenders, grand and systematic thoughts about nature. While the figure of the romantic naturalist — the wandering scientist overloaded with butterfly nets and specimen boxes — may remain laughably naive, we should ask whether the gap between a figure such as Lorenz Oken (a *Naturphilosoph*) and that of Alexander Humboldt (a natural scientist) is actually so wide. The largest gulf was not so much a divide between model and experiment but that, in the case of the former, many of the experiments were turned towards the implement of experimentation itself, that of the *Naturphilosoph's own body*. Oken and Humboldt used similar theories and both conducted physical experiments trying to discover the inner works of the relation between life, physics, geology, and minerology. Yet it is Ritter's overtly speculative tendencies which damn him (retroactively) as a *Naturphilosoph* while Humboldt, despite having shared conceptually romances, is considered a forefather of scientific investigation.

Whether one's model blinds one to the experienced peculiarities of the actual world, or whether the empirical undulations of sense experience are taken to determine the contours of one's model, Châtelet's emphasis on metaphorical dislocations indicates that this is a false choice. This does not mean that science and metaphor are the same, but rather suggests that the explosion of a category in its given domain (such as intelligence) does

---

45 Gilles Châtelet, "A Martial Art of Metaphor: Two Interviews with Gilles Châtelet" (1998), trans. Robin Mackay et al., *Urbanomic.com,* https://www.urbanomic.com/document/gilles-chatelet-mental-ecology/.

not proliferate metaphors in order to increase knowledge of that category. The metaphorical deployment of concepts has to remain adequately tethered to a conceptual weight that is agreed upon by cognitive consensus.

In essence, we cannot equate the inferential testing of a hypothesis, whether philosophical, artistic, political, or scientific, with the metaphorical drift of a concept (even one as big as thought). The metaphorical movement of a concept is more like an experiment that succeeds only if the metaphor disappears, thereby indicating an invariance across domains of inquiry. Or, if the breaking of the metaphor exposes a wider gap between domains than would be otherwise expected, we have a revelation of the devilish details teeming between fields and theories. Following this, we could ask after and interrogate each and every theoretical passage that proceeds to gift subjectivity, or intelligence, to other species. But based only on our shallow understanding of our own capacity to think, how would anyone explain the human metaphorization of other species as itself not particular to human thought?

Thinkers of the Romantic era, Schelling included, are often brought to task for seeing themselves, or at least their reflection, in the whole world, but I would argue that this reads the narrative backwards. The Romantics thought the natural world had an unbounded capacity to ground and generate both processes and things, so the question for them was, 'why do things take the forms they do?' Applying this question to thought, we can see that the Romantic approach is actually more cautious than many of the texts in the realm of plant thinking (and the posthumanities) mentioned above. If we are not careful, the ever-expanding constellation of posthuman turns will leave us in territory far more Romantic than any that the Romantics themselves explored or even dreamed of.

11

Figures

Lisa Dowdall

Call it the Chthulucene: this threshold at the edge of the present in which the monstrous, the chthonic, the tentacular, the horrific, and the weird abound. How to write the Chthulucene? Why not start here in the speculative mode that touches on the hidden, but cannot quite name it — that recovers terror and strangeness in the sym-poietic cascade of crisis and becoming.

Science fiction. Fantasy. Slipstream. Cli-fi. Horror. New Weird. Such stories estrange the world, rendering it and its agents both immediate and uncanny in that immediacy. From John Wyndham's triffids to Jeff Vandermeer's Southern Reach[1] and Ellen van Neerven's plant people[2] — weird stories that reimagine

---

1 The Southern Reach series comprises a trilogy of novels — *Annihilation, Authority,* and *Acceptance* — all published in 2014. Annihilation was adapted for film by Alex Garland and released in 2018. In the series, an unnamed biologist embarks on an expedition to a mysterious coastal environment dubbed Area X, where an ecological cataclysm is warping space and time. 'Southern Reach' not only describes the geography of Area X, but also the agency responsible for monitoring and researching the region. One common interpretation of the series is that alien life has begun to colonise Area X, causing plants and animals to mutate, often grotesquely or monstrously. However, another suggests that the region's natural ecology is spontaneously, yet wilfully, transforming into a 'terroir' — a term that connotes an ecology beyond comprehension, as well as an uncontainable terror rooted in the unknowability of ecosystems undergoing unpredictable transformation.

2 Ellen van Neerven, "Water," in *Heat and Light* (St Lucia: University of Queensland Press, 2014), 67–124. In the story 'Water' in van Neerven's

the interactions between plants and humans in the Chthulucene offer new ways of thinking, or, as Vandermeer claims, *feeling,* in rapidly changing and multi-species worlds.

Weird tales reinforce a 'visceral understanding...in and under the skin, as well as in the subconscious' — they render the Chthulucene *tangible* in that they expose what lies beneath the surface of Nature — what is felt before it is known.[3] For Vandermeer, weird tales "represent the pursuit of some indefinable and perhaps maddeningly unreachable understanding of the world beyond the mundane — a 'certain atmosphere of breathlessness and unexplainable dread' or a 'particular suspension or defeat of...fixed laws of Nature.'"[4] He sees this as a kind of haunting - storytelling that captures indefinable or unrecognisable events as they unfold: the 'progression of decay *in the moment.*'[5]

Responses to the insurgencies of the ongoing apocalypse demand more than science or ethnography. This kind of writing recalls what Muskogee Creek poet Joy Harjo calls 'skin thinking.' *We've been here before, thinking in skin and our pleasure / and pain feed the plants, make clouds. I see it with my eyes / closed.*[6] Skin thinking can evoke the 'deep embodiment' of the Chthulucene — for Harjo, the skin is 'flawed, scarred and embattled,' but also 'beautiful, capable, and trustworthy': it is the 'most basic location of our memories and our stories.'[7] Do weird tales — the

Heat and Light, the plant people are the ancient ancestors of traditional owners of the island region off southern Moreton Bay in Queensland, discovered during a project to transform the islands into an off-shore community called Australia 2, where indigenous people can apply to live.

3   Ann and Jeff Vandermeer, 'Introduction,' in *The Weird: A Compendium of Strange and Dark Stories* (New York: Tor, 2011), xv–xx at xv.

4   Jeff Vandermeer, 'Hauntings in the Anthropocene: An Initial Exploration,' *Environmental Critique,* July 15, 2016, https://environmentalcritique.wordpress.com/2016/07/07/hauntings-in-the-anthropocene/.

5   Ibid.

6   Joy Harjo, 'We Can See It with Our Eyes Closed,' in *A Map to the Next World: Poems and Tales* (New York: W. W. Norton, 2000), 101.

7   Robert Warrior, 'Your Skin Is the Map: The Theoretical Challenge of Joy Harjo's Erotic Poetics,' in *Reasoning Together: The Native Critics Collection,* eds. Craig S. Womack, Daniel Heath Justice, and Christopher

tales that bring us into breathless confrontation with the inexplicable life we too often cut ourselves off from but intrinsically
depend upon — create an embodied connection to the world?
Can skin thinking — thinking through flesh, through touch,
across boundaries — offer a way of situating ourselves in living
networks? Perhaps skin thinking suggests new aesthetic modes
for the Chthulucene. As Thom van Dooren and Deborah Bird
Rose write, 'stories are opportunities to test and explore different
modes of responsiveness, to "learn to be affected" in new ways.'[8]

The story shared here (see below), 'Figures,' is an experiment
in skin thinking — a speculative riff on the constantly evolving af-
filiations and assemblages that characterise vegetal life, especially
within periods of planetary flux. Ecological crisis is more than
terminal apocalypse. 'Figures' thus acknowledges the disastrous
conditions under which the generation of new modes of being,
becoming, and imagining (with and among Others) is possible,
and speculates on the transformative relationships between humans and plants in a rapidly changing biosphere.

∂❧

The blasted remnants of trunks, boughs, and roots lay petrified
in cocoons of ash, their skin burned black and flaking away. Piec-
es had been flung into the river where they lay half-submerged
with the water bubbling around them, thick and sulphurous.
The bedrock had cracked and gas spewed from the vents, turning the water to poison. Bloated fish bloomed on the surface and
swirled downstream, open-mouthed but mute. The humans
that once lived there had fled long ago, leaving the land to fend
for itself and die.

Three figures oozed through the cracks and flung themselves
onto the riverbank, their skin bubbling and their hair falling out.

B. Teuton (Norman: University of Oklahoma Press, 2008), 340–52, at
350.

8   Thom Van Dooren and Deborah Bird Rose, 'Lively Ethography: Story-
ing Animist Worlds,' *Environmental Humanities* 8, no. 1 (2016): 77–94,
at 90, https://doi.org/10.1215/22011919-3527731.

.

Slowly, they recovered and began to metastasise into almost-human forms: a young maiden with a headdress of quetzal tail feathers; a naked giantess with billowing breasts, belly and thighs; a woman with a sun-disc crown.

They had been conferring for many years; now, they agreed, was time to make a change. They began by sinking their fingers deep into the earth and mobilising the organic compounds they needed. Working with the phosphates, amino acids, and nucleotides, they slung hundreds of years of bio-evolution into fast-forward, shrouding the land in green fire. Eukaryotes, microbes, phytoplankton, algae: these were first. But the figures didn't stop there. They sent spore into the nutrient-dense atmosphere and brought the rain. Life accelerated: anthropods turned the soil to loam and peat, and new plants grew viciously, reaching higher and higher, twining together in new filaments covered in thorns and mycorrhizal fungus. Everywhere, plants erupted, spiking into the air like fierce rebuttals, all crowding towards the sun.

Happy with their progress, the figures slipped back into the river and dissolved into the vents, not bothering to seal them up; these they left as gateways for whatever, whoever, would come next. They oozed through the earth's crust together, moving north, where they knew they would find their next target: ripe for change.

ॐ

We came to Svalbard from all the continents, our bags full of seeds and pollen. We had seen our reefs dredged, our rainforests burned, and our coasts flooded. We exchanged uneasy glances when we saw that the plane was called The Beagle. Maybe this trouble all started back then, when we began to discover things that would have gone better left untouched, uncatalogued, unnamed.

We approached on foot, the wind chafing our faces and whining in our ears. There was no sun; the sky sagged over the mountains and the black rock was bare except for patches of grey slush, melting beneath the dense atmosphere.

I paused beneath the blunt concrete entrance jutting out of the permafrost as our guide fumbled off her glove to press her thumb to the touchpad. The façade vaunted Arctic light from its prisms of glass and fiberoptics, and as it licked the exposed skin on my face, I felt as though I, too, was being scanned and processed.

I could not shake this sense of surveillance as we passed through the circular, silent rooms that led deep into the interior — it was impossible to concentrate on what our guide was saying as we cut deeper into the recess of the mountain, down to where they kept the seeds. The words ricocheted off me. There was a throbbing in my teeth, in my eardrums, and in my belly, quickening as we approached the storage rooms. I wondered if I was ill. Zika. Dengue. Malaria. There were new strands all the time; vaccines couldn't keep up with nature's accelerated vectors.

Inside the vault, I stood with the other scientists and watched as staff catalogued the special palynomorphs I'd brought and entered them into the database — gymnosperms from the middle Mesozoic, *Ilex* from the late Cretaceous, *Myrtaceaea* from the Paleocene. The other scientists had brought more ordinary seeds, including genetically modified varieties: drought- and disease-resistant grains, vegetables, and trees. Mine, though rare and of historical value, were not of practical use, but no one was crude enough to say it. People in gloves and masks wrapped all the samples in foil and sealed them inside plastic containers, which they shelved in towering racks that reminded me of banks of computer servers. The air conditioning whined: the permafrost, even here, was melting and the climate control struggled to keep the vault at minus eighteen.

As I made my way back to the entrance, I felt it again, stronger now — as though something immense was gurgling beneath or around me, just on the other side of the walls. There was a whispering, too, like the sound of insects moving through leaf litter. I paused, sensing a pattern to it, a cadence verging on language, but our guide was punching the pin code into the panel at the exit, and when the doors parted the wind gasped through and cleared my head. We all took turns shaking hands with the guide and walked away beneath the reticulated lights of the installation back towards The Beagle.

My supervisor at the museum had asked me to take photographs for an exhibition on the palynomorphs and the seed bank, though I wondered who could possibly spend their money on the entry fee when water and food prices were rising all the time. The only reason we were still open was because staff came to work for free on the promise of their pay cheques one day cashing out.

Later, back at my hotel on the mainland, I flicked through the images I'd taken in the vault. They were all smudged and the glare of the fluorescent lights on the lens had impressed strange fingers of green and orange at the edges. I found I could not remember the names or faces of the people I'd met — not the guide, the other scientists or anyone else. When I tried, more fingers of light obscured them from me and if I strained to recall any specific features, the glare became unbearable and I had to shut my eyes and blink away the pain.

❧

I wound up staying north longer than I planned because there was an ash cloud disrupting the global flight routes. But I found I liked walking across the tundra in the middle of the night when it was still light out. My feet slithered on the moss as I made my way through the tangle of crowberry and bearberry down to the rush of the river. Sometimes I saw voles, sleek and plump with the early summer, slipping into their burrows, licorice root clutched in their jaws. I liked how the midnight sun cast a gold net across the river, and the deep red shadows among the groundcover of willow and cottongrass seemed to throb with a solar rhythm, as though the land itself had a pulse. I hadn't been able to shake the feeling of something breathing or speaking to me in the vaults where I'd deposited my pollens, but long walks helped me push it to the back of my mind. I had dreams, now, of walking up to the vault and finding the doors propped open, the tentacles of some chthonic beast spilling out and reeling me in.

I was taking my last midnight stroll before I flew home when I saw it: a shard of light lodged in the space between two ridges, too bright. I watched as it oozed across the sky and ran down the horizon in a gold sheath that spread across the river. I tried to run but stumbled on the rocks and sprawled on my belly. Wherever the light fell, thickets of grass and weed grew as if in a time-lapse. Soon, they had engulfed my arms, my legs, and my torso, until I was almost submerged. A hole opened in the bracken and I tried to fight my way towards it, but then I felt the scrub pushing me along with fingers of twig and thorn, and I dug my heels in, pushing back, *stop stop stop.* When I was scrabbling at the verge, clawing desperately at the plants that thrust me forward, I looked down and saw the chasm was filled with that viscous gold light that had appeared between the mountains. But I couldn't stop, and I tumbled over the edge and fell down and down, through the bottomless hole, choking on the light, which was thick with pollen and spores.

I landed on my back before the entrance of the vault, its electronic display malfunctioning and the lights blaring bare and white. Above, the sky: roiling, its edges cracked, and through it, long fingers of light, thick like treacle, bursting through, dripping down, swallowing the clouds. I saw thickets of saxifrage roiling and spreading, and I crawled forward, though the door that should not have been left open, and into the vault.

ॐ

Inside, plants had broken the walls and gnawed at the mountain from the inside out. The roots took me instantly, cocooning me in white webs of mycorrhizae like a caterpillar ready for pupation. I did not panic. I felt anaesthetised and let the plants do their work. They wrapped me inside a shell of fungus, and vines came to carry me to the higher branches. I saw other white cocoons swaying like fruit: a new source of energy. There was no pain or anguish. The fungus put me at peace.

I opened my eyes one last time. The world was flooded with pollen, and great webs of climbing vines — liana, moonseed, ivy — had latticed the sky, which was dotted with algal blooms. Halfway between here and there, in a vortex of light, I saw a stream of voles, all running so fast their bodies blurred and then there was only the appearance of speed, a grey streak with a thousand feet, that disappeared through a curtain of light. I smelled burning and glimpsed the world on fire, but the heat could not reach me there.

ॐ

In decrying the poverty of our nomenclature, Eileen Crist identifies the impulse towards, and the arrogance of, naming the present ecological crisis after ourselves: the Anthropocene. She states
that the present eco-historical moment erupts from mankind's
silencing of all Others, including plants. In the Western canon,
these Others do not 'speak, possess meanings, experience perspectives, or have a vested interest in their own destinies.'[9] Instead, these Others — the plants, animals, and all other organic
matter that comprises the biomass upon which all human activity depends — have fallen victim to the organised human project
of forgetting encapsulated by their unnaming. While previously,
these Others were understood to speak through 'primitive, symbolic, sacred, totemic, sensual, or poetic' registers, the language
of risk management and neoliberal production constructs the
natural world as external resource: climate change adaptation
and mitigation; ecosystem services; carbon pricing; natural capi-
tal (etc.).[10] Such language represents an atrophy of the biophysical
bonds between humans and Others in pursuit of a planetary con-
quest that places the human figure at the centre of the narrative.

Yet perhaps this language is also a ward, a kind of spell against
the adaptive and retributive tendencies of the natural world.
Nature, as Wendell Berry reminds us, 'has more votes, a longer
memory, and a sterner sense of justice than we do.' Biospheric
evolution is characterised by perpetual atmospheric and geo-
chemical disturbance. In its persistent expansion, life tends towards complexity, and is generative rather than entropic or adaptive. Yet such perspectives do not account for humans in their
timescales and thus do not fit within the anthropogenic nomenclature of the present. Human ethical perspectives towards the
earth shrink in the face of the autopoietic power of microbial
life. As J. Baird Callicott contends, there is no need to patronise
Gaia with human morality when organisms such as cyanobac-
teria are proven survivors, having weathered changes as drastic
as the Great Oxygenation Event 2,400 million years ago, which

9   Eileen Crist, 'On the Poverty of Our Nomenclature,' in *Anthropocene
    or Capitalocene? Nature, History and the Crisis of Capitalism,* ed. Jason
    Moore (Oakland: PM Press, 2016), 14–33, at 133–34.
10 Ibid., 134.

forced anaerobic organisms to flee to oxygen-deprived environments. Given this point of view, perhaps the present epoch could equally be dubbed the Chytridcene, after the flourishing of the fungus that is afflicting frog species worldwide. Or the Culicidaecene, after the mosquitoes and the vector-borne diseases that might flourish in warmer temperatures.

However, Donna Haraway's term 'Chthulucene' perhaps best captures the multi-species web of 'diverse, earth-wide tentacular powers and forces' that shape the more-than-human world. Haraway's term recognises the 'real and possible timespaces' of entities like Naga, Gaia, Tanagora, Medusa, Hanigasu-hime, and other tentacular beings, who speak in registers that, though silenced, have not yet completely disappeared.[11] These assemblages embrace a kind of kinship not captured by the monstrous figures of the renowned racist H.P. Lovecraft, though they reference its terrifying force. She argues that inter-species webs of speculation — storytelling, in short — help map connections between species. As Eduardo Kohn stresses, life is 'constitutively semiotic...life-forms represent the world in some way or another, and these representations are intrinsic to their being.'[12] This semiotic dynamic between species produces newness. It may be the space in which new ways of thinking and of writing through different sign processes become possible. Stories are, after all, 'of the world, not in the world.'[13]

Writing the Chthulucene does not mean writing the world as an apocalyptic space of terror. It means, instead, acknowledging its liveliness, its strangeness, and its immersiveness. This is different to ethnographic writing, which often plays the role of bearing witness. This weird writing, this skin thinking, reinforces how the world acts on humans in ways beyond cognitive understanding. Timothy Morton argues that fiction that encourages

---

11 Donna Haraway, 'Anthropocene, Capitalocene, Platationocene, Chthulucene: Making Kin,' *Environmental Humanities* 6, no. 1 (2015): 159–65, at 160, https://doi.org/10.1215/22011919–3615934 .

12 Eduardo Kohn, *How Forests Think: Toward an Anthropology Beyond the Human* (Berkeley: University of California Press, 2013), 9.

13 Donna Haraway, quoted in van Dooren and Bird, "Lively Ethography," 89.

'planetary awareness' must also involve an 'uncanny realization of co-existence with a plenum of ungraspable hyperobjects — entities such as *climate* and *evolution* that can be computed but that cannot be directly seen or touched.'[14] Perhaps the bio- or geophysical mass of the plant is another such object. This is not a rejection of an ethos of care based on situated, connected living with and among others, but instead broadens the teleology of life to embrace silenced Others and thereby decentres the human and rejects the name Anthropocene.

'Figures' is a story of the Chthulucene that works through the weird, through skin, and through speculation to evoke the entanglement of human and plant subjectivities. In the Chthulucene, weird stories figure strangeness itself as a way of being-in-the-world. Such stories resist systematisation and capture the inextricable connections between, and the signification of, all living things — including plants.

14 Timothy Morton, "Pandora's Box: Avatar, Ecology, Thought," in *Green Planets: Ecology and Science Fiction,* eds. Gerry Canavan and Kim Stanley Robinson (Middletown: Wesleyan University Press, 2014), 206–25, at 207.

III

Political Landscapes

12

The Colour Green

Prudence Gibson

In the beginning there was green: a chaos of plant cells.[1]

Human representations of nature, as green, are prolific. The history of the colour — as pigments mixed by artists, as iconic sculptural motifs of green figures, as environmental politics and as more recent philosophies of plant life — has influenced a battle between conventions of nature's expression and changing perceptions of the vegetal world. This chapter addresses the colour green as an aesthetic, cultural, and political tool.

Living cells, capable of performing photosynthesis, first appeared on earth more than three and half billion years ago.[2] Plant life was later charted in the creationist doctrine as the earth sprouted vegetation on the third day, when plants yielded seeds and trees bore fruit...and God thought it was good.[3] Conversely, Derek Jarman writes of the Garden of Eden (and of Adam and Eve's eviction from it, post apple-eating) and recalls the angry Adam hacking down the Tree of Knowledge to build the first house.[4] Such terrible irony: as the utopian garden was lost and with that first tree slaughtered by man's hand, as Jarman believed, we began our environmental demise. Climate change is biting at

1   Stefano Mancuso, *Brilliant Green: The Surprising History and Science of Plant Intelligence* (Washington, DC: Island Press, 2015), 6.
2   Ibid., 7.
3   1. Gen. 1:11 (King James Version).
4   Derek Jarman, *Chroma: A Book of Colour* (New York: Overlook Press, 1994), 37.

our heels, and all mythic and philosophical stories of 'green' can now be seen with the eco-eyes of hindsight and reclaimed as a vibrant slice of the colour wheel.

Green, as the vegetal, exists broadly across the surface of the planet as biotic matter: it extends from algae to apple tree, from underground fern to the canopy of a Tasmanian Pine, from nori weed to samphires (succulent halophytes). The greens of the sea, the river, the forest, and the grassy plains are the colours we know deeply and in a fundamentally psychological way. These green and natural things affect our mood and our primal urges to strive, to provide, to care. 'Green' affects our sense of wonder in the face of life. The fear of losing contact with the natural world is solastalgia, a neologism referring to climate-change-induced stress. How we can build a positive perception of *nature* as a construct of imagination or a material and sensual collective memory is a chronic problem in contemporary society.[5] It is due to the loss of green from our everyday habitats that greenness is more than a hue of nostalgia; it has also become a keen political weapon, an activated and dynamic arena of civic and civil debate. Thinking green is the same as thinking for *the long now,* where plans and concepts need to have longevity and long-distance strategic clout.

The Philosophies of Green

Green has conventionally been relegated to the back drop of human action. Nature as a wilderness is something 'over there' and far away from civilised living. Jeffrey Nealon charts the way plants have been considered in light of their excessive growth, for production, and for further generation. This is what has placed them on the lowest rung of the ontological ladder, following Aristotle's conceptions.[6] In *De Anima,* he asks, 'What is the soul of

---

5   Glenn Albrecht et al., 'Solastalgia: the Distress Caused By Environmental Change,' *Australas Psychiatry* 15, Suppl. 1 (Feb. 2007): 41–55, https://doi.org/10.1080/10398560701701288.

6   Jeffrey Nealon, *Plant Theory: Biopower and Vegetal Life* (Stanford: Stanford University Press, 2016), 31.

plant, man and beast?' and Nealon qualifies that this question is less about essence and more about differing capacities.[7]

Hearing green, eating green, thinking green, and representing green are all intrinsic to extended philosophies of the vegetal. Prior to any Christian texts, Aristotle spoke of how he believed plants were close to inanimate beings.[8] This lowly status of plants is misleading, however, as the term 'inanimate' refers to a lack of mobility rather than a lack of sentience. Aristotle's thinking reflected the ideas of the day that mobility, vast distances, or rapid movement across the surface of the earth was not associated with plants. However, seed passage (via wind) and expansive subterranean movement (via root growth) contradict Aristotle's position. This perception of plant life as less relevant than other species does not constitute the 'green thinking' that this essay provokes. The environmental, social, and cultural history of the colour green can be presented as more than a political emblem; more than a representation of nature.

If we think of green in Kantian terms, then we might understand the limits of the concept of the colour. If a leaf is given to us, as Kant explains in *Critique of Pure Reason,* then we understand the form, texture, and colour of a leaf.[9] Green things are described as green so that there is a consensus that the given colour, described as such, is in fact green. When Kant says, 'Nature is beautiful because it looks like art,'[10] he is calling our attention to how we fall in love with our human versions of the world in which we live. Kant's suspicion of this recognition of green as a colour is pertinent, as it disrupts the way we assume we understand perceptual experiences as a whole, and in particular how we understand our ocular experience of colour. Our perception of the colour green in nature as a colour of goodness, bounty, sustenance, and moral good is plagued, then, by our conditioning of all experiences as humans. If nature's laws are contingent,[11]

7 Ibid., 35.
8 Mancuso, *Brilliant Green,* 13.
9 Immanuel Kant, *The Critique of Judgment,* trans. John Bernard (Amherst: Prometheus Books, 2000), 187.
10 Ibid.
11 Ibid., 22.

as Kant says, then perhaps we need to connect experience with perception. Kant's cautious mistrust of green makes sense, even more so when bearing in mind the current associations of green as pure politics.

Any ocular misgivings regarding colour versus perception of colour are played out in colour blindness. Both my sons have been tested for and diagnosed with red/green colour blindness. The general physician used Dr. Shinobu Isihara's scanned plates of coloured dots which form shapes and numbers. Colour-blind people can distinguish between red and green, but not the same tones as those others see. The discernible features of saturation are different for them. In other words, they literally see the world differently. There are degrees of colour blindness; one end of the spectrum being where my sons sit, where they see different shades of red-green colour from others; and the other end of the spectrum where people only see shades of monochrome brown, a dreary fusion of red and green.

The colour-blind among us learn that the colour they see as grass, for instance, is green. In other words, we are trained to understand and perceive colour. The opportunistic side of me then wonders: if we are so impressionable and so open to forming associations between what we see and how we perceive it, then is there a way to make people understand and perceive our environmental plight more keenly? In other words, can the colour green be used to shift our perceptions of 'humans in the world' to 'the world in humans'? This requires a dismantling of boundaries of life as lived by humans to include life as lived by all things.

Eating Green

Vegans follow an ethical life by not eating any produce from any living animal or insect. They eat a lot of green. What will we do now that new plant science proves that plants have sensory capacities, cognitive-like behaviour, and communication skills? Natalie Angier brings to task the ethical vegans and the moralist vegetarians by reminding us that plants exhibit sensory capacities — hearing, smelling and talking.[12] Discovering that plants have sensory

12 Natalie Angier, 'Sorry, Vegans, Brussel Sprouts Like to Live, Too,' *The*

capacities, including being able to sonically 'hear' the reverbera-tions of a caterpillar eating their leaves and responsively trying to curl up its leaves, is disturbing.[13] It is also a reality check to dis-cover that acacia trees emit a poisonous chemical during drought times when oxen over-eat their leaves, to warn down-wind acacias of the imminent threat and also to kill the oxen. The problem of discovering these new high-capacity behaviours of plants creates questions regarding the ethics of eating them.

Michael Marder tackles this sticky issue at the very end of *Plant Thinking* and suggests we eat everything but with care and ethics. His advice is 'if you want to eat ethically, eat like a plant.' He suggests that we don't have to eat inorganic minerals but that what is needed is a 'complete and concerted de-commodification of vegetal life.'[14] So, this is an effort to eat with a green ontology (in this case a sense of fairness and of equal relevance) and not to homogenise what we eat. The plant replenishes us but it has a greater function in the world than as mere nourishment for us.

Gary Francione, who has written widely on animal rights and proclaims an abolitionist vegan approach to eating, participated in an interesting debate with Michael Marder on this issue.[15] Fran-cione stated that 'If plants are not sentient — if they have no sub-jective awareness — then they have no interests. That is, they can-not desire, or want, or prefer anything. There is simply no reason to believe that plants have any level of perceptual awareness or a mind-like quality that prefers, wants, or desires anything.'[16] This position devalues the rights of any form of life that cannot prove its own sentience. Marder responds to Francione: 'It does not make sense to me to advocate something clearly unethical — a total instrumentalization of certain living beings, or plants — in

New York Times, December 21, 2009, https://nyti.ms/2mv39up.

13 Daniel Chamovitz, *What a Plant Knows: A Field Guide to the Senses* (New York: Farrar, Straus and Giroux, 2013).

14 Michael Marder, *Plant-Thinking: A Philosophy of Vegetal Life* (New York: Columbia University Press, 2013), 185.

15 Gary L. Francione, 'Debate with Professor Michael Marder on Plant Ethics,' *Animal Rights: The Abolitionist Approach,* November 3, 2016, http://goo.gl/B41gRL.

16 Ibid.

the name of ethics — a complete de-instrumentalization of other kinds of living beings, or animals. In such advocacy, the end does not justify the means, but the means annul the end.'[17]

What these discourses highlight is the green methodology of shifting models of ontology away from a human-centred view to a multiple species view. Plants, like humans and animals, engage in non-conscious determination regarding their growth. This does not mean a decision is not made.[18] For Marder this is an elemental and philosophical call for a re-structuring of nature ontology; of the food-chain model of being.

The Colour Green

Green, the colour, has facilitated shifts in art history as well as philosophy and geology. It exists as a pigment on paper and as oil paint mixed on canvas since its 19th-century industrial development. Green is taken from below the earth's surface in biotic forms as part of the formations of a deep geology such as the magical malachite. Malachite is a rare semi-precious material that is so mesmerising it incites deep envious desire. Or there are the green-stained stromatolites, rock-like structures that are living fossils. As Bryson says, stromatolites are 'living rocks – quietly functioning replicas of the very first organic structures ever to live on earth. You are experiencing the world as it was 3.5 billion years ago.'[19]

Likewise, green appears as scientific play: it is conjured in cathode ray experiments where a charged electric impulse (cathode ray) is presented to tubes with slightly varying gas. The lower the gas present, the greener the light fluoresces that is reflected in the glass tube.[20] Fluorescence is naturally green. Green also appears

17 Ibid.
18 Prudence Gibson, 'Pavlov's Plants: New Study Shows that Plants Can Learn from Experience,' *The Conversation,* December 6, 2016, https://theconversation.com/pavlovs-plants-new-study-shows-plants-can-learn-from-experience-69794.
19 Bill Bryson, *Down Under* (New York: Doubleday, 2000), 310.
20 'Crookes Tubes,' *The Cathode Ray Tube Site,* December 5, 2016, http://www.crtsite.com/page7.html.

above the earth's surface, high in the atmosphere in the form of the vibrant hues of the Northern Lights.

'Green' has become an increasingly potent subjectile force in science-centred contemporary 'nature art' or bio-art. Think of American artist George Gessart, who bred green plants for art as early as the 1970s,[21] and of Brazilian artist Eduardo Kac[22] whose transgenic co-species experiments changed our understanding of the delineations between human and plant. Both have left a poignant mark on the art-nature scene, blurring the boundaries between the species of plant and human. Land art, plant art, trans-species (human-plant), eco-art: all these praxes follow a green discourse, they participate in a green contract of drawing awareness to tracts of land, and also represent themselves in art within the prism of a green or environmental conceptual theory. It is this nexus of all three green elements that makes new iterations of environmental art the colour of political force.

Writer and natural scientist Johann Wolfgang von Goethe (1749–1832) believed there were only two pure colours: blue and yellow, but that magenta had a non-spectral, essential role. [23] If darkness and light interact, and shadowed colour must be added to a full circle, as Goethe proposed, then these two main colours of blue and yellow might meet most obviously at the point of green. Goethe felt the prismatic fringes of any given prism were where all the colours could be derived.[24] His experimental mode of inquiry and his methodology acknowledged the experimental mediation of the subject and the object, that is, the perceiver and the perceived.

The colour green as a field of inquiry, then, can be both a method and a theory of inquiry — the green in art and the green of art, the green in politics and the green of politics, the green in

21 George Gessart, *Green Light: Toward an Art of Evolution* (Cambridge: MIT Press, 2012).

22 Eduardo Kac, ed., *Signs of Life: Bio Art and Beyond* (Cambridge: MIT Press, 2006).

23 Neil Ribe and Friedrich Steinle, 'Exploratory Experimentation: Goethe, Land and Colour Theory,' *Physics Today* 55, no. 7 (July 2002): 43–49, at 43, 46, https://doi.org/10.1063/1.1506750.

24 Ribe and Steinle, 'Exploratory Experimentation,' 44.

philosophy and the green of philosophy. Goethe's years of observation, poetry and theoretical writing, sometimes published together, are an example of how experience and perception might correlate somewhere in between the subject and object in art.[25]

Green is a loaded word with extended associations that can't be undone unless we first understand them. An enquiry into its etymology as a colour, a pigment, and a natural material helps to resuscitate the force that has always powered this wondrous colour. Vigorous growth and grass are the associated ideas connected with the word 'green.' Green is growth; it is the green light of permission (go!); it is the stimulus to change and to move forward and it is a tender space of the yet-to-ripen. Axioms or clichés surrounding the colour green abound and consistently suggest desirability:

Green is good,
It's not easy being green,
Moving on to greener pastures,
The grass is always greener on the other side,
Oh, she is so green.
(etc.)

Green, as a colour of aesthetically high stakes, achieved newfound interest in 1775 when the Swedish apothecarist Carl Wilhelm Scheele began isolating chlorine and experimenting on chlorine compounds before at last turning his attentions to the chemical properties of arsenic. He soon had a green compound copper arsenite which he manufactured as 'Scheele's green.' The paint colour was used by Turner's 1805 sketch *Guildford from the Banks of the Wey* (1805) and in Edourd Manet's *Music in the Tuilieries Gardens* (1862). Manet's was a late use of Scheele's green because it was out-foxed by the better compound, discovered by Wilhelm Sattler. The 'copper aceto-arsenite, whose brilliant green crystals are made via the reaction of verdigris dissolved in vinegar with white arsenic and sodium carbonate.'[26] Otherwise

25 Johann Wolfgang Von Goethe, *The Metamorphosis of Plants* (Cambridge: MIT Press, 2009).
26 Philip Ball, *Bright Earth: The Invention of Colour* (London: Penguin

known as emerald green, it became more commercially available by 1822.[27]

Surely life in the nineteenth century had enough mordant troubles, what with its high mortality rates and short life spans, without manufacturing poisonous colours. The arsenic content of these arsenite green colours, used in wallpapers, proved to be gravely hazardous. Naturally, paint releases faint dust particles when brushed or knocked. If exposed to rising damp conditions, the pigments would start to decompose and release an arsenic gas. Napoleon Bonaparte is rumoured to have died from his emerald green paint.[28]

Green also has historical infamy as a mode of coloured room. A room of green! There are Malachite Rooms in Castello Chapultepec, Mexico and in The Hermitage, Moscow. These palatial rooms are designed and constructed using the earthy substance, malachite. Malachite is extracted as a semi precious geological specimen from deep in the ground. As a mined material, it of course has imperial and economic baggage. Used as decoration for Russian and South American excess, this gives Malachite a quite particular 19th-century colonial imperial power.

This brings to mind the colonial trend of collecting specimens as an expression of imperial power — the attainment of knowledge and the kudos of ownership — and as a way of spreading tentacles of influence into far-flung places. Of course, these trips of botanical collecting were more than a means of obtaining science. They were also a means of reconnoitre, that is, finding plants that had medicinal value that could be harvested for a profit. In more recent post-colonial times, Ayahuasca trips in Peru continue this tradition. Ayahuasca is a natural ceremonial drug, taken to enhance your experience of the world. Its pursuit has started to cause concern for the Peruvian government. This tourist experience offers journeys into the jungle to try out the hallucinatory ayahuasca plant.[29] The ayahuasca hallucinogen is

Books, 2001), 174.

27 Ibid.

28 Ibid.

29 Ella Damiani, 'Deadly Warning on Peru Tea Travel,' *Traveler,* August 4, 2013, http://www.traveller.com.au/deadly-warning-on-peru-tea-travel-

made is by using several species of the genus mixed together. It is believed that local Peruvians could find the appropriate shrub leaf (*chakruna*) to mix with the vine root (*caapi*) by listening to the plants communicate with one another.[30] Recent plant research regarding plant communication by chemical emissions,[31] which looks at the opening and closing of leaf nodes, and the information passed amongst undergrown roots via mychorrhizal communications, make this Peruvian myth believable.

Green Mythology

If green matter exists beneath the earth's surface, and it can be transformed/created by alchemy as an artist's choice of pigment, so too it has had significance in other, more mythological modalities. Green, in the shape of the Green Man, has a long and apotropaic history. The Green Man is an iconic image that has acted and performed as an important variation of the 'wildman,' a cautionary symbol, a sign of fertility, virility, and growth, as a warning against the gates of hell. So, the image of the Green Man has been considered in Western and Eastern thought as both benevolent provider and ominous threat. In ecclesiastical and secular buildings alike, the iconic image of the Green Man appears as gargoyles and interior architectural design features. This paradoxical figure entered mythology, pagan worship, and finally the Christian church. Imagery of this interaction reaches back in European history to early architectural gargoyles and to German manuscript illustrations from as early as the 12th century.

As Carolyn Dinshaw writes,

My ultimate interest in analyzing the Green Man is to explore ideas of interrelations between human and non-human that — even as species boundaries are broken and

---

2r6ga.

30 'Ayahuasca-Plant Spirit Medicine,' *Medicine Hunter,* November 3, 2016, http://www.medicinehunter.com/ayahuasca.

31 Monica Gagliano and Michael Renton, 'Love Thy Neighbour: Facilitation Through an Alternative Signaling Modality in Plants,' *BMC Ecology* 13, no.19 (2013): 1–6, https://doi.org/10.1186/1472-6785-13-19.

traversed — acknowledge the histories of subjugation and devaluation enabling that human/ non-human distinction in the first place. My goal, then, is not only to trace the afterlife of this medieval imagery but also, and most importantly, to 'think with' the Green Man myself in order to develop a framework for understanding human / non-human relations.[32]

The late filmmaker Derek Jarman, who was also a renowned for his garden landscaping, refers to the woods being reclaimed via the Green Man: 'These woods were the home of the Green Man whose lichen-covered face stares at you from a roof boss in the church. The Green Man moves slowly like the sloth, which is green with algae.'[33] He reminds us not to forget that not all green is good. There are poisons in your hedgerow, and deadly agency in your brewed herbs. Green Aconite, Deadly Nightshade, and Cuckoo Pint will *do you in.*

Norwich Cathedral has a number of leafy heads — nine visages with oak, maple, strawberry, buttercup, or gilded hawthorn leaves. Richard Mabey reads these foliate faces as, in one case, a 'gigolo' and in another, a 'diabalo.' He refers to them as 'symbolically sinful' and 'undoubtedly having a theological status.' He cites Kathleen Basford, a scholar who has worked with the history of green men, as creating an admonitory interpretation.[34] Mabey traces Basford's research into 8th-century theologian Rabanus Maurus's interpretation of Green Man's leaves as sins of the flesh from lustful and wicked men, whereas William Anderson sees the Green Man as a more general universal figure of Gaian connection to the earth.[35]

32 Carolyn Dinshaw, 'Black Skin, Green Masks: Medieval Foliate Heads, Racial Trauma, and Queer World-Making,' in *The Middle Ages in the Modern World: Twenty-First-Century Perspectives,* eds. Bettina Bildhauer and Chris Jones (Oxford: Oxford University Press, 2017), 3.

33 Derek Jarman, *Chroma: A Book of Colour* (New York: Overlook Press, 1994), 38.

34 Kathleen Basford, *The Green Man* (Suffolk: Boydell and Brewer, 1978).

35 William Anderson, *Green Man: The Archetype of Our Oneness with the Earth* (New York: Harper Collins, 1998).

While Anderson's interpretation makes more sense from a contemporary point of view, as it allows for the historical changes from Satan-like terror to more bucolic and wine-guzzling naughtiness to develop, his argument for the leaves emanating from the mouth still needs to be discussed. The attraction of plant imagery in the form of a human-hybrid face (foliate face) began as a seasonal worship. With each new quarter, fruit and berries would arrive, small crops would be harvested, and herbs would be gathered. These gifts were worshipped and mollified. This entered culture through processions, Morris dances (folk music with bells on their shins), and architecture.[36] The pagan worship included both praising and fearing the concept of a green man, a monster that may come out of the woods in spring to rape the women. This leads on from a long history of mythological rapes by the gods. Green Man was a figure of fertility but also of bounty and fecund promise; The Green Man of summer.

They reflect a wish to dominate nature and to guard humanity from evil. Beginning as pagan images, the church soon adopted the Green Man as a means of converting the heathens, appealing to their base framework of belief. The widespread use of these apotropaic symbols is interesting — across Britain, Spain, France, Turkey, etc. The Green Man appears as an emblem on inn signs across Britain by the 16th century. Not just a symbol of fertility and sexual prowess or strength, he was a Bacchus-like figure, a jester, and someone to lead processions and pageants. In the 17th century, the Green Man appeared in association with Distilleries, such as drunk woodmen (wildmen).[37] The Wildman or Green Man became iconic as 'sans god' — the necessity of god to keep evil and devils at bay. The Wildman was typically stupid, but the Green Man was pleasantly stupefied by his intoxicating liquors. So there was a linear shift from Wild Man to Green Man of revelry.

The Green Man, as symbol of irrepressible fertility, potential evil, and finally of bacchanalian fun, has an indeterminacy to it. There has been very little documentation of the Green

36 Brandon Centerwall, 'The Name of the Green Man,' *Folklore* 108 (1997): 25–33, at 26.

37 Ibid., 28.

Man image that has existed for over two thousand years, in some churches outnumbering images of Christ. Jarman notes the related green mythology:

> But other legends rose out of myth. The Green Knight comes to King Arthur's court, his hair and complexion green, riding a green horse, and carrying an axe of green gold. He commands Gawain to meet him at the Green Chapel at the spring solstice. The Holy Grail was formed from an emerald struck from the crown of Lucifer by the archangel Michael...a green chalice.[38]

While the Green Man is a separate entity from Robin Hood or the Green Knight, different from the Swamp Thing or The Hulk, there are some characteristics in common, such as a connection with the wilderness — that which cannot be contained. Green Man is both good and evil.[39] We must be reminded that Green Man is more than a malevolent gargoyle.[40] He is an elusive figure whose mystique provokes our imagination.

The Politics of Green

Have you ever leaned against a paper bark tree and pulled at its papery surface, listening to the sound of the wind shuffling through its leaves, not thinking about whether that tugging of its bark caused a sensory effect in the tree system? Have you ever thoughtlessly snapped off a rose bush branch to smell the intoxicating aroma that sends you into olfactory bliss, not thinking about whether this might elicit a response of chemical activity? I am guilty. Now, with all that we know about communication via chemical emissions in plants as signals, for example, via Suzanne Simard's work,[41] and with all that we know about their sensory

---

38 Jarman, *Chroma,* 38.
39 Richard Hayman, *The Green Man* (London: Shire Publications, 2015), 11.
40 Ibid.
41 Monika A. Gorzelak, Amanda K. Asay, Brian J. Pickles, and Suzanne W. Simard, 'Inter-plant Communication through Mycorrhizal Networks

capacities via the work of Chamovitz,[42] it is the time to deeply consider or re-orient green politics as a social, cultural, and ethical phenomenon in all its iterations.

There is no possibility of turning back the damage of multiple mining sites, careless logging, overuse of land, and erosion from clearing and fracking. In the 1970s, the Western Australian government had a policy where any owners were allowed to clear native bush land of up to one million acres per year in order to develop more farming land. Called the Iron Ball Taxonomy, these kinds of legislations caused early friction between farmers and 'greenies.'[43] The tension between green activists and farmers was especially peaky in the 1980s and 1990s, but things have slowly changed.

Val Plumwood reveals the fundamental issues that plague various green political parties around the world:

> What might loosely be called 'green theory' includes several subcritiques and positions whose relationship has recently been the subject of vigorous and often bitter debate, and which have some common ground but apparently a number of major divergences. The debate seems to have revealed that the green movement still lacks a coherent liberating theory, and raises the question of whether it is and must remain no more than a political alliance of convenience between different interest groups affected differently by the assault on nature.[44]

Plumwood also makes the point that exploitation and disregard for the environment via high technology agriculture, high-yield farming, and sales and licenses for mining to foreign countries

Mediates Complex Adaptive Behaviour in Plant Communities,' *Annals of Botany Plants* 7 (2015): plvo50, https://doi.org/10.1093/aobpla/plvo50.

42 Chamovitz, *What a Plant Knows*.

43 Giovanni Aloi, 'Gregory Pryor: Postcolonial Botany,' *Antennae: The Journal of Nature in Visual Culture* 18 (2011): 24–36, at 26.

44 Val Plumwood, *Feminism and the Mastery of Nature* (London: Routledge 2003), 13.

not only damages the ecosystems, but also damages its parts. In other words, it's not just the land itself that is left with high levels of toxin, extreme erosion, dirty water runoff, agronomy deterioration and water table subsidence etc. These damages are quantifiable but so are the people that are exploited in the making. The farmers who are forced to sell. The bird life that must leave their habitat. The miners who have to bear the separation from families for months on end. Or the fauna and flora that are completely devastated. Promises of regeneration are hollow, being expensive, finite, and poorly regulated. It's impossible to recreate a thriving ecosystem just by planting some saplings and never returning to check on progress. Waterways are ruined and insects are long gone. Plumwood says, 'We die of the product (the destruction of nature) and also of the process (technological brutality alias technological rationality serving the end of commodification).'[45]

Plumwood's idea is that the lack of unity both internationally and within the Greens Party in Australia is caused by a lack of focus about what to do and how to do it. There are economic complexities to mining that make the concept of a domination over nature sound a little precious. There is no strong leadership suggesting alternatives that are powerful enough to make a difference. Perhaps there are too many of us, the deep ecologists, and not enough of them, the social ecologists. We could follow Plumwood's advice and address both the product and the process of ecological assault and create a politics of care that attends to both.

The big question is whether politics can lead the charge for change. Or do we instead need a subtle, sub-political operation of 'green' conversion? Although our perceptions of green life may remain intact (most humans care for the greenery in their lives), the experience of anthropocentric human life (the damage humans have caused to nature since Industrialisation) suggest the incapacity of humans to stem the flow of neo-liberal decision making and overuse of resources, which leaves only a fetid stench.

Green politics is young. For instance, Australia's Greens party is only 24 years old. Many green political parties are susceptible

45 Plumwood, *Feminism and the Mastery of Nature,* 13.

to the forces of economic and political pressure, and they are under duress to be effective as well as moral, to lead a nation as well as follow more ethical lines of governance. These quandaries make it difficult for green groups to flourish.

There are legal issues surrounding plant (nature) rights and they are growing in a tumescent way but there are still no legal precedents in Australia, as there are in Switzerland, New Zealand, Ecuador et al. The Greens Party is young in Australia yet still one of the earliest protagonists around the world. The United Tasmanian Party was the first to run candidates in 1972 and were the first group to espouse green ideals. The successful fighting of the flooding of the Franklin Dam in Tasmania in 1978–83 was a landmark event. The German Green Party was established in 1983 and were the first political party based on green politics of social justice environmentalism and non-violence.

More recently in Australia, 'wild law' is being discussed in the context of extending current environmental laws away from human actions and to better reflect that the environment has rights. Professor Brendan Mackey, of the Fenner School of Environment and Society at the Australian National University, says that wild law was the 'next step in the evolution of environmental law....This is about how law needs to evolve so that it's adequate to meet these big environmental challenges we are facing.'[46] Michelle Maloney, a researcher at Griffith University's Socio-Legal Research Centre and advisor of the Australian Earth Laws Alliance, says, 'Wild law suggests we look at the world as a community of subjects — that we are only one of many players in the ecological sphere.'[47] Her expertise is in earth jurisprudence, or the theory of law, which is a commons-based approach that is centred on the earth and moves her to work towards a governance system that is eco-centric. Cormac Cullinan, influenced by 'Should Trees Have Standing' by Christopher Stone, has pub-

---

46 Graham Readfearn, 'Calls for Equal Legal Rights for Nature,' *The Sydney Morning Herald,* September 16, 2011, http://www.smh.com.au/environment/calls-for-equal-legal-rights-for-nature-20110915–1kbit.html.

47 Brendan Mackey, 'Earth Jurisprudence: Building Theory and Practice,' paper presentation, 3rd Wildlaw Conference, Brisbane, Queensland, Australia, September 16–18 2011.

lished *Wild Law: A Manifesto for Earth Justice*,[48] which calls for using systems theory and indigenous systems to build on the small number of wild laws already in place around the world.[49]

A Green Reminder

Earth jurisprudence is slow, but paying attention is always the first step. We can't hear plants and we can't speak to them. Sometimes we don't even notice, until someone reminds to look a little harder, or tells us to listen with a more attuned ear. The most exciting moment is when we see 'green' for what it really is, as something we couldn't see before. The effect is startling.

For instance, one May morning, during the Sydney Writers Festival May 2016, I stood on a bed of mulchy leaves, surrounded by low-slung branches from a huge fig tree. An original creek had been cemented in and straightened, to run from the ridge down to the harbour. By good fortune, there was an incline where Australian poet Eric Avery stood, so the trickle of natural stream water was a constant passage of sonic time.

He read his poem, speaking to the giant fig tree rather than us (a cluster of poetry acolytes). After Bach had danced across his violin to concert standards, there was another poem. And then, Avery began to move his bow in a repetitive allegretto across the strings of his violin. Back and forth, up and over, before joining his instrument with an Aboriginal song learned from his grandfather. This combination of Bach-like reverie and almost moaning of indigenous song which exists on a minimal register with an earthy range created something disruptive. In fact, it was a merging of two cultures, both earthbound, that I had never heard before in tandem. He used his violin like clapping sticks, like a didgeridoo. He found voice from the reverberations of the tree,

---

48 Cormac Cullinan, *Wild Law: A Manifesto for Earth Justice* (White River Junction: Chelsea Green Books, 2002).

49 Michelle Maloney, 'Introduction to Earth Jurisprudence and Rights of Nature,' paper presentation, Wildlaw Workshop, Darwin, Northern Territory, Australia, May 17, 2013, http://www.earthlaws.org.au/wp-content/uploads/2013/03/Michelle-Maloney_Introduction-to-Earth-Jurisprudence.pdf.

the rustling of the leaves, and the endless flow of water. The song did not rise to a crescendo nor did it mimic a narrative arc with repeated choruses. Instead it existed alongside the tree, winding around its trunk and fluttering around its branches.

The music Avery played was green. He played 'to' the tree. He played 'for' the tree. In other words, there were flows of energy in Avery's playing that moved beyond the violin and beyond his voice. It was a pattern of green-coloured reverberations that pulsed in the bark, under the fallen leaves, behind the reaching branches. These energies had a colour on this day that was decidedly a deep time green, dark and heavy with the history of aboriginal massacres and stolen land. Yes, Avery's music and singing seemed to offer a redemption. He cooled the red of anger into a green of memorial. He created a sound that matched the glade, in its changed and transfigured form.

But that wasn't the surprising part of the green experience. There was yet something to discover that reminded me to take more care, to peer closely and replace a surface view of nature with a deep ecology view: It was when Avery finished playing music that he told us the place where we stood was a massacre site of indigenous people. He explained that the grand old fig tree was not the original tree for that spot. Instead, before white invasion, a paper bark gum tree had been there. *Couldn't we see it,* he asked? *What did he mean?* The poetry lovers looked at each other, bemused, befuddled yet again by our invader whiteness, our inability to see what was in front of us. Patiently, Avery gestured up towards the branching off of the tree and then I saw it.

The limbs of another tree, inside the fig tree, growing out of it. High canopy branches of paper bark were just visible where foliage met bluer skies. The fig had choked the old paper bark and had completely subsumed the entire circumference of its trunk. But still the paper bark had survived. Not symbiotically, the Gardens curator explained but in tandem, without destroying one another. The metaphor was obvious. Avery sang and played, on an equal ontological footing as his double tree. He sang to it, with it. Not for us.

The Green End

So, to finish, a personal story. When I was small, my mother gave me a full set of Derwent coloured pencils. I loved the waxy touch of the crayon tip; I inhaled the woody smell of the pencil length. I was drawn to several colours such as amethyst, rose and acqua, but viridian green was my favourite. It was that strange sea green-blue that you never really see in the sea; Close to a dark sage, but more saturated. I used it in my drawings for trees and for grass, for clothes and for walls. I used it for flowers and for cars, for signposts and for dog leashes. It soon became a stub among its tin of giants, too small to grip, left as a reminder of the full colour wheel. Its place in the case stood out as an abused and overused pencil, now no more than a sad little butt of chromium oxide. Handing these pencils down to my daughter, she has all the colours except that viridian green. I used it too much.

My part in a 'green contract' is to voice the story of the myriad tales of the colour green, to participate in critical plant studies, and to aid an extension of those studies into aesthetics — visual art, mythology, and philosophy. By thinking green, we may yet discover a connection with the earth we couldn't perceive before.[50]

50 Marder, *Plant-Thinking*, 185.

13

Persons as Plants: Ecopsychology and the Return to the Dream of Nature

Monica Gagliano

Introduction: The Hero's Mythical Journey

> *In the human spirit, as in the universe, nothing is higher*
> *or lower; everything has equal rights to a common cen-*
> *ter, which manifests its hidden existence precisely through*
> *his harmonic relationship between every part and itself.*
> — Goethe, *Ernst Stidenroth*[1]

With the provocative title *Plants as Persons,* Matthew Hall's brainchild had stirred up an exciting discourse on the perception and the action of people towards plants, and more generally, Nature. In sharing my excitement over this book with a friend, I was asked whether the word *persons* is 'proper English' and whether it is even reasonable to equate plants to people.[2] So let this essay

---

1 Johann W. Goethe, 'Ernst Stiedenroth: A Psychology in Clarification of Phenomena from the Soul,' in *Goethe: The Collected Works, Volume 12, Scientific Studies,* ed. Douglas E. Miller (New York: Suhrkamp, 1998), 45–46.

2 In his book, Hall clearly specifies that the view of plants as persons is not concerned with projecting human-like faculties where they do not exists, but rather with relating to these other-than-humans as living beings who have their own perspectives and ability to communicate in their

be the journey that starts there, at the origin and significance of this word; a journey that weaves its way through the powerful threads of Silverstein's storytelling[3] to nurse the Western rational mind from the bigoted Aristotelian idea of the inferior nature of plants to the timeless and soul-full reality of plants as teachers experienced by indigenous healers and shamans across the globe. And from the world of shamans, so beautifully embroidered with magic and deep truths, let this journey bring us back to the scientific world of the Western mind, but with a new much-needed perception of what humans call 'Nature.' And just like in T.S. Eliot's poem 'Little Gidding,' let this be a journey that ultimately returns us to the place from where we started, but which we now truly know for the first time.[4]

Linguistic Heritage and the Human Condition: What is a Person?

Generally, the term 'person' is used to indicate a human being. However in its origin the word, derived from the Latin word *persona*, which in turn was most probably derived from the Etruscan word *phersu,* which referred to the masked actors that appeared in theatrical performances where the mask described the character an actor played on stage. I find the epistemology of this word to be particularly intriguing, because its original meaning is still interwoven with our current thinking, so much so that it has been retained virtually intact within the Jungian framework of modern psychoanalysis. Indeed Jung referred to the *persona* as the outer face of the psyche, the mask through which human be-

own way. Matthew Hall, *Plants as Persons: a Philosophical Botany* (Albany: SUNY Press, 2011), 105.

3   Shel Silverstein (1930–1999): American poet, composer, cartoonist, and author of children's books.

4   One of *Four Quartets* written in 1942 by T.S. Eliot on the main theme of time and eternity, *Little Gidding* exemplifies the cyclic progression of human understanding. Each of the four Quartets derives is name from a place which was particularly important to the American poet. Little Gidding is a village in the historic county of Huntingdonshire (now Cambridgeshire), which Eliot visited in 1936. Thomas S. Eliot, *Four Quartets* (London: Faber & Faber, 2001).

ings act out their roles as their relate to each other and the world around them. While the mask lubricates and eases our social exchanges in everyday living, this role-playing game comes with the ever-present danger of identifying one's true Self with the mask (or several masks). When we fall for it, we shrivel behind the mask or ego-image of our mental and emotional states where we can only see and experience the distorted shadows of things,[5] slipping down towards a sort of *psychological mummification.*[6] Because life lived behind all these masks becomes a very lonely and unfulfilling affair, we inevitably strive for the opposite state of being that leads to true psychological development, guiding us back towards the experience of the Self and the acceptance of everything 'as is' (rather than what we think it should be). Now, if the drama of life (as we perceive it) is the special ingredient that makes a *person,* then plants are no persons. Plants live no dramas and require no psychoanalysis to unlock otherwise closed doors in their emotional lives, as we do. And this is so because plants are at peace with being exactly what they are, plants.[7] By being truly immersed in the matrix of Nature, plants 'know' what their place in Nature is, but do we?[8] So, allow me to share a story.

5   In Book VII of the *Republic,* Plato presents one of his most famous analogies, the Allegory of the Cave. Plato viewed the human condition through the analogy of chained prisoners, who can only see the distorted shadows of reality on the wall of a cave. Plato, 'Republic,' in *Plato: Republic,* Loeb Classical Library Volume 276, ed. and trans. Christopher Emlyn-Jones and William Preddy (Cambridge: Harvard University Press, 2013), 514a–517c.

6   Peter O'Connor, *Understanding Jung, Understanding Yourself* (Richmond: Methuen, 1980), 66.

7   If we were to categorize plants according to human standards, they would be described as unitive beings living in the universal paradigm of the undifferentiated field of consciousness. For a user-friendly description of the Wilber's *unitive* state as well as the other developmental stages of consciousness, see Susanne Cook-Greuter, *Ego Development: Nine Levels of Increasing Embrace,* 2005, http://www.integralchurch.se/media/9levelsofincreasingembrace.pdf.

8   Re-situating the human being in the living world by understanding our place and task on this planet is the focal domain of Philosophical Ecology. For example, see Erazim Kohak, *The Embers and the Stars: A*

Storytelling: From a Giving Tree to the Pyramid of Life
(Upside-Down)

This story goes something like this.... Once there was a huge apple tree and a little boy. Every day, the boy would come to the tree to play. The boy would climb up the trunk, swing from the branches, play with the leaves, eat the apples, and take a nap under the shadow of the tree. And the boy was happy. And the tree was happy. As time went by, the boy grew older and was no longer interested in playing around the tree. Instead he wanted money to buy things and asked the tree for help. Because she loved the boy very much, the tree was delighted to offer him all her apples, so he may sell them to make money and be happy. So the boy climbed the tree, took all the apples, and did not come back for some time. Then one day, the boy returned, this time wanting a house and asking the tree for help. Because she loved the boy very much, the tree gladly offered all of her branches to the boy, so he may use them to build a house and be happy. The boy cut all the branches off, took them away to build a house, and did not come back for a long time. Then once again, the boy returned feeling sad and unhappy. He wanted a boat to take him away and so he asked the tree for help. And again, because she loved the boy very much, the tree happily let him cut her down so he may build a boat in which to sail away and be happy. And the boy cut her down to a stump, built a boat and sailed away. It took many years for the boy to return to the tree. Now an old and tired man, he only wanted a quiet place to sit and rest. 'Well, an old tree stump is a good place for sitting and resting. Come boy, sit down and rest,' said the tree. So the boy sat down and rested, and the tree was very happy.

This is the story of *The Giving Tree* by Shel Silverstein, who certainly wrote it for children, but even more so for adults. In fact, whether at first glance it looks just like another bedtime story, both children and adults find this tale especially moving and inspirational because it speaks to us of unconditional love.[9]

Philosophical Inquiry into the Moral Sense of Nature (Chicago: University of Chicago Press, 1984).

9   The word 'love' is not used here to denote a human value or construct

That is the kind of love that places no limits and does not set any conditions on what it should be. That is the kind of love that Nature, which is overwhelmingly made up of plants, offers freely and which human beings symbiotically depend on to survive[10] and so deeply ache for to be happy.[11] On the stage of life where we

that we may project on to how plants feel or relate to us. Instead, it refers to the idea that plants together with non-human animals are indeed endowed with their *own* personal way of expressing feelings. Darwin himself discussed the topic of animal emotions in *The Expression of the Emotions in Man and Animals* (London: John Murray, 1872) and also claimed that 'the lower animals, like man, manifestly feel pleasure and pain, happiness, and misery': see Charles Darwin, *The Descent of Man and Selection in Relation to Sex* (London: John Murray, 1871), 39. Moreover, recent scientific research has provided evidence that animals feel a full range of emotions, including fear and love: for example, see Marc Bekoff, 'Animal Emotions: Exploring Passionate Natures,' *Bioscience* 50, no. 10 (2000): 861–70, https://doi.org/10.1641/0006-3568(2000)050[0861:AEEPN]2.0.CO;2. This is somehow unsurprising given that we share common neurochemicals, such as serotonin and testosterone, and even brain structures, such as the hypothalamus that are important in the expression and feeling of emotions like anger, for example. Thus, the word 'love' clearly does not describe an exclusively human domain; the real question should not be about whether animals experience emotions or feelings but rather *how* they experience them in the privacy of their mental states. In regards to plants, the state-of-affair is truly not much different; plants exhibit cooperative and altruistic behaviours similar to those seen in animal social systems. It is a given that they have their *own* way of expressing their concern for the welfare of others, but so do humans. Based on the rapidly mounting scientific evidence of the amazing animal-like feats plants are capable of, I suggest it would be wise to assume that they do 'love' until proven otherwise.

10 In principle, our symbiotic relationship with plants is of a commensal nature, where plants provide us with oxygen, food, shelter, clothing and fuel amongst other goods, while they are neither helped nor hurt. However, it stands to reason that an excessive number of commensals (e.g., uncontrolled increase in the human population) on a single host (e.g., our forests as a whole) will indeed hurt the host and the relationship will slide towards the parasitic.

11 Glenn Albrecht, Gina-Maree Sartore, Linda Connor, Nick Higginbotham, Sonia Freeman, Brian Kelly, Helen Stain, Anne Tonna, and Georgia Pollard, 'Solastalgia: the distress caused by environmental

all play, I believe no human being can truly deny plants their role as nurturers of the human physical and emotional subsistence. Yet according to the Western hierarchical understanding of the natural world, those motionless and insentient beings are clearly of an inferior nature to animals and (of course) humans, and are therefore relegated to the bottom of the pyramid of life. So what is going on here?

Let me share another story. In early 2010, I went to a little village near the seaside in the Philippines and there, I met William. He was a very playful and energetic man, and a well-regarded psychic surgeon.[12] Because of our respective natures, I almost incessantly asked questions on his work and he gave almost continuous and clear explanations on it. During one of our numerous exchanges, he described to me the nature of plant, animal, and human beings as they are seen from the *astral* plane or the plane of existence that modern physics calls the '9th dimension.'[13] In this emotional hyperspace, plants are indeed the simplest beings as they exclusively embody the most refined energy of love. Animals are more complex because they express love as well as fear. And finally humans, certainly the most multifaceted, embody the energy of love, fear, and doubt. According to William, doubt is the root of all our *dis-ease* states, which include both ailments manifested in the physical dimension and the discomfort expressed emotionally, and it is the cause of our emotional inadequacy that prevents us from truly loving. It was immediately clear that my academic understanding of life hierarchies needed significant adjustment: who was I to rule out the possibility that the Western mind got the pyramid of life upside down?[14]

change,' *Australasian Psychiatry* 15, no. 1 (2007): S95–S98, https://doi.org/10.1080/10398560701701288.

12 Psychic surgery is widely practiced in the Philippine Islands, but it is also performed in Indonesia, Central Africa, and Brazil. During psychic surgery, the body is opened with the bare hands of the healer. Tumours, body tissue, a blood clot, or any unwanted obstruction are removed painlessly from inside the body, without the use of anaesthesia and while the patient is conscious.

13 William A. Tiller, *Science and Human Transformation: Subtle Energies, Intentionality and Consciousness* (Walnut Creek: Pavior, 2007), 56.

14 This has parallels with writing in East Asian Buddhism, which sees

Role-reversal: Plants as teachers and the solution to the environmental crisis

For millennia, plants have been regarded as animated, superior intelligent beings, honoured as teachers by many cultures. In the Americas for instance, dozens of indigenous groups still revere plants for the psychological and spiritual impacts they have on both individuals and communities. In late 2010, I was fortunate to find myself in the Amazonian jungle under the nurturing guidance of a Peruvian shaman, where I had a brief but direct experience of this plant teacher-human student relationship that, until then, I had considered just an interesting concept. The teacher-student dialogue is developed through a specific *die-ta*.[15] This is a period of apprenticeship spent in isolation in the jungle, during which the student observes total sexual abstinence and a very strict diet, while ingesting parts of the teacher plant at varying interval depending on the species. It is during such *dieta* that the initiate learns how to connect with the spirit of that particular plant, which will instruct him/her through visions and songs[16]. Indeed, the communication between humans and plants is established through a non-dualistic language of sound; and, shamans must learn the song that each species of plant possesses for the teaching to take place.[17] In Peruvian shamanism, in par-

plants as enlightened beings, or 'perfect yogis.'

15 Luis Eduardo Luna, 'The Healing Practices of a Peruvian Shaman,' *Journal of Ethnopharmacology* 11, no. 2 (July 1984): 123–33, https://doi.org/10.1016/0378-8741(84)90035-7.

16 In the Western world, this kind of shamanic work is often equated to the use of the psychoactive herbal brew, known as ayahuasca. And indeed, the 'ayahuasca movement' in the West has gained incredible popularity over the last few decades. Yet, all *vegetalistas* (i.e., plant shamans) are adamant about the crucial importance of the *dieta* and insist on the fact that the real work of becoming familiar and sensitive to the spirit of the plants and their teachings takes place during the isolating period of the *dieta*. Because of this, attending to ayahuasca ceremonies alone will not take the student very far.

17 Robert Greenway, 'The Wilderness Effect and Ecopsychology,' in *Ecopsychology: Restoring the Earth Healing the Mind,* eds. Thedore Roszak, Mary E. Gomes, and Allen D. Kanner (San Francisco: Sierra Club

ticular, the plant teachers reveal themselves during the *dieta* and gift the shaman with their songs, called *icaros*. And today still, shamans are above all people who sing and, through chanting, endeavour to establish and retain a strong ecological and spiritual connection with individual plant species, so that they may be taught, for example, how to diagnose and treat specific illnesses.[18] My personal journey into the world of Peruvian plants and their shamans turned out to be an extremely fruitful and rich experience; yet upon my return home to Australia, it was even more interesting to learn that there is no need to go to these far away lands of shamans to experience plants as teachers.

Recently, plant spirit medicine man Phil Roberts pointed out to me that plants are in fact mentoring us on how to find solutions to our human problems in spite of and within our concreted western world of cities and technology. Phil sits next to a plant on the verge of an ordinary suburban street, quiets his mind and then waits patiently to be invited in for an 'internal' conversation with the spirit of the plant. And it is within this meditative space that the plant delivers its *medicine* to him and for him to use with the people that come to his clinic. Indeed being 'whole' rather than divided by fear and love, plants are to modern humanity a unique and wholesome source of medicine in all facets. This is why our learning from plants does not have to be limited to an understanding of their chemical properties that heal the physical body. Of course, we already know that plants offer humans more than physical healing; we already know that they are a constant source of inspiration, and through this we have already learnt, for example, how to bind fabrics together (like the tiny hooks found on the surface of burdock seeds, which have inspired the creation of hook-and-loop fasteners, commonly known as Velcro) or harness energy more efficiently (like the recently designed biomimetic heliotropic solar panels that mimic the way plants gradually tilt towards the sun to optimize solar energy capture).

Books, 1995).

18 Luis Eduardo Luna, 'The Concept of Olant as Teachers among Four Mestizo Shamans of Iquitos, Northeastern Perú,' *Journal of Ethnopharmacology* 11, no. 2 (1984): 135–56, https://doi.org/10.1016/0378–8741(84)90036–9.

Yet, plant teaching extends far beyond the pragmatism of the material world; it heals the mind by piercing through the rich drapery of appearances (made of energy and consciousness) that we recognize as physical realities, but which both modern science and ancient wisdom agree on describing as a *Dream*. Within this dream, plants have one simple teaching for us, whether it is delivered through our devotion to gardening on the weekend or our venturing into the jungle to apprentice to indigenous shamans: they teach us to move past the illusion of duality that restricts modern life to the rhythm of Time, and enter a level of *entangled* reality where there is no time and no separation into self and other—hence no conflict, no destruction, no ecological crisis.[19] Why then, just like the boy in *The Giving Tree,* do we seem to be so obstinate about living dysfunctionally in apartheid with plant life and hence perpetuating a state of crisis?

In the view of indigenous people around the world, the relationship between humans and Nature, specifically plants, is an unequivocal one of respect. In the words of Australian Aboriginal elder and custodian of Uluru as well as beautiful friend, Uncle Bob Randall:

> We live in Kanyini! The word Kanyini means being responsible with unconditional love for all living things and each one of us need to live a life of caring. It means appreciate all things that care for us in their many ways; from the air we breathe,

19 Plant research has recently shown that fundamental processes like photosynthesis (and possibly sound production), may be of a quantistic nature, where atoms and molecules are 'in sync' with each others moving exactly together in space and time in an 'entangled' reality. Yet beyond plants, a closer look to Nature reveals that such collective 'in tune' behaviour is in fact an essential aspect of all life and it is found at all levels of biological organization from the symbiotic cooperation of the internal organelles of the eukaryotic cell to the evolution of organismal colonies and societies, like those of many animals including humans. Despite the general idea that biological evolution is the outcome of fierce competition among selfish parties, the evidence indicates the complex web of life is a system built on minimal conflict and instead on the substantial cooperation of units working together to create more complex systems while maintaining their own individuality at the same time.

the water we drink to the plant people that gives us life and the many animals whose lives are taken so that we can live. They are all full of love, full of Kanyini and we too need to reach that level of living our life moment by moment, learning to really care for each other so that there are no strangers in our neighbourhood, there are no strangers in the town we live in, no strangers in the cities, no strangers in the world. We are all one family[20].

Because of this *unitive* ability to feel at one with life and see the dignity of all manifestations of life, this view of the world cherishes and accepts all beings 'as is' in a non-controlling and non-hierarchical way. Away from such eco-psychological wisdom also known as the Dream of Nature, most of us experience the dualistic world of industrialized Western societies and its conventional mind, which by definition is characterized by the concepts of isolation (the self) and conflict (the others). Such mind is indeed incarnated in the grand myth of modern Western science, based on the unquestioned assumption that subject and object are separate and the blind belief that we can control Nature through proper scientific methods and analyses. Clearly through the lenses of this conventional mind of maximal separation between subject and object, we believe reality to be something external to ourselves, made up of solid, permanent objects waiting to be scientifically measured, analysed, and controlled for our gain. While this may indeed be how a fully-grown and functional adult is defined and accepted within the current model of modern society, I am intrigued by the fact that such a scientific mind frame neatly corresponds to the Piagetian *formal operational stage* representative of the cognitive development of 11–16-year-old children, also known as the adolescence period — when humans start developing the ability to think about abstract concepts and start exhibiting a capacity for logical thought and deductive reasoning. As such, we may simply recognize that the modern Western mind is at an immature developmental stage, still naïve of the fundamental inter-connectedness of all phenomena and just like a young and irresponsible adolescent, it is focused on externalizing and

20 Bob Randall, personal communication (Uluru, August 2012).

projecting outwardly the internal delusion of separation and the associated turmoil. Then the current crisis, whether perpetuating environmental abuse or other destructive behaviour, is the outer manifestation of this inner distraught state, which can only be resolved by learning who we are and how we fit into the rest of Nature, thereby moving beyond adolescence into the powerful and responsible time of adulthood.

Personally, I believe we are experiencing this growth right now; in fact, we now recognize our destructive capacity and have already acted by creating, for example, natural parks to protect natural habitats and their species from our own devastating activities. These protected areas are places where we can be in harmony with Nature; although it is true that they still occupy only a relatively small portion of the continents, it is also fair to acknowledge that we have only 'woke-up' to this necessity in the course of the last century. We are now actively restoring forests and recycling paper; countries such as Costa Rica have shown great example of 'adulthood' by investing funding and resources, previously devoted to their military industry, towards the conservation of their land, protection of their forests, and education of their people. Successful programs for the conservation and sustainable use of biodiversity already exist in many countries, which have now also developed comprehensive legal frameworks to implement such programs effectively.

Moreover, Earth jurisprudence, a network that contributes to granting rights and legal standing to Nature and hence actively offering viable solutions in support of the health of ecological systems, is now a reality around the world. Despite the continuing destructive activities such as mining, fracking, polluting, and deforesting, I believe that the rise of programs and initiatives like those described above is a clear indicator of the change that is currently happening as part of our evolution as a species. So, are we finally moving beyond adolescence and becoming responsible adults? Ironically, just as the young boy in *The Giving Tree* does, it seems we need to go around in circles a few times before discovering that the salve of peace, solace, and contentment is simply attained by listening to the invitation of the tree, and once again, sitting in the Dream of Nature, yet with a mature post-conventional and unitive mind. After all, isn't it true that the hero's journey found in so many narratives around the world is completed when the hero hears their own story and the emerging wisdom returns the hero home?

14

Rooted

Justin Clemens

The Greek for tree is dendron,
Dendrites neurons' branched projections
Sparking to soma. The phrenology
Of diaphragms spores the hidden lights
Of twinned breath, the dendritic cells
Bifurcating to bans of the bond
Between adaptive and innate.
I am a lichen. A photo is synthesis
As space and time inner sense
And translation ice in the night
Shattering the word vessels.
No plants in the waste but gods.
The trees are gone. Kin are cloned
With fungal hyphae that penetrate
The mass of the root. Smut and rust
Runnels wreathe the rare wraiths of rain.
Rats race through the fibrous homorrhea
Of vegetal percepts, hypnopompic,
Heliotic, the ciliated protozoans
Of feast. Agony the brain that thinks
Only itself in the fire of deprivation.
Trees talk to each other about the forest
That they are, unions of divisiveness.
Small beasts with ball joints swing large
Across the first entropy of axons.
Symbiotic each becomes a heart
Pulsing in a labyrinth of bone,
Green and dying in an earth lake of blue.

15

Agricultural Inventiveness: Beyond Environmental Management?

Lucas Ihlein

In 2014, I began working on a collaborative art project called *Sugar vs the Reef?* The project came about following an invitation from John Sweet, a retired farmer and active community worker in the Queensland town of Mackay. Sweet's hunch was that the involvement of artists in a complex environmental management problem might help to catalyse positive transformations in the sugar cane industry, which is often accused of polluting the pristine waters of the Great Barrier Reef with agricultural run-off.[1] This chapter is based on some of the early field research for *Sugar vs the Reef?* and my task is to present the inventiveness of three change agents: two human and one non-human. The first is Simon Mattsson, a sugar cane farmer in Mackay, and a founder of Central Queensland Soil Health Systems (CQSHS). The second is Allan Yeomans, director of the Yeomans Plow Company on the Gold Coast and inventor of the Yeomans Carbon Still: a device for measuring carbon sequestration in soil. The third change agent has been around for millennia: the humble plant — specifically grass — and the complex soil community of which grasses are an integral member. While presenting the inventiveness of these three change agents together here, I also want to point to

---

1 *Sugar vs the Reef?* is a collaboration between artists Lucas Ihlein, Kim Williams, and Ian Milliss, together with farmers and community members from Mackay, Queensland. See Lucas Ihlein et al., 'About the Project,' *Sugar vs the Reef?*, http://www.sugar-vs-the-reef.net/about/.

some of the factors that have thus far inhibited the broader up-take of their inventions. I do so in the hope that identifying such barriers might be a small positive step beyond the paternalistic discourse of environmental management, and towards the formation of more dynamic relations in social and ecological systems between humans and plants.

The Great Barrier Reef, Sugar Cane Farming, and Soil Health Systems.

The bleaching of the Great Barrier Reef (GBR), which received widespread media coverage in early 2016, [2] brought attention to the harmful effects of global warming on coral ecosystems.[3] Besides climate change, the major factors affecting the health of the reef include fishing, coastal development, and run-off from terrestrial agriculture.[4] Due to the abundance of land used for growing sugar cane in the GBR catchment along the Queensland coast, this industry has come under particular scrutiny. The most obvious impact of sugar cane farming derives from run-off, as nitrogen-based fertilisers, soil sediments, and pesticides are carried by heavy rainfall into adjacent creeks and rivers and out to sea.[5] The addition of agricultural nitrogen to the GBR ecosystem

---

2 Michael Slezak, 'The Great Barrier Reef: A Catastrophe Laid Bare,' *The Guardian,* June 6, 2016, http://www.theguardian.com/environment/2016/jun/07/the-great-barrier-reef-a-catastrophe-laid-bare.

3 The world's oceans have begun to increase in temperature, as well as becoming more acidic as they absorb carbon dioxide from the atmosphere. Warming waters can trigger 'coral bleaching' — the process by which coral polyps eject the zooxanthellae algae with which they exist in symbiosis. If the water remains too warm for too long, the zooxanthellae will not return, and the coral will die. Increasing acidity weakens the calcium carbonate skeletons of the coral. This process is described succinctly in Callum Roberts, *Ocean of Life: How Our Seas Are Changing* (New York: Penguin, 2012), 96–108, 191.

4 Great Barrier Reef Marine Park Authority, 'Great Barrier Reef Outlook Report 2014,' *Great Barrier Reef Marine Park Authority,* http://hdl.handle.net/11017/2855.

5 Nearly 70,000 tonnes per year of agricultural nitrogen runs into the Great Barrier Reef, as well as approximately 14,000 tonnes of phospho-

helps to increase the population of Crown of Thorns starfish, which predates on coral. This weakens the resilience of the coral and its ability to bounce back from periods of higher than normal temperatures.[6]

The sugar cane industry has been subject to carrot and stick legislation to encourage farmers to reduce the amount of run-off from farms, and significant improvements have been made through the adoption of Best Management Practices (BMP) over the last 30 years.[7] Improved practices for sugar cane now include: cutting green, the elimination of the traditional pre-harvest burning; trash blanketing, the application of sugar cane mulch onto the surface of the soil; minimum till, the reduction of soil-disturbing tillage practices; and the application to the soil of mill mud, a nutrient-rich substance that is a byproduct of milling. The use of these and other BMP methods — such as the increased efficiency of fertiliser application by GPS-guided tractors — can improve the health of the soil and minimise its tendency towards erosion, thereby reducing the nutrient, herbicide, and sediment run-off significantly. However, the uptake of BMP by sugar cane growers is still insufficient to meet the federal government's *Reef Plan 2050* requirements of an 80% reduction in run-off by 2025.[8]

rus and at least 30 tonnes of herbicide. These chemical inputs produce tangible detrimental effects on the coral reef ecosystem. See Jon Brodie et al., 'Terrestrial Pollutant Runoff to the Great Barrier Reef: An Update of Issues, Priorities and Management Responses,' *Marine Pollution Bulletin* 65, nos. 4-9 (2012): 81–100, https://doi.org/10.1016/j.marpolbul.2011.12.012.

6   'Backgrounder: Impact of Land Runoff,' *Australian Institute of Marine Science,* http://www.aims.gov.au/impact-of-runoff.

7   'About Smartcane BMP,' *Canegrowers,* http://www.smartcane.com.au/aboutBMP.aspx.

8   Lara Webster, 'Queensland's Cane Industry Milestone Tarnished by Ongoing Criticism of Great Barrier Reef Run-off,' *Queensland Country Hour,* ABC Rural, April 11, 2016, http://www.abc.net.au/news/2016-04-11/queenslands-cane-industry-milestone-tarnished-by-criticism/7315730; Queensland Government, *Great Barrier Reef Report Card 2015: Reef Water Quality Protection Plan,* State of Queensland, 2015, http://www.reefplan.qld.gov.au/measuring-success/report-cards/2015/assets/gbr-2015report-card.pdf.

Mackay farmer Simon Mattsson has been agitating for sugar cane farming practices to improve well beyond BMP standards: he began experimenting with no-burn harvesting in 1986, and stopped tilling for fertiliser application the following year. However, despite his adoption of these improvements, from the late 1990s, Mattsson noticed a pattern of declining yields in his annual sugar crops.[9] This led him to a long period of research and experimentation, including practical on-farm trials and observations, alongside a survey of published literature on regenerative agricultural systems. In 2013, Mattsson was the recipient of a Nuffield Scholarship, enabling extensive field trips to explore holistic farming systems in eleven countries. Upon his return to Mackay, Mattsson established Central Queensland Soil Health Systems (CQSHS), an affiliation of farmers dedicated to exploring the crucial role of soil ecosystems in agriculture.

In his Nuffield Scholarship report, Mattsson outlines the principles underpinning his experiments in sugar cane farming.[10] Aligning himself with an international movement known as regenerative agriculture, Mattsson focuses on soil health. The principles are summarised as follows:

1. Minimise mechanical soil disturbance.
2. Maintain permanent organic soil cover.
3. Maintain a living root in the soil.
4. Plant diverse crop species in sequences and/or associations.

The common agent connecting all of these principles is the plant. Sugar cane is classified as a perennial C4 deep-rooted grass, and in nature such grasses tend to grow in a close relationship with a diverse network of other species, each of which provides aboveground and sub-soil services to the overall community.[11] Indus-

9   Simon Mattsson, *Making the Most of Your Soil's Biological Potential: Farming in the Next Green Revolution* (Nuffield Australia, June 2016), viii, http://www.nuffieldinternational.org/rep_pdf/1467606487Simon MattssonreportFINAL.pdf.
10 Ibid., iii.
11 David A. Wardle et al., 'Ecological Linkages Between Aboveground and Belowground Biota,' *Science* 304, no. 5677 (June 11, 2004): 1629–33,

trial monoculture cropping, by contrast, grows sugar cane in isolation from other plant and animal species, which actively works against the development of this diversity. As a result, monoculture cropping requires nitrogen-based fertilisers to supplement the nutrients which would otherwise have been made available to the plant's roots by a diverse sub-soil ecosystem. Monocrops also require chemical pesticides and herbicides to suppress species other than the target crop. While they may be successful in knocking back a known weed or parasite, chemical inputs always have unintended side effects, such as killing beneficial nematodes and fungi.[12] Thus in the case of conventionally farmed sugar cane, a C_4 grass is being asked to survive without the network of other plants, fungi, and micro-organisms that in nature would be working together to cycle nutrients and continually re-establish multi-species equilibrium. This weakens the sugar cane and makes it prone to further attacks from pests. The result is a spiral of dependence, requiring increased chemical inputs from the farmer, with the risk of these chemicals being picked up by heavy rainfall and transported as run-off from the farm to the reef.

In his experiments, Mattsson has attempted to 'emulate nature' by planting a range of brassicas (such as daikon radish) and legumes (such as peanuts) in amongst his sugar cane.[13] The daikon, with its very large root, is able to reach down into the earth and break up compacted soil. If left in the ground, it will decompose and contribute much needed carbon-based organic matter to the soil. Peanuts and other legumes such as soya beans provide the additional service of taking nitrogen from the atmosphere into the soil via bacteria, called rhizobia, which are located in nodules on their roots. From the point of view of the

https://doi.org/10.1126/science.1094875.

12 Graham Stirling et al., 'Yield Decline of Sugarcane: A Soil Health Problem Overcome by Modifying the Farming System,' in *Soil Health, Soil Biology, Soilborne Diseases and Sustainable Agriculture: A Guide* (Melbourne: CSIRO Publishing, 2016), 165–86.

13 Mattsson, *Making the Most of your Soil's Biological Potential*, 31. Mattsson's multi-species intercrop trial has so far involved the following species: radish, turnip, chickpea, soybean, common vetch, cereal rye, and oats.

farmer, this reduces the need for chemical fertilisers. Healthier sugar cane plants result from the diverse sub-soil community associated with multi-species cropping, with the effect that the soil becomes enriched with carbon-based biological matter and acts like a sponge, reducing run-off and erosion.[14]

Barriers to the widespread adoption of Regenerative Agriculture in the Sugar Cane Industry

While experiments like Mattsson's are relatively new in the sugar cane industry, they have been a feature of other kinds of progressive farming (particularly in pasture grazing) for a long time. One of the major factors inhibiting widespread adoption of multi-species cropping is the superstructure of the sugar cane industry itself. Unlike vegetables or fruits, which require only sorting and packing for market, the sugar cane plant needs to go through an intensive industrial milling process after harvesting. The cane is crushed to extract the juice, then evaporated and crystallised, and the crystals are separated from the mother liquor using a centrifuge. The dried sugar may then be refined into different market varieties. In Australia, more than 80% of sugar produced is exported, so bulk storage, shipping, and the price fluctuations of international markets are also major factors which constrain sugarcane farming methods.[15]

The industry tends to be very centralised, with mills setting the harvest timetable for all the surrounding farms. The milled sugar from each farm is bundled and sold as a commodity product, without any system of provenance connecting a packet of sugar on the supermarket shelves back to a particular farm. The efficiencies required for these processes mitigate the wider uptake of multi-species cropping: growing diverse species can slow down the monocrop harvesting process, and require the farmer

---

14 Ibid., 3.
15 Australian Government Department of Agriculture and Water Resources, 'Sugar,' *Australian Government Department of Agriculture and Water Resources,* February 25, 2015, http://www.agriculture.gov.au/ag-farm-food/crops/sugar.

to connect with new markets for non-sugar crops such as legumes and brassicas.

Since 2015, Mattsson has tried to address these challenges by growing a dual crop of sugar cane and sunflowers in alternating rows.[16] Planted at the same time, the sunflowers (an annual species) quickly take advantage of the available sunlight, germinating and growing up faster than the sugar cane (a perennial species). This also functions to shade out some of the weeds that might emerge in the early stages of the sugar cane crop. The sunflower plant contributes to the flourishing of sub-soil biological diversity, which benefits the health of the sugar plant, by establishing its own rhizosphere (the zone surrounding the roots) within which an abundance of bacteria, fungi, nematodes, and animal life forms cohabit. Finally — and this is significant for the economy of such an experiment — because of their rapid growth and maturity, the sunflowers are ready to harvest well in advance of the sugar cane. A harvester can move through the field, lopping off the heads of the sunflowers while the sugar cane is only half-grown. The sunflower seeds are processed and sent to market, while the sunflower stalks are left to decompose in the field, providing further carbon-based biological matter for the health of the sugar cane plant.

Plants and farmers working together as change agents

At the time of writing, Mattsson's experiments are still in progress, and the efficacy and economy of this dual crop has not yet been scientifically proven.[17] However, given that there are over four thousand sugar cane farms in Queensland, the impact of

16 Lucas Ihlein, 'Sunflowers as agricultural and cultural change agents,' Lucas Ihlein et al., *Sugar vs the Reef?*, September 7, 2016, http://www.sugar-vs-the-reef.net/sunflowers-as-agricultural-and-cultural-change-agents.

17 Mattsson is currently collaborating with three soil scientists — Graham Stirling, Susanne Schmidt, and Jay Anderson — who are studying the impact of his multi-species cropping method on the population of nematodes in the sub-soil environment.

his work with plants could be wide-reaching.[18] Continuing to practice as a sugar cane farmer, and demonstrating that alternative polycropping methods are not only possible but also economically advantageous, Mattsson can push the industry to evolve, find new markets, increase overall yields, and improve soil health.[19] Such human-plant partnerships may in fact become a necessity for survival of any agricultural practice which wants to remain viable in the mainstream carbon economy of our short term future. A discussion of this economy forms the basis of the second part of this chapter.

The Engineer, The Carbon Economy, and the Role of Plants

I now want to introduce the entrepreneurial research of an engineer, Allan Yeomans, who is working to facilitate Australia's transition to a carbon economy, and who believes this will drive financial (and soil health) benefits for farming communities. Over the past decade, various Australian proposals for a carbon tax, carbon emissions trading scheme, or carbon price have been proposed.[20] Despite the diversity of proposed systems, all these schemes hold in common the notion of a *carbon economy*. Because of the tangible cost of the effects of human-induced global warming, a future economy of this sort would measure, quan-

18 Australian Sugar Milling Council, 'Australian Sugarcane Industry Overview,' *Australian Sugar Milling Council,* http://www.asmc.com.au/industry-overview.

19 If one of the goals of an action is cultural transformation, then the definition of a *yield* can be expanded beyond tonnes per hectare of sugar. Elsewhere, I have touched on this issue of yield from a Social Ecology perspective. See Lucas Ihlein, 'PA Yeomans and Social Ecology,' in Lucas Ihlein and Ian Milliss, *The Yeomans Project,* October 31, 2011, http://www.yeomansproject.com/pa-yeomans-and-social-ecology.

20 The only scheme actually implemented — the Labor government's Clean Energy Act (2011) — was subsequently repealed in 2014 after a change of government. See Alexander St John and Juli Tomaras, 'Australian Renewable Energy Agency (Repeal) Bill 2014,' *Parliament of Australia: Parliamentary Business,* Commonwealth of Australia, October 17, 2014, http://www.aph.gov.au/Parliamentary_Business/Bills_Legislation/bd/bd1415a/15bd035.

tify, and assign financial value to the cycling of carbon in the atmosphere. To date, the atmosphere has been treated as a free resource, or commons, which can be exploited without being properly accounted for.[21]

However it seems inevitable that globalised trade systems will soon force into existence a system in which carbon dioxide emissions will become part of the total accountable costs of goods and services.[22] It is possible that this system will pay individuals or organisations that are able to reduce the stock of greenhouse gases in the atmosphere. But how, exactly, could such payments be organised? Allan Yeomans, the director of Yeomans Plow Co. on the Gold Coast, Queensland, has been working towards a plant-based solution for this problem for the past decade.

Yeomans' father Percival Alfred (P.A.) was the inventor of Keyline, a method for the design and management of dryland farming in Australia. Keyline, unlike conventional models of agriculture imported from Europe, is responsive to the specific requirements of the Australian climate. Keyline design involves laying out a farm according to its topography and landforms, strategically situating dams and irrigation channels to maximise the soil's capacity to store moisture.[23] Keyline farming also involves the use of a deep-ripping subsoil implement to assist with this process — the Yeomans Plow — which allows air and water to penetrate below the roots of pastureland without violently inverting the soil. Now in his eighties, Allan still runs the Yeomans Plow Company, having inherited his father's inventive and entrepreneurial spirit.

21 Ottmar Edenhofer et al., 'The Atmosphere as a Global Commons – Challenges for International Cooperation and Governance,' *Mercator Research Institute on Global Commons and Climate Change,* June 2013, http://www.mcc-berlin.net/fileadmin/data/pdf/Final_revised_Edenhofer_et_al_The_atmosphere_as_a_Global_Commons_2013.pdf.

22 John Fialka, 'China Will Start the World's Largest Carbon Trading Market,' *Scientific American,* May 16, 2016, http:// www.scientificamerican.com/article/china-will-start-the-world-s-largest-carbon-trading-market/.

23 Lucas Ihlein, and Ian Milliss, 'P.A. Yeomans and the Art of Landscape Design,' *World Water Day Symposium,* March 22, 2012, http://waterwheel.net/media_items/view/1474.

In the context of the carbon economy, Allan Yeomans' agricultural heritage is significant. One of the possible ways to remove carbon from the atmosphere is by working with plants to perform the function of sub-soil sequestration. This can be achieved by a variety of methods. Yeomans' Keyline system, Peter Andrew's Natural Sequence Farming, Allan Savory's Holistic Management, and Joel Salatin's Polyface farming are all members of a family of agricultural systems which claim to build soil carbon. The way this works in a grass and cattle system is described by P.A. Yeomans in his book *Water for Every Farm*.[24] Grasses in pastureland photosynthesise using energy from the sun. Photosynthesis allows the grass to put on weight (growing leaves and roots), while drawing carbon dioxide and nitrogen from the atmosphere. When the plants reach maturity and begin to produce seed, cattle are sent in to intensively graze them. Grazing gives the grass plants a shock, and they drop a large proportion of their roots below the soil surface. The dead roots decay and contribute to the build up of soil organic matter, 58% of which is carbon.[25]

Recent developments in regenerative grass and cattle systems also recommend the use of mob-grazing or cell-grazing, where the herd is kept in a very small enclosure with lightweight mobile electric fences. The cattle are moved regularly (daily in some cases) by shifting the fences, grazing intensively, eating the leaves of all the plants (not just the more palatable ones) and depositing manure within the fenced area.[26] This contributes to the rapid regeneration of the grasses, which through repeated cycles of growing new roots and then dropping them, build a deeper layer of topsoil rich in carbon content.

24 P.A. Yeomans, *Water for Every Farm: Yeomans Keyline Plan* (Southport: Keyline Designs, 1993).

25 Edward Griffin, 'What is Soil Organic Carbon?' *Government of Western Australia Department of Agriculture and Food,* November 18, 2016, http://www.agric.wa.gov.au/climate-change/what-soil-organic-carbon.

26 This process has been described as 'mimicking nature,' insofar as wild herds of cattle on grasslands constantly move through the landscape, and stick together tightly as a defence against predators. See Jody Butterfield et al., *Holistic Management Handbook: Healthy Land, Healthy Profits* (Washington, DC: Island Press, 2006).

Allan Yeomans experimented with this type of pasture grazing together with his father in the 1950s. Long before carbon was an element of global currency, a common qualitative testing practice was to use a shovel to extract a cube of soil in order to inspect the depth of root penetration, and check for the presence of earthworms. More recently, as a design engineer and author, Allan Yeomans has been developing a method to assist with the quantitative measurement of soil carbon on a much larger scale. His self-published book, *Let's Pay Our Farmers to End Global Warming,* has two functions — operating as a passionate call for action and as a practical guide, or protocol, for how a soil carbon sequestration payment system could work. [27]

Yeomans' protocol (simplified here) works as follows. The land of any farmer who wishes to be paid to sequester carbon needs to be first baseline tested to determine its starting carbon content. This is done by collecting a set of samples randomly distributed across the paddock in question (Yeomans has invented an augur device to collect the samples reliably and with repeatable consistency). The soil samples are cleared of live plant matter, after which they are put through a series of sieves to reduce soil particle size to 2mm. The resulting sifted soil is then placed in the Yeomans Carbon Still (a special oven with an inbuilt weighing scale) and heated to just over 100 degrees Celsius, to evaporate any water content. After evaporation, the soil is weighed, and the Carbon Still heats the dry sample to 550 degrees Celsius, at which temperature the carbon content burns away. The soil sample is weighed again, and the difference between the first and the second weights indicates the amount of carbon in the sample. A final calculation is made by multiplying the sample size to work out the soil carbon content of the whole paddock.

If this protocol is repeated each year (the farmer having in the meantime applied regenerative agricultural methods), it would be possible to determine the incremental increase in soil carbon content from the baseline measurement. This change is what

27 Allan Yeomans, 'Let's Pay our Farmers to End Global Warming: Protocols and Test Apparatus for Reward Based Agricultural Soil Carbon Sequestration and How and Why it Works,' *Yeomans Plow Co.,* http://yeomansplow.com.au/10-carbon-still-soil-test-system/.

would be used in determining the payment to the farmer for soil sequestration services.[28]

Barriers to the Widespread Adoption of Soil Carbon Sequestration Measurement

In *Let's Pay Our Farmers to End Global Warming,* Yeomans describes a number of factors which slow down the implementation of his soil carbon sequestration measurement system. These can be grouped into the following categories: technical complexity, cost effectiveness, and legislative problems. The first category, technical complexity, relates to the difficulty in designing a workable protocol (set of procedures) by which soil samples could be collected and analysed.[29] The second category, cost effectiveness, includes the expense of performing and monitoring the soil testing procedures, as well as administering payments to farmers.[30] There is little motivation for implementing a system of payments to farmers if the cost of doing so outweighs the benefits of the service. The third category, legislation, is a blockage at a higher level: until a global carbon economy becomes a legal reality, and passes into national law in Australia, the collective will to solve the other limitations will not gain momentum.[31]

28 A comprehensive description of this 'loss on ignition' method of testing soil carbon content is published at Allan Yeomans, 'Soil Carbon Tests. Big Cheap & Easy,' *Yeomans Concepts,* 2016, http://yeomansconcepts. com/1-soil-carbon-tests-big-cheap-easy.

29 Yeomans proposes that his Carbon Still protocol (which requires no specialised skills and can be performed on-farm) will address this gap.

30 At approximately 10,000 Australian dollars (AUD), Yeomans argues that the Carbon Still could pay for itself after only ten soil testings. Yeomans proposes that a group of farmers could collectively purchase a still, and thus bypass the current expensive government soil testing regime.

31 One of the organisations working to accelerate the legal acceptance of carbon accounting is Carbon Farmers of Australia. I called director Louisa Kiely to ask about the difficulties Yeomans was experiencing in having his Carbon Still accredited. Kiely advised that the standard process for accreditation would involve selecting a piece of grazing land, paying to have the soil baseline tested for carbon content via the current government protocol (which could cost approximately AUD 100 per hectare),

Yeomans is an innovator working with plant-based soil systems to create positive environmental and social transformations. Beyond the limitations outlined above, one of the fundamental barriers Yeomans describes is the existence of a disciplinary demarcation in how research is defined. For Yeomans, it is his practical experience as a farmer and engineer that has enabled him to identify problems, trial solutions, and report on insights. However, he does not belong to one of the special social groups (politicians, academic scientists, or media makers) whose voices are heard in discussions around climate change mitigation, and in his book he repeatedly expresses frustration in his attempts to bring the Yeomans Carbon Still to wider attention.

Conclusion: Beyond Environmental Management?

In this narrative about innovation and the barriers to change, I have focused on the work of two human change agents collaborating with plants to transform industrial agricultural systems: to improve crop yield through soil health (Mattsson), and to perform a global service by facilitating the sequestration of carbon dioxide from the atmosphere (Yeomans). Despite the crucial role played by plants in each of these processes, human action is given priority in the way my stories are told. In each case, plants are managed by humans and marshalled towards a human-centric goal. Perhaps this is to be expected: we humans are more practiced in telling and hearing stories in which we are the protagonists.

In my own research as an artist beginning to work at the edges of agriculture and engineering, I have noticed the prevalence of the term 'environmental management,' and I have begun to use this language myself. It's practical: environmental management has widespread acceptance in scientific research and policy development, where the priority is to report on what is

and then using the Yeomans Carbon Still to test the same piece of land. If identical results are generated, then the Carbon Still will be in a position to apply for accreditation as an approved carbon measurement system. See Carbon Farmers of Australia, 'What is Carbon Farming,' *Carbon Farmers of Australia,* http://www.carbonfarmersofaustralia. com.au/About/what-is-carbon-farming.

knowable.[32] We want soil micro-organisms to be observed under a microscope, we want yields that can be quantified with precision (tonnes per hectare of sugar), and we want rates of carbon sequestration to be precisely determined in a given area over a known period of time. These are all environmental management processes. The results of these processes — usually reported in peer reviewed academic journal articles, or filtered through government funding schemes — are the tools for generating positive changes for 'the environment.' And yet, implementation of the recommendations of this knowable research — as shown in each of my case studies above — can be painfully slow. So what is going on? If we *know* what works, and if we are still not able as a society to do what we know works, then it can only be assumed that *factors beyond the knowable* must be at play. It is at this point that environmental management as a strategy of control starts to break down. How might we invent alternative ways of generating change?

One approach which attempts to find a way of framing human and nonhuman relations beyond the management paradigm has emerged from the field known as the environmental humanities. The writing of scholars like Val Plumwood and Deborah Bird Rose is exemplary of this approach.[33] Their work

32 As an indicator of the widespread use of this term, two major international journals use it in their titles: the *Journal of Environmental Management and Environmental Management,* both of which started publishing in the mid-1970s. In its journal scope description, *Environmental Management* has the following: 'As the principal user of nature, humanity is responsible for ensuring that its environmental impacts are benign rather than catastrophic.' Similarly, the *Journal of Environmental Management* outlines its goals: 'As governments and the general public become more keenly aware of the critical issues arising from how humans use their environment, this journal provides a forum for the discussion of environmental problems around the world and for the presentation of management results.' Both of these journal scope descriptions outline an instrumental relationship to 'nature,' where humans are its 'users' and 'managers.'

33 Martin Mulligan and Stuart Hill, *Ecological Pioneers: A Social History of Australian Ecological Thought and Action* (Cambridge: Cambridge University Press, 2001), 276–89.

describes the position of humans in a world where we are not always the managers, but rather in relationship with a multiplicity of non-human species. By necessity, a decentred form of philosophy must embrace diverse modes of knowledge. This is a complex intellectual endeavour, and its influence is percolating throughout the humanities. However, I have yet to hear these ethically decentring ideas being used *practically* by scientists researching the Great Barrier Reef, nor by politicians tasked with environmental portfolios — and certainly they have no currency in the mainstream media. There is a gulf between *environmental management* (humans attempting to control nature) and the *environmental humanities* (humans trying to think their way towards a reciprocal relationship with nature, or indeed to move beyond the culture-nature divide). Is it possible to bridge this gulf? What new practices might be needed for this endeavour?

While it is still at an early stage in its development, this is one of the areas of focus for *Sugar vs the Reef?* The method of socially engaged art employed by the project shuttles between the outcomes-focused priorities of environmental management on one hand, and the deliberately non-instrumental ethics of the environmental humanities on the other. Socially engaged artists do this by embracing their own disciplinary ambiguity.[34] Their way of working allows practical experiments in the field — such as collaborations with farmers and engineers working with the materiality of plants and soil — to co-exist with unresolvable philosophical, ethical and aesthetic discussions. These experiments and stories are published side by side in the project blog, and are embodied in the various public collaborations which will constitute *Sugar vs the Reef?* over its lifespan. One of these in-

---

34 In his influential book on Socially Engaged Art, artist and educator Pablo Helguera discusses the importance of disciplinary ambiguity: 'Socially engaged art functions by attaching itself to subjects and problems that normally belong to other disciplines, moving them temporarily into a space of ambiguity. It is this temporary snatching away of subjects into the realm of art-making that brings new insights to a particular problem or condition and in turn makes it visible to other disciplines.' See Pablo Helguera, *Education for Socially Engaged Art Practice: A Materials and Techniques Handbook* (New York: Jorge Pinto Books, 2011), 5.

volves the planting of a dual crop of sugar cane and sunflowers in the Mackay Botanical Gardens, in collaboration with Simon Mattsson and members of the Australian South Sea Islander Community, whose descendants were forcibly removed to Australia in the 1860s to work as indentured labourers in the sugar cane fields. This cross-disciplinary group will work together to map the topography of the terrain, test the soil, plant and tend the cane, and eventually harvest and process it. The multi-year duration allows a set of collaborative processes around the life cycle of a plant, and all its accompanying species both above and below the soil, to slowly develop. The sugar cane crop-as-artwork thus transcends its normal role as a functional element in an industrial system, and becomes instead the fulcrum, and physical site, for dialogue around a host of economic, social, cultural, and environmental issues. In planning these events, and in reflecting on the collaborations between farmers and engineers with non-human lifeforms like sugar cane, I am searching for a form of social-environmental catalysis which goes beyond management, and into a more reciprocal relationship between humans, plants, and social/ecological systems.

16

Trees as Landlords and Other Public Experiments: An Interview with Natalie Jeremijenko

Susie Pratt

In 2012, while I was an art medic-in-residence at the Environmental Health Clinic in New York, the director of the Clinic, Natalie Jeremijenko, showed me her designs for a co-working office space in a tree. The plans were still in the early stages, but what caught my attention was her articulation of how a tree would be set up as the landlord of the office. The rent people paid for using the co-working space would be put in the service of its own interests, for example to improve soil quality or for companion planting. The TREExOFFICE, as she called it, was to be installed in Socrates Sculpture Park as part of the exhibition Civic Action — this was the first of many iterations of this intervention. I was curious to talk with Natalie to find out how the project had evolved. What is it like to have a tree as a landlord? How did tenants behave? How can a tree engage a community to serve it's own and collective interests? How can public experiments, such as TREExOFFICE, help to re-imagine and re-design our relationship to natural systems?

Jeremijenko is currently an Associate Professor in the Visual Art Department, New York University, and is also affiliated with the Computer Science Department and Environmental Studies program. She has pioneered the academic field of socio-ecological systems design and has had numerous international exhibitions. Previous infamous experiments include: the Bureau of Inverse

Technology (including what is arguably the first drone artwork), howstuffismade.org, One Trees (an installation of 1,000 cloned trees arranged in pairs in different urban micro-climates, to demonstrate environmental impacts), and feral robotic dogs that sniff out environmental hazards. Natalie and I spoke in May 2016. What follows is an edited transcript of our conversation.

Susie Pratt: Plants have long been active agents in your work. What are some of the key issues you are grappling with right now?

Natalie Jeremijenko: I would argue that one of the biggest challenges of the 21st century, in terms of urban design and urban planning, is the reintegration of vegetation back into the urban environment in such a way that we create benefits and improve environmental health. We've got this demonstrated technology for improving air quality (the number one human health risk), which is leaves, and this technology is inexpensive and delightful. Air quality is implicated in not only asthma and cardiovascular issues, but also in the breast cancer epidemic, diabetes, obesity and all of the major health issues. Even your life span is better predicted by how close you live to a major arterial road, rather than any genetic markers. Air is our fundamental commons. It is also the thing that ties us to plants and the exchange of carbon. It is a shared intimacy—breathing in and breathing out, and vice versa.

SP: While I was artist/medic in residence at the Environmental Health Clinic (xClinic) back in 2012, you were just about to launch the first TREExOFFICE in New York, a co-working space in a tree and owned by the tree. You've now launched different versions in New York, Berlin, and London, for the London Festival of Architecture (late 2015). What is your thinking behind this project?

NJ: So the idea of the TREExOFFICE is that we have the creative agency to design our urban environments, to design our work spaces and urban infrastructure. A co-working space in a tree, and owned by the tree, is an invitation to consider, not just because it is a more efficient allocation of workspace, but also as a collective de-

sign challenge, which is to reimagine and redesign our relationship to natural systems. What's more delightful than working in a tree?

It introduces the idea that green spaces could be productive spaces, not just leisure spaces but fundamentally part of a healthy ecosystem and lifestyle, not just a decorative addition which enhances your real-estate value. We are exploring what is possible, and that's what the tree office is interested in. Its interested in new systems that don't degrade the soil, that don't degrade the air quality, but improve human and environmental health.

SP: What was your inspiration for the TREExOFFICE, and the notion of a tree as landlord?

NJ: There is this wonderful legal precedence that exists in Athens, Georgia which is 'the tree that owns itself.' In 1832, Col. William Jackson willed an oak tree to itself. Poetically and imaginatively, the entity of the tree was in fact an entity that had rights, and autonomy, and was self-directed, and in every way seemed recognisable as something that could own itself. So he willed the tree and the 8 foot by 8 foot plot of land around it to itself.

Unfortunately the tree died, but the scion of the original tree was planted by the Junior Ladies' Garden Club on the same plot in 1946. What the Junior Ladies' Garden Club did was test heritability laws, and so they demonstrated that the tree was perfectly capable of inheriting the land. The tree that owns itself now continues to own itself. This idea that we can extend rights to non-humans is made concrete and possible.

Does it make sense to have a tree as a landlord? When you haven't paid they will text, 'I'm not going anywhere until you've paid.' For me, it makes perfect sense to have a tree as a landlord; in fact it makes more sense to have a tree as a landlord than anything else- certainly instead of some absent holding company in the Virgin Islands. In a sense, the fictional entities that become landlords in contemporary financial culture require much more imaginative leaps of faith than the fact of a tree being a landlord.

SP: How much did it cost for a desk space in the London TREExOFFICE in Hoxton Square? What did the tree landlord charge?

NJ: So we had it worked out at 15 pounds for half a day and there were 14-15 desk spaces, very inexpensive to have a nice little powered, delightful place to work, with the best views in London, really the best office in London.

Rupert, who is the arborist for Hackney Council, which is where the London Tree Office was, has 60,000 trees under his care and a budget of 60,000 pounds per year for the care and maintenance of every one of those trees. That's a pound per tree, these magnificent plane trees, they define London, they make it breathable, visually they are what we recognise, and yet they get a budget of a pound a year. It raises questions of how much these living organisms are valued in this economy, or rather how badly these organisms are valued.

The council was very keen to have a revenue generating scheme in their park, but they were very keen to hold the money. I was in this very difficult struggle with them — the profits go to the tree.

SP: Once this relationship is established, with the tree as landlord, it invites questions of what will the tree do with the money? Is this what you intended?

NJ: Everyone who sees the TREExOFFICE says well, why are we paying the tree? What is the tree going to do with it? And this is where it became a really nice space to have this conversation. The tree is obviously going to spend its profits on the tree's interests and what exactly its interests are is up for debate. Discussing this with council members and other not-for-profits was interesting.

By extending rights discourse to the tree, and by taking it seriously as a landlord with its own interests, it raises questions: What would be in the interests of the tree? What does a tree want? How will it spend its profits? To be able to see from that point of view, to be able to understand the complexity of an urban ecosystem from the point of view of a non-human, I think, is a powerful way for us to understand interests and our relationship in/with natural systems.

Also, I like working in the tree; working in a tree is delightful. This is a radically different way of developing shared urban space in our health interests and in the interests of the environment. If a tree in New York City receives a municipal salary of $400+ for 80 *years of service, it is very low paid worker in that paradigm. But, if it is a landlord in a public park generating $1000 a month —if we see it as an asset, as a revenue generator, as an entity that is generative —this is a very different view of natural systems. It's not the view of a park as an image or pastoral site of leisure, it is a view of a much more complex interrelationship. I think we can use this shift in valuation to change the urban environment, air quality, and climate.*

SP: The TREExOFFICE is now more than just a co-working space. You've also designed in waste-to-energy systems in the form of xKITCHEN and cloud data storage. How do these different projects fit together? Why link office space, waste, energy, and cloud data storage?

NJ: If we were to address one thing that would radically transform, poverty, pollution, energy efficiencies, air quality, we would deal with waste. Waste is completely wasted. So, the idea is that under the TREExOFFICE is a community kitchen —xKITCHEN. People can bring their own waste —their paper waste, all the waste that is generated from the TREExOFFICE, and their food waste, and they can put it through the kitchen to produce locally generated clean energy and sequester carbon.

In all urban contexts the biggest waste system is paper and packaging. We put it through a process called pyrolysis, heating plant matter in the absence of oxygen, to generate natural gas, syngas, you can use it to run any turbine, it's a clean energy. And you also get a by-product, biochar, a type of charcoal which can be stored in the ground as a way to remove carbon dioxide.

The second biggest waste stream that goes through the TREExOFFICE, but also through any other knowledge institutions, is food waste. We put the food waste into an anaerobic tank where there is no air getting in to generate methane, like in landfills, but that methane is of course gas, which you can again use, just like you can use natural gas. In this way we deal with it locally and sensibly instead of the crazy way municipalities distribute it and often triple truck it, degrading everybody's cardiovascular health. Distributing waste wastes waste, it makes no sense.

So, the two major waste streams become two sources of clean energy which both of course produce a co-benefit — syngas and bio-char in the case of pyrolysis and methane gas in the case of anaerobic digestion. And then if you take the biochar and you work that into an urban soil, not only are you sequestering carbon, but it also improves soil fertility. Plant a tree and you sequester carbon for maybe 100 years, but we need to be thinking about sequestering carbon at a high rate, for thousands of years, which is the aim of xKITCHEN.

So that's how the TREExOFFICE powers itself and improves health. The waste is systemically remediated through this energy system that sequesters carbon and improves soil fertility; it demonstrates that we can in fact design shared infrastructure so that it doesn't degrade our health but systematically improves our human health and our environmental health.

SP: And how does this tie into cloud data storage — the other service the TREExOFFICE provides?

NJ: One of the biggest demands for energy is in cloud data storage, and most people don't think about how their Instagram images, Facebook posts and tweets are internet services that rely on cloud data storage. Cloud data storage is the fastest growing area of the digital economy and they are more polluting than the entire airline industry.

The TREExCLOUD data storage service offers cloud data storage that improves human and environmental health rather than degrading it and it does this by using clean energy from local waste. To ensure health improvements, the capacity of TREEx-CLOUD data storage is indexed to the leaf area index of the trees, so if you want more data storage you increase the leaf area. Leaf area index, is the ratio of leaves over one square meter of ground area. As I was saying to begin with, leaves are the only demonstrated technology for improving urban air quality in any cost effective way and they also are a very good proxy for health (leaf area index not leaves, not tree count), because it's the complexity of the canopy structure, not a single tree that indicates a healthy complex community.

So this is my big claim, we can actually change the global cli-mate by how we recycle our waste, and do it in the benefit of hu-mans and non-humans. If we do it everywhere it makes sense for the local benefits of air quality improvements.

SP: While I was at the xClinic, you were researching agent-based modelling and mutualistic organisms, where two organisms (of different species) form a relationship that benefits both species. How has that research fed into The TREExOFFICE and associated services?

NJ: The TREExOFFICE is a way of concretising the mutualistic relationship. We have a biological and social contract with plants that I think is intuitively understood, but it is a fundamental mu-tualistic exchange of bodily fluids that we breathe out what they breathe in and vice versa.

When I was reading a paper on agent based modelling, they said it might be a good idea for us to model mutualistic organ-isms —after all, they account for about 95% of the world's biomass. I was struck by that, I had heard a lot about mutualists, but I had never seen the 95% number put on them and (by further research that's a conservative estimate), but all the forests, all the corals, all the flowers, pollinators —these are all mutualists.

Mutualists are a subset of biotic organisms not just living be-side each other, but benefitting from each other's presence; they reproduce more and live longer in each other's presence. So there is a very measurable benefit to be associated with these other organ-isms. And we are locked in this absolute beneficial relationship with vegetation and it's critically important to see that in the con-text of urban ecosystems.

The idea that mutualism is the fundamental relationship has really become a theme song of mine, because there are so many political, design, and conceptual ramifications. It is such a produc-tive term and concept —the idea that most of the world is a mutu-alistic system. On first approximation we've heard so much about predator-prey relationships, competition of resources, parasitism, all of these other forms of relationships. But the mutualism that is the fundamental relationship, it's so common that it is unseen.

So everything that we used to think of as a cost-benefit analysis becomes a benefit-benefit analysis.

SP: I saw that you had linked the TREExOFFICE and these projects under the framing of the Museum for Natural Futures rather than the Institutional framework you created in 2007 — the Environmental Health Clinic. How is the museum operating? What is the framework?

NJ: Having set up the Environmental Health Clinic in 2007 as my conceptual framework, I framed my work with the idea that the best proxy for human good is human and environmental health, that it trumps the economic arguments of pro-development or political arguments. Health is the way, if it improves your health and mine and increases biodiversity —you can't find anyone who is anti-health. It is a way of being able to say this is what we use as our measurable proxy of the common good. But there is still a complete lack of education about the possibilities that are available to us. The understanding that we have we have to act from and from the fact that we know that increasing the leaf area index will significantly improve human and environmental health. It's irresponsible for us not to use that knowledge to design urban systems as if we didn't know that.

The whole fundamental idea that the Museum of Natural Futures is about is that we can design our shared infrastructure, not only to reduce food miles and reduce petrochemical fertilisers and reduce pesticides and pollution and waste, but we can design shared infrastructure so that it improves human and environmental health, so that it increases biodiversity, improves water quality, and increases our human health. That's the fundamental idea the Museum of Natural Futures is trying to show with examples like the TREExOFFICE —here are concrete examples, small scale, implementable now, that can aggregate into really significant benefits that actually shows us what mutualistic systems design actually looks like, how you can do it. It is about orientating the commons of scientific knowledge towards the future. We can design these systems and we can aggregate those small actions into collective action to reimagine and redesign our relationship to natural systems.

17

Gardening out of the Anthropocene: Creating Different Relations between Humans and Edible Plants in Sydney

Jennifer Mae Hamilton

Perhaps it is in the space of artists' gardens that we might learn what might be able to take root in the ruins of Anthropocene thinking.
— Natasha Myers[1]

One way to critique the kind of technocratic development signified in the term 'Anthropocene', to challenge the problematic anthropocentrism of the concept, and also to maintain a cogent response to the environmental crisis at the same time, is to imagine how society could leave a different kind of trace in the fossil record. Donna Haraway has called for the Anthropocene, or 'Capitalocene,' to be as thin a layer as possible — what stratigraphers call a "boundary event" rather than an epoch.[2] Following her, scholars are trying to theorize what it would mean and what

---

1   Natasha Myers, 'From Edenic Apocalypse to Gardens Against Eden: Plants and People in and After the Anthropocene,' in *Infrastructure, Environment and Life in the Anthropocene,* ed. Kregg Hetherington. (Durham: Duke University Press, in press).

2   Donna Haraway, 'Anthropocene, Capitalocene, Plantationocene, Chthulucene: Making Kin,' *Environmental Humanities* 6, no. 1 (2015): 159–65, https://doi.org/10.1215/22011919-3615934.

it would take to make a qualitatively different earthen layer.[3] How to dig ourselves out of this mess? Natasha Myers proposes the idea of the 'Planthroposcene,' not as a new epoch *per se,* but as a new methodology for living with plants.[4]

Undoubtedly people already live with and are, indeed, alive *because of* plants. The entire financial system currently relies on plants, from the fossilized plant matter in plastics to our daily bread. The problem is not that humans live with plants, but the dominant mode of that relation in western capitalist, settler colonial societies. At the very least, plants do not receive adequate acknowledgement for their labors.[5] Plants arrive in the lives of many humans already transmogrified into commodities like energy, food, fibre, or aesthetic objects. While humans have always instrumentalized plants for survival, a growing body of work criticizes the current global, fossil fuel intensive, corporatized agricultural model. These kinds of instrumentalism are evidently profitable for certain conglomerates and deliver necessary nutrients to many, but certainly not all, people. At the same time,

3   See Anna Tsing, *The Mushroom at the End of the World: The Possibility of Life in Capitalist Ruins* (Princeton: Princeton University Press, 2015), 19–25. See also events such as the Anthropocene Feminisms conference held at the Centre for 21st Century Studies' (http://c21uwm.com/anthropocene/) and Feminist, Queer, and Anti-Colonial Propositions for Hacking the Anthropocene series, organized by Astrida Neimanis (2016) in collaboration with Jennifer Hamilton (2017, 2018), (https://compostingfeminisms.wordpress.com)

4   Myers develops this term (and discusses the spelling) in 'Photosynthetic Mattering Rooting into the Planthroposcene,' paper presentation, European Association for the Study of Science and Technology (EASST) and the Society for the Social Studies of Science (4S) Conference, Barcelona, Spain, January 4, 2017, https://www.academia.edu/28312965/Photosynthetic_Mattering_Rooting_into_the_Planthroposcene_4S_EASST_Talk_Barcelona_Elements_Thinking_Panel. Haraway's own future epoch is the 'Chthulucene': see Donna Haraway, *Staying with the Trouble: Making Kin in the Chthulucene* (Durham: Duke University Press, 2016).

5   The term 'labour' is starting to be applied to non-human entities to characterize their role in the economy. See Jennifer Mae Hamilton, 'Labour,' *Environmental Humanitie*s 6, no. 1 (2015): 183–86, https://doi.org/10.1215/22011919–3615970.

however, such practices are widely understood to be problematic in a range of ways, including the scale of waste produced by this system,[6] and the exploitative and unjust elements of the corporate monocultural model.[7] For Myers, the Planthroposcene invites humans to open themselves up to plants differently. In this new world order, humans might eat plants, but we also might be materially and psychically altered by a new awareness of and responsiveness to the ways in which plants sense the world.[8] Such awareness, Myers contends, challenges human exceptionalism and anthropocentrism.

Given that eating is a matter of necessity, the concept of opening one's self to plants differently gives rise to the big and pragmatic question: how? How to materially create a world where one does not have to be on a meditation retreat to notice that a sunflower tracks the sun throughout the day and night?[9] In my own work here and elsewhere, I am interested in how to disentangle one's self from current resource-intensive urban systems without entirely abandoning the progressive social, ethical, and political projects that cities enable.[10] This essay explores one small aspect of that much larger project, by investigating a series of artists' experiments with edible plants in Sydney, Australia. In this

6 See, for an example of food waste characterized as an ecological issue in Australia, Leah Mason, Thomas Boyle, Julian Fyfe, Tanzi Smith, and Dana Cordell, *National Food Waste Assessment: Final Report* (Ultimo: University of Technology, 2011). This report was prepared by the Institute of Sustainable Futures for the Department of Sustainability, Environment, Water, Population and Communities.

7 See, for example, Vandana Shiva, *Stolen Harvest: The Hijacking of the Global Food Supply* (London: Zed Books, 2000).

8 Natasha Myers, 'Conversations on Plant Sensing: Notes from the Field,' *NatureCulture* 3 (2015): 35–66.

9 This is Myers' example of how plants relate to the world differently in 'Conversations on Plant Sensing' (36).

10 My own collaborative life-practice in this regard is called Earlwood Farm. This is a flawed and partial attempt to live in the city differently. To make kin, career and social life, eat a plant-based diet and, all the while, resist and enact a critique of the dominant systems that govern that life. It is nothing if not ambitious! I occasionally blog about it at http://www.earlwoodfarm.com.

Fig. 1. Screen Grab of my live Google Map of the different gardens. For more images and links go to https://www.google.com/maps/d/viewer?mid=1MfqcqArjXF1O_mkBOkbDOdb1yDY&.

chapter I show how these projects operate critically both within a larger, epochal imaginary and also *in situ* on the eastern seaboard of Australia.

* * *

The projects discussed in this chapter were or are situated in inner Sydney during the first decade and a half of the twenty-first century. They are all either gardens in artist run initiatives or are set up as installations within a gallery or institutional setting. They all involve growing and caring for plants in a soil medium and their eventual harvesting for human consumption.[11] Given

11 See for example, *2. Field Work,* an exhibition by Lisa Kelly and Dennis Tan, at Chrissie Cotter Hall in Camperdown (2008), two installations and events by Makeshift (a collaboration between Tessa Rappaport and Karl Logge), including *Make-do Garden City* and *Gwago Patabá-*

the abundance of examples and the limited space of this chapter, I focus primarily on the three projects that were durational art installations — *Tending, Food Forest,* and *Girl Shed III* — and draw on other examples where relevant. [12]

I call these projects the durational and edible live art gardens of inner Sydney. First, 'durational' specifically references the contemporary performance art of live acts that endure across times longer than the 'normal' one or two hours of a happening or theatre show. [13] In this case the duration recognizes the active and ongoing human labors of care, but also the ways in which the plants live in time, across months or years. Secondly, although they are not commercial food-growing operations, all the examples are engaged in growing food for potential human consumption.

gun___we will eat presently (2010), the Artist as Family Food Forest at St Michael's churchyard in Darlinghurst (2010-), *Tending* garden by Dr Lucas Ihlein and Diego Bonetto, funded by Professor Ross Gibson, on the grounds of Sydney College of the Arts (SCA) in Lilyfield (2010–11), *Tending III* in a different courtyard of SCA (2014–2016) voluntarily developed by students and staff, the collaboration between Kirsten Bradley and Nick Ritar of Milkwood Permaculture and the managers of the artist-led community space 107 Projects known as the *107 Rooftop Garden* in Redfern (2014–), a year-long artist residency at Air Space in Marrickville involving the redesign of the small back courtyard into a durational work known as *Girl Shed III* by Dr Sarah Newell (2014–2016) and a small permaculture-inspired garden at Frontyard, a council-owned house-cum-community artist run initiative run by a board of volunteers including Clare Cooper and Dr. Alexandra Crosby (2016-). The final four examples, *Tending III, 107 Rooftop, Girl Shed III,* and *Frontyard* were all still being actively cared for at the time of writing; whereas the exhibitions or tenure on the sites had ended in the former examples. That said, while *Tending* and *Food Forest* are no longer being regularly cared for, some of the plants are still growing. The day I visited *Tending,* for instance, I took home a pocketful of kaffir lime leaves, and I spied mint, strawberries, mulberries, and parsley amidst a range of citrus plants at the *Food Forest.*

12 These projects can be explored via the map above; a link is in provided in the caption of Fig. 1.

13 Kenneth Pickering, 'Durational Performance,' in *Key Concepts in Drama and Performance* (Basingstoke and New York: Palgrave Macmillan, 2010), 152.

The edibility of these gardens is important because they provide a counterpoint to the wider agricultural economy which nourishes the human laborers in urban centers, especially where artists offer their 'audiences' a take-home snack pack which changes their engagement with the work itself. Finally, 'live art' is a widely used term for socially engaged performance practice,[14] which suggests that these kinds of durational happenings have a politically-oriented dimension; they are not only trying to represent an issue. In the garden, artists are modeling, at least temporarily, a life practice that, in the process of making, challenges the boundaries between professional art as a form of wage labour exchanged for an aesthetic object and artistic creation as literal, temporal world-making, or world building.[15] Categorising my examples in this way serves to foreground the socio-political creative process that is opened up by the gardens. In focusing on art, rather than strictly agricultural or community garden projects, I am given access to the conceptual tool kit of contemporary art practice and the ideas through which the art-gardeners theorize their practice. In sum, these projects are evidently exploring, representing, and living out more than just a new, urbanized human-plant relation; they also propose a life-practice where humans have different relation with plants, cultivating a new kind of urbanism. In exploring the concepts and practices that emerge from food growing as art and considering the site specificity of my examples to Australia's largest city, this chapter outlines the specificities of the gardens and theorizes the worlds they propose. I will show how these gardens occupy a marginal space between art, farming, plant-growing, and the economy, while actively living the paradox of the city, simultaneously participating in and critiqu-

14 See Deidre Heddon and Jennie Klein, eds., *Histories and Practices of Live Art* (Basingstoke: Palgrave Macmillan, 2012).

15 This claim is big and relates to each artwork differently, so it is beyond the scope of this chapter to trace the nuances work by work. The artists that are trying to enact this claim in the most fulsome sense work in the collective Artist as Family. Patrick Jones, one member of the group, theorised their practice in full in 'Walking for Food: Regaining Permapoesis,' PhD diss., University of Western Sydney, 2013, https://issuu.com/permapoesis/docs/walkingforfood_cmp.

ing urbanized life and culture. In cultivating relationships with plants, these artists critique extant standards of living and modes of development but at the same time recognize their own debt to the current system.[16]

This chapter addresses the challenge of how to 'read' difference into, for instance, lettuce planted in the *107 Rooftop,* or at *Girl Shed III,* or in a non-creative context. I spoke to most of the gardens' caretakers in order to understand what they were trying to do given the similarities in the process and outcome of a food garden. Many of them commented it was an attempt to not just represent or model a different way of being in the world, but actually practice that in a lively and disciplined way. More detailed reflections on individual practices are recalled in various ways below. Given that the gardens are not for sale, and the edible aspects not commodified, extrapolating meaning from the artists' lively collaborative processes with plants and each other is paramount. Where possible, I physically visited the gardens and explored their digital roots online across various blogs, social media platforms, review essays and image galleries.

What Is a City?

The gardens are located within a few kilometers of the financial and governmental center of a sprawling metropolis. The site-specific care called for by the gardens require/d the artists to pay new attention to the particularities of the soil and the different needs of seeds, seedlings, and mature plants, in terms of sunlight, water, and nutrients, and also in relation to the urban infrastructure and bureaucracy that had to be pried apart to make space for the plants. One pair of artists were enmeshed in the history and architectural legacy of a colonial psychiatric hospital and the politics of a university's lease on valuable but heritage protected land (*Tending*); another artist negotiated a sublease from private

16 Kathryn Yusoff's essay 'Queer Coal: Geneaologies in/of the Blood' informs this argument insofar as she suggests that we need critiques that start in the mix of what is already happening, rather than proposing a break free from the lifestyles we love. See Kathryn Yusoff, 'Queer Coal: Geneaologies in/of the Blood,' *philoSOPHIA* 5, no. 2 (2015): 203–29.

gallery directors and grappled with unaccommodating light-industrial architecture and toxic legacies of inner-city factories (*Girl Shed III*); the collective Artist as Family sought approval from Aboriginal elders, the Church and the City (*Food Forest*); and another waited months for a lift to be repaired in the building to comply with Council's accessibility policy before planting on the rooftop courtyard could begin (*107 Rooftop*). In other words, these gardens were not guerilla projects shirking the rules and regulations of these highly managed places, they became spatially, temporally, and legally part of the city.

Under the imaginary provided by the concept of the Anthropocene, cities can no longer easily be considered separate from nature or 'purely' cultural spaces; instead they are material transformations of the world. The task is now to interrogate ethical and material implications of such alterations and, as Haraway argues, imagine a way of marking the earth in different ways.[17] Before the popularization of the geological concept, Erik Swyngedouw defined the city as a 'cyborg', expanding on another of Haraway's concepts, as a way of accessing and politicizing the natureculture of urban space. For Swyngedouw the city is a 'metabolic circulatory process that materializes as an implosion of socio-natural and socio-technical relations organized through complex political, social, economic, and cultural relations.'[18] Swyngedouw describes cities as materializations of 'political visions [that] are, therefore, necessarily also ecological visions.'[19] In this regard, any project aiming to intervene in or resist the dominant political mode of the city, 'must, of necessity, also be an environmental project (and vice versa).'[20] From this perspective, the gardens become parts of the cyborg body of the city, perhaps enzymes that aid in the way the metropolis digests the world or a new kind of lens for refocusing the urban ecological vision. As mini-political ecologies in themselves as well, the gardens can also

17 Haraway, 'Anthropocene, Capitalocene, Plantationocene, Chthulucene,' 159–65.

18 Erik Swyngedouw, 'Circulations and Metabolisms: Hybrid (Natures) and Cyborg (cities),' *Science as Culture* 15, no. 2 (2006), 105–21, at 114.

19 Swyndedouw, 'Circulations and Metabolisms,' 114.

20 Ibid., 118.

be conceived as political in the sense that they materially represent alternative ways of living and working in cities.

The dominant ideological model structuring the ongoing development of Sydney is neoliberal settler colonial capitalism. Parts of city that were once publically owned and managed by the state are being readily transferred into private hands and developed as residential and commercial space and, most scandalously, roadways like WestConnex and casinos in Barangaroo. In these transactions, public green spaces are simultaneously being created and destroyed. For instance, a large parkland was designed to represent the native plants that once lived on Barangaroo headland and ameliorate a public who lost a slice of harbor side land to private developers and investors. At the same time, the Royal Botanical Gardens and Domain Trust is sacrificing part of their land for a hotel to produce revenue for the rest of the gardens. Meanwhile, sections of public parkland built on an old rubbish tip are slated for conversion into a motorway off ramp. The edible art gardens need to be understood as strange and hitherto unnamed cells within the wider cyborg body, a body that is selling off its collectively owned parts. In this regard, at the same time as producing new kinds of green space open to emergent publics, the embodied and physical labors of gardening also invite questioning into the dominant modes, means, and purposes of work in the urban knowledge economy.[21]

When it comes to critiquing urbanization, recourse to pastoral and pre-lapsarian fantasies are common. Conceptualizing gardens as mini-Edens or zones of retreat from the 'hustle and bustle' will fail to understand how the gardens are entangled with and respond to the wider urban system and contemporary moment of which they are a part. As Haraway argues, 'discourses of natural harmony, the nonalien, and purity,' are 'unsalvageable

---

21 This critique of labour practices in a knowledge economy is developing in my work in multiple ways. For my other work in this regard, see the reference in footnote 5 and also my article 'Labour against Wilderness and the Trouble with Property Beyond *The Secret River*,' *Green Letters* 20, no. 2 (2016): 140–55, https://doi.org/10.1080/14688417.2016.116606 6. I also keep a blog about the garden at my shared rental house located at http://www.earlwoodfarm.com.

Fig. 2. Artist as Family, *Food Forest* (2010). Photograph taken in 2016 from Albion Street. St Michael's Church and rectory also in shot.

for understanding our genealogy in the New World Order.... It will not help — emotionally, intellectually, morally, or politically — to appeal to the natural and the pure.'[22] These gardens are not surfaces representing and aestheticizing ideas, but durational and experimental engagements with place. Drawing on a feminist politics of labour and care work, Maria Puig de la Bellacasa argues that 're-learning' how to enrich soil without petrochemically produced synthetic additives and instead working with biotic and abiotic matter, the slower and embodied labors of human care workers on biodynamic or permaculture farms 'cannot be understood as a nostalgic return to a pre-industrial landscape, nor one that chooses to ignore pre-industrial unsustainable relations with soil. The present reconfigurations of human-soil relations for the inheritors of industrial revolutions will have to be *unique* to an epoch and timescape where the re-

22 Donna Haraway, *Modest_Witness@Second_Millennium Female-Man©_Meets_OncoMouse™: Feminism and Technoscience* (New York: Routledge, 1997), 62.

creation of ecological tradition faces global breakdown.'[23] The same can be said for the gardens in question here. The *107 Roof-top* is a training ground for city dwellers to grow food in small spaces like balconies and courtyards of medium density residential developments. At Frontyard they practice the conceptual art of 'futuring'[24]-gardening in tandem with these theoretical discussions, while at *Girl Shed III,* Newall explored strategies and techniques for living within the city, not as a means to escape it. They are similarly wedded to their particular sites: *Tending* was designed to build new community connections in an art school and worked with the sandy, nutrient poor soil of the grounds, while *Gwago Patabágun___we will eat presently* was a historical provocation about food crisis located on the grounds of the MCA, which was also the site of the first British colony in Australia and is now a popular tourist zone. And in *2. Field Work,* Kelly's preoccupation with slow life practice and Tan's focus on questions of Singaporean identity and national security merged to think about food, life, and design across cultural boundaries. If any of these projects reference Eden or pastoral idealism, it is long after the fall and without any hope of escape from the political and industrial transformations of nature we know as cities.

23 Maria Puig de la Bellacasa, 'Making Time for Soil: Technoscientific Futures and the Pace of Care,' *Social Studies of Science* 45, no. 5 (2015): 1–26, at 19.

24 In my interview, Alexandra Crosby suggested that the collective had some trouble communicating the idea of 'futuring' to the wider non-specialist community, but in practice it is quite straightforward. 'Futuring' workshops involve sitting and collectively planning how to respond to issues and imagine what the world will look like in 10, 20, and 50 years from now on account of these hypothetical responses. In a professional context, this activity would be known as 'scenario planning,' but its objectives are different at a grassroots level: exchange with Alexandra Crosby (janitor at Frontyard), June 30, 2016, Marrickville, New South Wales, Australia (digital recording).

Sydney's Edible and Durational Live Art Gardens in Historical and Contemporary Global Context

A city is often defined by what it is not — it is not the bush, the forest, or the farm — but the contemporary settler colonial, neo-liberal political moment and the grand historical narrative of urbanization intersects in surprising ways with these inner-city gardens. Sydney has an extraordinary history of being a lush and fertile zone full of coastal and marine vegetable and animal life for consumption by local indigenous people,[25] and a complex subsequent history of failed colonial farm projects and later second-wave migrant market gardens. But dominant practice in Sydney, and of the few cities that dot this vast continent,[26] is to pave over and develop open space into office skyscrapers, retail malls, residential apartment complexes, and suburbs. Today if gardens are constructed they are usually retreats from the office, or as recreational spaces; with a few exceptions such as Pocket City Farms, they are not for food growing. Market gardens do still exist within the Sydney basin, but are constantly under pressure from residential developers.[27] When edible plants are planned and planted in the inner city now, they become historical objects on display, not a proposal for an alternative way of living. On a headland just west of the Sydney Harbor Bridge, the newly constructed Barangaroo Reserve — a green-space designed to offset the transformation of other public space into offices, multi-million dollar apartments, and a casino — contains many edible species of Australian 'native' plants, including *Cissus hypoglauca* (native grape), *Dianella revoluta* (blueberry lily), and *Tetragonia tetragonioides* (New Zealand Spinach or Warrigal Greens). They are planted as

25 For a paradigm shifting study of indigenous farming practice see Bruce Pascoe, *Dark Emu, Black Seeds: Agriculture or Accident* (Broome: Magabala Books, 2014).

26 For an exploration of how the continent itself held back development of larger swathes of the nation, see Libby Robin, *How a Continent Created a Nation* (Sydney: UNSW Press, 2007).

27 Sarah James, 'Protecting Sydney's Peri-urban Agriculture: Moving Beyond a Housing/Farming Dichotomy,' *Geographical Research* 52, no. 4 (2014): 377–86, https://doi.org/10.1111/1745-5871.12048.

living museum installations, representing plant life that lined the headlands and foreshores of Sydney Harbor before colonization, with past uses of these plants made public through aboriginal education tours. But all uses are memorializing the 'past.' In contrast, Sarah Newall of *Girl Shed III* specifically suggested that her garden was for the 'future,' imaging a new role for the urban artist, who might have to incorporate food growing in and for the future.

As responses to larger processes, the art gardens explored here can be understood as one dimension of a new global movement advocating edible plant-growing or urban farming in developed cities. To call plant-growing in cities a 'new movement' will seem historically naïve to some, which is partly true. In Sydney, there are many sites around the inner city which, until relatively recently, were for the growing of edible food. Food for human consumption has grown in valleys now lined with homes and apartments, since long before colonization. Backyard chickens were common in the 1950s because centralized caged egg production was not. In urban Australia, the suburban block was designed to enable a practice of nostalgia for food growing and enabled citizens to idealize a past rural lifestyle.[28] My own tramping around inner suburbs, with an eye for edible plants, reveals established private food forests in backyards. Since the development of Earlwood from farmland estate into suburb during the mid-twentieth century, olive trees have been planted in the streets while front yards sport healthy lemons trees for the making of preserves to compliment the cooking of first generation Mediterranean migrants from Greece and Lebanon.[29] Thus, in one sense, there is nothing new or innovative about this 'movement'.

In recent years, however, there has been an observable rise in urban agricultural projects in developed cities like Brooklyn,

28 Andrea Gaynor, *Harvest of the Suburbs: An Environmental History of Growing Food in Australian Cities* (Perth: University of Western Australia Press, 2006).

29 A project exploring food growing in the inner suburbs through walking and looking is 'Mapping Edges' (http://www.mappingedges.org/) by Ilaria Vanni and Alexandra Crosby at the University of Technology, Sydney.

Atlanta, Vancouver, Berlin, and Sydney, with many books published on how-to farm cities and rooftops, alongside new kinds of private gardening courses and community-supported farms.[30] These projects are trying to reclaim what the city has already paved over or transformed from functional to aesthetic green space, as well as continuing to work against further development. These projects represent people pushing back against a monstrous present, rather than an expressed ignorance of prior practices. These farming and art projects also incorporate, often quite openly and moralistically, responses to the environmental crisis, food insecurity, history, rising living costs, critiques of mainstream urbanization, and the structure of the labor market in a knowledge economy.[31] Indeed, although public green spaces are shrinking, urban development is expanding, and residential dwellings are tending towards densely packed apartments rather than freestanding homes, and there are enough urban agricultural projects in developed cities to identify this as a trend building on and altering extant twentieth-century allotment style spaces, suburban plots, and established commercial market gardens. Indeed, Jeffrey Hou theorized the global phenomenon of contemporary urban community gardening and farming as a form of 'insurgent placemaking,' in contrast to what he calls 'institutional placemaking.'[32] For Hou, urban gardening embodies 'a distinct and alternative mode of placemaking that stands in contrast to the predominant practice of planning and design that defines the relationship between

---

30 See, for example, Novella Carpenter and Willow Rosenthal, *The Essential Urban Farmer* (London: Penguin, 2012); Curtis Stone, *The Urban Farmer: Growing Food For Profit on Leased or Borrowed Land* (Gabriola Island: New Society Publishers, 2015); and Annie Novak, *The Rooftop Growing Guide: How to Transform Your Roof into a Vegetable Garden or Farm* (New York: Random House, 2016).

31 For a critique of organic agricultural practices and urban farmer's markets, see Julie Guthman, 'If They Only Knew: The Unbearable Whiteness of Alternative Food,' in Alison Hope Alkon and Julian Agyeman, eds., *Cultivating Food Justice: Race, Class and Sustainability* (Cambridge: MIT Press, 2011), 263–82.

32 Jeffrey Hou, 'Urban Gardening, Insurgent Placemaking: Public, yet Personal; Organized, yet Informal,' lecture presentation, Rachel Carson Centre, Munich, May 24, 2013, https://vimeo.com/69297731.

cities, environments and their users.'[33] Given the ways in which already developed cities are growing further by privatizing the commons, the urban farm can be seen as transnational movement responding to a widespread issue.

Although hitherto unnamed, the edible live art garden is a global phenomenon, too. Writing in the *Village Voice,* Martha Schwendenner catalogues and historicizes recent garden art in New York and considers it as a form of land claim similar to the Occupy Movement[34]; meanwhile, in Brussels, an art collective is designing an art festival around the establishment of a new community garden and education space.[35] However small in scale, most of these projects should be seen as creative responses to what Cheryl Lousley calls a 'farcical cultural moment when environmental knowledge circulates so *readily* but is dissociated from any particular political project of social change.'[36] None of the gardens address the ecological problem at scale. Indeed, at the *2. Field Work* installation, Lisa Kelly foraged mulberries from trees around inner Sydney backyards and placed them on a table for her audience to eat. When situated in the context of a global crisis, the action seems ridiculous or pointless and in no way a viable systemic response. But in the face of systemic inaction or, indeed, the expansion of fossil fuel exploration and mining, all buoyed by an ideology of growth, eating a foraged mulberry felt more like an act of systemic resistance than a gesture of hopeless nihilism. Puig theorises taking time for slowly building up soil communities as, 'acts of care [that] can be considered as a kind of resistance'[37] against the dominant technology-driven pace of post-industrial, monocultural agriculture. Read in this light,

33 Ibid.

34 Martha Schwendenner, 'Gardening Art Grows into Activism in the Age of Occupy,' *Village Voice,* June 11, 2016, http://www.villagevoice.com/arts/gardening-art-grows-into-activism-in-the-age-of-occupy-7172081.

35 See, for instance, the Brussels-based *Le Jardin Essential,* http://www.parckdesign.be/projects/ateliers-du-jardin, and also https://www.flickr.com/photos/parckdesign2016/sets/72157668950677325.

36 Cheryl Lousley, 'Ecocriticism and the Politics of Representation,' in Greg Garrard, ed., *The Oxford Handbook of Ecocriticism* (Oxford: Oxford University Press, 2013), 155–171, at 156.

37 Puig de la Bellacasa, 'Making Time for Soil,' 7–8.

although eating a foraged mulberry is a farcically small act, it is only too small if we are expecting every act to figure as a comprehensive and scalable solution to, say, the problem of carbon emissions from the global food system. Via Puig, however, we can understand it as a local act of resistance and also communal proposal for finding alternative economies and ways of relating.

The primary difference between an edible live art garden and a commercial or community urban agriculture project is economic. Funded by crowdfunding, government grants, or other odd jobs, art gardens are liberated from the need to produce vegetables as commodities and thus the gardeners are able to focus on other questions at the same time as growing food. In a small-scale, community-supported agricultural business (CSA) — such as, for instance, the 'Love is Love' farm at the housing co-op Gaia Gardens in DeKalb County, Atlanta — the managers work on the farm and pay their employees with profits made on vegetable box subscriptions and farmer's market sales. The funding for other art gardens came largely from grants or personal income: an Australian Research Council Grant funded *Tending*;[38] *Girl Shed III* was supported by free rent of the courtyard and the artist's paid employment at a community arts center;[39] and the Australia Council supported many of Makeshift's projects.[40] Being freed of the necessity to have a clear and calculated yield of edible plants, either for food or income, these gardens can be explorations in what it would mean and what it would take to actually live in a different relation to plants, animals, and the city. The answer is not straightforward. Issues such as polluted ground water, toxic soils, high land values, the high cost of living, and dwindling and contested open space make farming in cities difficult, if not physically and financially impossible. The purported undesirability of subsistence living and the modeling

38 Lucas Ihlein (artist), exchange with the author, July 11, 2016, Callan Park, New South Wales, Australia (digital recording).
39 Exchange with Sarah Newall (artist), July 7, 2016, Marrickville, New South Wales, Australia (digital recording).
40 Exchange with Tessa Zettel (Makeshift artist), July 13, 2016, Brussels/Earlwood, New South Wales, Australia (digital recording of Skype session).

of a global living standard on the idea of being liberated from such hard labor[41] practices means that an equitable future model of farming needs to interrogate other elements of life and work as well. The creative space opened up by the edible live art garden thus utilizes the privilege of not having to labor for income or subsistence to play with what it would be like to grow food as part of living.

Similarly, while Ihlein and Crosby cite the gardening method 'permaculture' as an influence, they are by no means orthodox practitioners. Permaculture or 'revolution disguised as gardening'[42] is a principled practice, with three central maxims — earth care, people care, and fair share — and twelve principles including things like 'obtain a yield' and 'observe and interact'.[43] Orthodox permaculture projects are specifically concerned with meeting necessity through personal labor and equitable community building, following the rules, but those who closely observe the principles tend not to live in cities. The more famous permaculture farms, like David Holmgren's Melliodora, are in rural areas. The grid of the city, the pipes, roadways, and concrete, not to mention the scarcity of available land and cost of living, make adherence to all the principles difficult. Artist as Family practice a creative adaptation of permaculture Jones calls 'permapoesis,' which is a strict and creative attempt to shun the fossil fuel economy, but they live in the rural Victorian town of Daylesford.[44] In other words, it is far more difficult to be an orthodox permaculture practitioner in the city. While the Milkwood group members

41 Well beyond the scope of this chapter is an investigation and critique of particular models of human development and living standards. The data is collected by the UN here: http://hdr.undp.org/en/content/human-development-index-hdi.

42 Despite the niftiness of the maxim, it is hardly a 'disguise' or even really a 'revolution' when t-shirts sporting the quote are available for sale on Amazon, although I imagine those really adhering to the principles don't actually buy the t-shirt.

43 The permaculture principles were first developed by Bill Mollison and David Holmgren, but they now the circulate widely in print and online. See, for example: https://permacultureprinciples.com/principles/.

44 Patrick Jones, "Walking for Food: Regaining Permapoesis," PhD diss., University of Western Sydney, 2014.

Fig. 3. Sarah Newall, *Girl Shed III* (Winter 2016). The official residency has ended; there is not much sunlight in the concrete courtyard of an old industrial warehouse. Image by Author

have become leading figures in permaculture training, they make money through education rather than growing for market. The *107 Rooftop* is an educational platform for their permaculture courses rather than a strict permaculture project in itself; meanwhile, 107 Projects rent the garden and adjacent conference room out to corporations like Telstra and government bodies like Urban Growth NSW, as a bespoke background for business-as-usual conferences in order to subsidize the funding of the art space.[45] On the one hand, *Tending* was written up on the Milkwood blog as 'Sydney's best kept secret permaculture garden'[46], but on the other Ihlein and Bonnetto were by no means religious followers of permaculture principles. As their own blog reveals, in contrast to the strict and long-term planning required of permaculture projects, *Tending* was quite unstructured in its plans, with the gardeners letting the garden evolve in dialogue with whomsoever

45 'Rooftop Garden & U1,' http://107projects.org/upstairs-107/.
46 Kirsten Bradley, 'Sydney's Best Kept Secret Permaculture Garden,' Milkwood, September 4, 2011, https://www.milkwood.net/2011/09/04/sydneys-best-kept-secret-permaculture-garden/.

showed an interest in it. While many of the directors at *Frontyard* have participated in Milkwood's courses, their garden similarly is not strictly designed and managed with permaculture principles. Crosby reported having to remind people to harvest food from the garden. Nonetheless, Crosby suggested that the principle 'observe and interact' has come to relate both to the garden and the rest of the community space. For Crosby, the health of the plants becomes an index of the health of the space.[47] If the plants are growing well, the community is too. Permaculture thus functions as a guide and ideal that orients the visions of the artists, but does not become orthodoxy.

These art gardens make no systemic structural challenge to dominant modes of food consumption and production, but they can represent ideas about grassroots methods for tackling the problem. At the level of art practice, then, the edible live art gardens of Sydney can all be understood as participating in the long tradition of the happening, the durational performance, or the live, socially engaged installation. They are on the margins of art and non-art, variously crossing over into community service, educational tool, grant 'outcome,' and activism. Reflecting on another farm-related art project, Ihlein considers such work as 'operating at 1:1 scale' and thus, such 'art does not represent the world in a separate, miniaturized version of itself, but rather participates in the world as it is, enabling a slightly shifted sensory and cognitive perception of reality.'[48] Edible live art gardens are creative happenings that exist on the edges of art practice. These gardens participate simultaneously in aesthetic production, community building, and activism; and they draw on methods and materials largely considered outside of art. At the same time, these gardens come to represent a critique of the dominant narrative of civilizational history and the currently prevailing mode of urban development. It is only as art that these gardens are ca-

---

47 Alexandra Crosby (Director of Frontyard), exchange with the author, July 7, 2016, Marrickville, New South Wales, Australia (digital recording).

48 Lucas Ihlein, 'The Yeomans Project: Peri-Urban Field Work,' *Axon Journal: Issue 8, Creative Cities* 5, no. 1 (2015): 1–14, http://ro.uow.edu.au/lhapapers/1995.

pable of expressing, thinking, and, indeed, materializing all these things at once.

Site Specificity

The gardens wrote another layer on the palimpsest of their locations. Each artist or collective had to navigate a range of indentations and marks made by prior and current 'stakeholders' and a suite of concomitant legal and bureaucratic constraints.[49] Moreover, with the exception of *2. Field Work,* which included foraged berries from Marrickville, and the Makeshift installations, which were potted and portable, the plants in these art works were put into the ground or planter boxes and literally rooted to their place. Thus, more than just buildings and employment agreements, the materiality of the site (weather, soil, plants, and labor practices) produces the works. As well as participating in wider historical and political narratives, the site specificity makes the garden projects intensely local responses to the global environmental crisis. Instead of trying to capture the world, local concerns and questions about global issues can be publically mobilized via the lived process of caring for plants and, at the same time, represented insofar as it is on display in an experimental, non-didactic, and community-oriented way.

All the gardens were situated on Gadigal or Wangal Country, but only Artist as Family reported seeking permissions from the original custodians of the land.[50] The *Food Forest* was an attempt to produce a garden that addresses local historical violence together with contemporary ecological questions. When I asked

49 I am hesitant to use the term 'stakeholder' as it is a newspeak that is often found in corporate documents when describing community consultation processes. If stakeholders can be grouped, labeled and, in one way or another, consulted, large-scale development projects can more easily navigate actually competing ideas about how the site will be used in future. At the same time, it is a term that accurately and expediently describes how there are lots of people with different stakes in sites around cities.

50 Personal communication with Patrick Jones and Meg Uhlmann. July 2016. Email.

them about site specificity, they were clear about their attempt to materially represent pre-colonial land relations. Their aim was not to do so by planting 'bush foods' and trying to recreate the past with plants, but in thinking differently about process, relations between people and place, and modes of land occupation:

> More than site-specificity our work is concerned with inspiring the possibilities of access to land for community resource regeneration contiguous with Aboriginal economies pre-1788 and agrarian economies throughout the world where private property doesn't dominate land-people relations. While the site's history and politic is of course central to the work — no discussion of land or site in Australia can disappear the lie of terra nullius, and thus permission to plant *Food Forest* using some traditional foods was requested from the Gadigal nation — community accessibility to land for the purposes of free organic food was the central focus. Thus, the making public of private (church) land became an exciting possibility through relationship building.[51]

Although it is not visible in the traces of the garden itself, in establishing the *Food Forest,* they activated local communities, bureaucracies, and layers of history in new ways in an attempt to materialize their concepts.

Developed as a commission from Sydney's Museum of Contemporary Art (MCA) exhibition In the *Balance: Art for a Changing World,* their contract enabled them to choose where the garden was located. This freedom was, ironically, limited by their concept outlined to a work that was not restricted to the exhibition timeline and instead could endure beyond its closure. This desire for a permanent tenure for *Food Forest* meant they had difficulty actually finding a place not contested, differently used or, more importantly, slated for a particular kind of redevelopment. They wanted to work with The Settlement, an aboriginal community activist organization based in Redfern. But wider corporatized government plans to redevelop the Redfern

Fig. 4. Diego Bonetto shoveling soil in the courtyard of an old psychiatric hospital-cum-art school, constructing a no dig sweet potato garden at *Tending* in 2011. The cart from Makeshift's project *Gwago Patabágun___we will eat presently,* in the background. Image by Lucas Ihlein.

area[52] meant the vision for *Food Forest* could only ever be temporary. The *Food Forest* came to be situated at St Michael's in Darlinghurst after the Church's land was suggested because it was public-facing private land (see Fig. 2) but owned and managed by the Church with relative autonomy, and no foreseeable redevelopment plans. Approval came quickly, first from the Church and then the City.

The extent to which Artist as Family's conceptual hope for an engagement with pre-colonial agrarian economies[53] material-

---

52 This redevelopment has been widely responded to by the arts community, see, for instance, the activities of Squat Space and the exhibition 'There Goes the Neighbourhood.'

53 Pre-colonial land relations are not often thought in traditional agricultural terms; indeed, the land enclosure that defines such practices are often defined against indigenous 'hunter/gatherer' societies. Bruce Pascoe's landmark and multi-award winning book *Dark Emu Black Seeds: Agriculture or Accident* (Broome: Magabala Books, 2014) is an example

ized in the Forest itself depends on one's perspective. During the MCA exhibition, these ideas were represented via discussions and activities of the artists on site and in the program and catalogue. In the public archive on the MCA website, however, the work has been reduced to just an 'off-site community garden...for producing food.'[54] Despite the various plants still growing, there is no signage at the church today outlining the ideas or history. The attempt to build an ongoing community relationship to place that could clear a path to a different way of being with the past, present, and future by way of the forest was to some extent thwarted by the process after the time of exhibition. Jones and Ullman reported difficulty in finding custodians to tend the Forest beyond their tenure on the site. The concept needed ongoing human labor, but willing volunteers were hard to come by in the urban economy. The attempt to break down the wall between public and private land, and troubled land-relations more generally, was also thwarted by reports of churchgoers trying to bring outsiders who came to tend the garden into 'the fold.' Thus, with no one really shepherding the process beyond the end of the exhibition, and the Artists, who live in rural Victoria, unable to maintain a regular practice of tending themselves, the Food Forest struggles and thus comes to represent the difficulty of materially mobilizing these concepts in the contemporary urban economy.

Sarah Newall reported a similar issue with finding an inheritor to her project at Air Space's courtyard in Marrickville. *Girl Shed III* was established as a project with personal questions at the fore, but also as an ongoing residency space. She committed to a year of praxis and the establishment of the space, but no one has continued her project. Again the plants and worms lure her back to the site intermittently, but it is still waiting for the next girl to come along. That said, the project was site specific for entirely different reasons to the Artist as Family. In establishing the *Girl Shed III* installation and residency, Newall suggests she was motivated by an existing practice preoccupied with rethinking

of work that is changing that narrative.

54 'In the Balance: Art for a Changing World', *MCA*, http://www.mca. com.au/collection/exhibition/536-in-the-balance-art-for-a-changing-world/.

domesticity and functional art and a desire to redress the gender bias in the idea of a 'man cave.' She shares a home with her partner about five minutes from the site of *Girl Shed III*. They have turned their garage into an exhibition space for outsiders to occupy and explore.[55] Thus *Girl Shed III* spatially functions as an extension of her backyard. But instead of a 'man cave' where the point is, apparently, to escape domestic drudgery by playing video games, watching sporting matches away from 'women and female sensibilities,' as the cliché laden Wikipedia entry on the subject suggests,[56] *Girl Shed III* aimed to make a second domestic space. In the rubric of the 'man cave,' Newall escapes the carbon-intensive Marrickville home for a self-sufficient parallel domesticity. She constructed garden beds, a worm farm, a rocket stove, and a tiny house with bed, table, and rainwater harvesting system. The site specificity bred difficulties, however, because the gallery, in an old light industrial warehouse, is sandwiched between other concrete cubes. The courtyard was not designed for humans to live in and receives little to no sunlight in winter and full sun in summer. In trying to stay in the house overnight and practice her idea, she was chased home by mosquitoes and a loud industrial fan from the adjacent warehouse. As we talked about the successes and failures of her work, we were entertained by a chorus of Ibis that live in the date palms that line the remnant industrial sites around Marrickville.

Tending emerged from a different pragmatic and conceptual zone to *Girl Shed III,* but was equally complicated by the site.[57] Having just completed his PhD, an unemployed Lucas Ihlein was thinking about going back on the 'Dole' (The Australian Government's unemployment welfare scheme). With no prospects in the art or academic world at the time, he thought to try and use his privilege to conjure some work. The well-networked Ihlein contacted Ross Gibson, then recently appointed Professor at Sydney College of the Arts, and asked if he had any work.

55 See *Marrickville Garage,* https://marrickvillegarage.com/.

56 'Man cave,' https://en.wikipedia.org/wiki/Man_cave (last modified July 6, 2015).

57 A history of the site is documented in a comment on the *Tending* blog by Ross Gibson at: http://www.tending.net.au/greeting-the-yard/.

Tending emerged from Ihlein's profile as an artist in need of a job, merging with an excess of grant funding, combined with a kernel of an idea from Gibson. The idea was to create a garden space for creating new kinds of interdisciplinary art practice in an institution known for traditional craftsmanship. Access for *Tending* was negotiated by Gibson, primarily with the University of Sydney administration and facilities management, but also with community activist groups like Friends of Callan Park.[58] Ihlein recalled how the original idea was to have the project situated on the edge of the school's property, near a public street and footpath. This was conceived in response to ongoing issues with the college in terms of its real and perceived insularity. The art school's reuse of a psychiatric hospital designed to separate people from society made interaction with the public physically difficult. By placing the garden on the edge of the property, as a site of activity, experimentation, conviviality, and liveliness, the idea was that the garden could act as a bridge between the wider community and the art school. The siloed disciplinarity of the school could also, in part, be attributed to the structure of the hospital, which meant that painting, drawing, ceramics, and photography were all located in discrete wards of the hospital. Thus, at the same time as opening the school to the public, the street-side location would have meant that people from the school would have walked through the space en route to their respective studios and, potentially, have encouraged people from different disciplines to get involved in the activities, thereby breaking down boundaries.

But Ihlein recounted how the edge-land desired by the gardeners was institutionally controversial and perceived by some community conservation groups as an attempt to 'soften' the land for a more radical redevelopment. Gibson ended up 'compromising' the space and was situated in the exercise yard of the former hospital, a space designed much like a prison, walled on all sides with a single, lockable door enabling access.[59] The garden was behind a closed door, accessible only when the gardeners were present.

58 See *Friends of Callan Park,* http://www.callanpark.com.
59 Lucas Ihlein, recounting the development of the project, in discussion with the author, July 11, 2016, Callan Park, New South Wales, Australia (digital recording).

In many ways, then, the garden became the opposite of what was intended and itself was cloistered within the walls of the school, making the artists literal gatekeepers to the space and outsiders either oblivious to or intimidated by its presence.

Although the architecture seemingly thwarted any loftier conceptual hopes that Gibson, Ihlein, and Bonetto brought to the garden, what emerged was a version of that vision. They hoped to facilitate a space that, unlike the rest of the institution and grounds, was not governed by a master plan and could be managed according to the whims of the community that grows up around it. They conceived of themselves as caretakers, but not ruling or managing the space.[60] The locked door and isolated courtyard troubled the aim to produce food and build connections with interested parties, but this did not stop interesting convergences emerging from the project. However small the scale, one of the most interesting stories they recalled in an interview, but which is also retained on their blog, is that of Betty. Betty is a migrant from Indonesia who lives in Marrickville and, at that point, was the manager of the SCA Café until midway through the project when her contract was not renewed. She donated plants, a compost bin, and her own expertise to the garden. So rather than painters using the space for inspiration or photographers exercising their macro lens, which was in part the plan of the garden, it was a professional staff member that crossed into the workspace of the academic.

Although the circumstances that brought each of the gardens together are different, these artists are all navigating a postcolonial city undergoing rapid privatization, redevelopment, and gentrification, with a growing fiscal and ecological cost of living. The marks of the zeitgeist are apparent in different ways in all of the projects traced above — from Betty's redundancy and Ihlein's post-PhD unemployment, to the racial divide between migrant service worker and white Australian artist; from Redfern's redevelopment and the peripheral role of the land-rich Christian church in the colonial city to art spaces weathering high-rental costs in unaccommodating industrial warehouses in suburban backstreets, to the warm albeit temporary nature

60 Ibid.

of the communities that spring up around all of these projects. These similarities in the projects can be understood as pushing back against the City's dominant ambition to grow and develop in a particular manner.

If the city is a cyborg, what kind of cyborg is contemporary Sydney? In an essay in Cordite poetry review, Ross Gibson listed adjectives for Sydney: 'aqueous. Shiny. Shifty. Stupid. Braggart'.[61] In this list, Gibson implies a watery city, which lacks self-awareness, as if the sun reflecting of the network of waterways blinds it or, in particular, the wealthy and powerful with water views. But it is a sprawling city, whose dominant mythology is firmly located in and around the shiny CBD and the harbor, but that sports much more diversity than such a myth cares to represent. Such a sentiment is explored by the poets of western Sydney such as Maxine Beneba Clarke, Peter Polites, Michael Mohammed Ahmed and Luke Carmann as well as artist Vanessa Berry, who has spent the last four years documenting urban ruins to form an encyclopedia of other perspectives in the project *Mirror Sydney*.[62] In her book-length memoir on the city, Delia Falconer cuts into the dichotomy between the blind glamour and sprawling diversity, suggesting that Sydney's nature is actually reflected in its intellectual history, one that is 'paradoxical, visionary [and...] iconoclastic.' But, she suggests, 'at the same time, and this is part of its paradoxical nature, you would be hard pressed to find elsewhere thinkers as palpably earth bound.'[63] She cites the city's famous poets and authors, Kenneth Slessor, Patrick White, and Ruth Park, as iconic place writers whose works turn on the relation between the physical and the metaphysical. In other words, the intellectual traditions, in which I would include artistic practices, have developed as responses to Sydney's particular and pe-

---

61 Ross Gibson, 'Blustertown,' in Astrid Lorange, ed., *Cordite Poetry Review* 38, no. o: Sydney, http://cordite.org.au/ekphrasis/blustertown/.

62 For a rundown of this emerging set of artists, see Luke Carman, 'Revelators, Visionaries, Poets and Fools: The Palimpsest of Sydney's Western Suburbia,' *Southerly Journal,* May 7, 2015, http://southerlyjournal. com.au/2015/05/07/revelators-visionaries-poets-and-fools-the-palimpsest-of-sydneys-western-suburbia/.

63 Delia Falconer, *Sydney* (Sydney: New South, 2010), 5.

culiar paradoxes. The city is, perhaps, a cyborg where the head does not really understand what the tail is doing. Within an intellectual tradition that is both idealistic and substantial at the same time, in the heart of a hilly city, built on stolen land that is surrounded by salt water and crisscrossed by brackish polluted waterways, these artists work against a dominant trend. Sydney is building itself up as a capitalist knowledge economy and a retail and administrative hub, with an IKEA that holds the record of being the largest retail shop in the southern hemisphere. Sydney is also selling off peri-urban farmland to residential developers and building massive new highways as other cities turn to public transport. It is in this specific context that these artists are spending time and resources seeking responsibility for plants.

Conclusion: A Path to the Planthropocene?

In their reflections on the relationship between art and gardening, the artists noted a distinction between the spatio-temporal zone occupied by gardens or living plants and more conventional modes of artistic representation, such as sculpture, drawing, or installation. This distinction was both important and political for the artists. Sarah Newall used to crochet plants and she openly reflected on the difference between exhibiting a crocheted plant in a gallery and growing a living plant as part of an installation. While her family always had a garden, Newall cautiously described the transition from crocheting flowers as art to growing plants as moving from the simulacra to the real. Regardless, both the flower represented in yarn and vegetal plants were art. But her response imagined the works as having a different relationship with human time, invited different kinds of labor, and thus implied a different kind of politics: '[The crocheted flower] feels like it has nostalgia and [is] drawing on the past,' while the living plant is involved in a practice that is 'thinking about the future, the future that we need to think about.'[64] While the flower would take a period of time to make, once it was in exhibition, the labor was over. In *Girl Shed III,* however, Newall needed

---

64 Sarah Newall (artist), in discussion with the author, July 7, 2016, Marrickville, New South Wales (digital recording).

to consistently tend the garden over the course of her residency. Conceptually, Newall reported nostalgia for gardens of her personal past manifest in her crocheted work, which shifted into a more direct engagement with the collective future in the growing of plants. Inspired by the minimalist functional art of Donald Judd and explorations of the 'social construction of necessity' by Andrea Zittel, Newall's turn to constructing mini-worlds evidently does not contain the same nostalgia as with the earlier plant sculptures. The nostalgia for the gardens also reflected a care for living gardens of her memory, but it seems she identified a need for living gardens to become part of her creative labor or they could literally be gone forever.[65] So, for Newall, shifting to working with living plants was a creative and political experiment asking questions about how to actually live out the ideas she had previously just represented.

The shift in Kirsten Bradley's art practice echoes some of what Newall said, only it occurs at a more industrial scale. Prior to establishing Milkwood, Bradley and Ritar were part of a creative trio known as Cicada, who constructed audio/visual installations that temporarily repurposed and redesigned public spaces. Their most high-profile work was in the prestigious Primavera Exhibition at the Museum of Contemporary Art. Entitled *Re_Squared* (2003), the installation occupied the forecourt and surrounds of Australia Square in the City's Central business district. When they moved to Milkwood farm near Mudgee in 2007, Bradley initially envisaged a life of growing plants on the family property alongside maintaining an international career creating art. But, in many ways, the plants won the battle for their attentions, and they ended up ostensibly leaving the 'art world,' such as it is, and

65 In this formulation, nostalgia occupies a privileged space in the world where loss is merely personal, rather than total. For instance, nostalgia is for a lost time of one's own experience, but it is something that could still be experienced by others. Nostalgia in this sense could be of an older person, long married, but nostalgic for the heady days of early romance. That can remain nostalgia because such heady romance is still possible for others. In Newall's conceptualization of climate change, perhaps the garden nostalgia risked becoming not something that others could be able to have and thus it needed to be worked for/fought for.

setting up a private permaculture school. Nonetheless, Bradley initially suggested that gardening was effectively the same thing as art in her mind. Later in the interview, when pressed to articulate the specifics of the creation of gardens in urban spaces, like the *107 Rooftop,* rather than audio/visual installations like *Re_Squared,* a temporal difference emerged. While both a garden and an installation are long term projects that produce a unique 'stacking (of) time and space in all...different ways,'[66] the legacy of the artwork is different to that of a garden. Bradley said that she hopes the garden will influence people in an 'ongoing... physical and environmental sense.'[67] The formal art installations, which were sometimes only set up for a few nights, the artist must hope that it lives on in the minds of the audience. The idea of remaking space temporarily suggested by the AV installation becomes a literal and enduring recreation in the construction of a garden. While Bradley reported some audience feedback from the MCA work that suggested they had achieved some success in the intangible zone of audience apprehension and new meanings about public space enduring beyond a single night, the liveliness of the plants in the garden creates new meaning, spatial transformation, and redesign that materially and conceptually endures.

In almost all cases, the idea that the plants call you back, endure in space, require tending, and care was not just a concept but a meaningful relationship that grounded the artists in place and motivated their work. Given that industrial agriculture is one of the most carbon-intensive, polluting, and wasteful industries in the world, transforming most ways life, it is deeply ironic and potentially tragic that one of the markers of the standard of living in the developed world is liberation from laboring for subsistence or necessity or, in other words, relief from a responsibility to plants. This is presumably because the care work involved in acting upon responsibility is often boring, tedious, and hard. As Puig imagines in relation to soil care, 'anybody who has been involved in caring for children, pets, or elderly kin, knows that

---

66 Kirsten Bradley (director, Milkwood Permaculture), in discussion with the author, June 29, 2016, Milkwood Farm/Camperdown, New South Wales (digital recording).

67 Ibid.

the work of care takes time and involves making time of a particular kind. Care time can be enjoyable and rewarding, but also tiresome, involving a lot of hovering and adjusting to the temporal exigencies of the cared-for.'[68] Cities promise a privileged relief from all kinds care work for the greater middle class, but here the middle class artists are divesting from that privileged post and returning to care for the plant.

Aside from the sole farmer driving the combine harvester, there are two readily available images of a different kind of human-plant relation: one is of an impoverished non-Western farmer, suffering a life of servitude to plants, with sunburnt skin, aching joints, and soil embedded in the cracks of aging hands. The other is of a happy Westerner choosing a good life of servitude to plants, buoyed by wealth, power, and privilege. While Sydney's edible and durational live art gardens might be understood and problematized in relation to the latter, the artists explored are evidently practicing something quite different, without glorifying the former. In Sydney, like other wealthy cities, small-scale market gardens are being sold for housing developments,[69] and at the same time, there is a movement both within the mainstream and counter culture to 'green the city' with gardens and farms. From a counter-cultural perspective, these artists are exploring this paradoxical situation using plants as medium and raised bed and pot-plant gardening as methods to think with plants in order to understand what it actually would take to relate to or, indeed, respond to plants differently in a highly urbanized metropolis. Neither adopting the identity of impoverished, or well-to-do, farmer, in these instances, the durational labor of tending a live art garden begins to map out a pathway for humans into the Planthropocene.

68 Puig de la Bellacasa, 'Making time for Soil,' 17.
69 See David Mason and Ian Knowd, 'The Emergence of Urban Agriculture: Sydney, Australia,' *International Journal of Agricultural Sustainability* 8, nos. 1–2 (2010): 62–71, https://doi.org/doi:10.3763/ijas.2009.0474.

Contributor Biographies

Andrew Belletty is an Indian born Australian resident artist who works with cultural, traditional and ecological acoustic knowledge and practices, and has been an influential voice in cinematic sound design since 1995. His current research is based on Aboriginal ideas of Listening to Country through a *situated listening* model, that extends to vibrotactile sensitivity as a critical component in the complex corporeal connections to place made by audible and sub-audible energies.

Tamryn Bennett is a poet and Artistic Director of Red Room Poetry. She has exhibited poetic projects across Australia, Switzerland and Mexico. Her collection *phosphene* is published by the Rabbit Poetry with other poems and essays appearing in *Five Bells, Nth Degree, Cordite, The Drunken Boat, ImageText,* and *Image [&] Narrative.* Tamryn is the co-creator of the 'Plant Symphony' with composer Guillermo Batiz.

Baylee Brits is adjunct researcher at UNSW. She was co-editor of the anthology *Aesthetics After Finitude* (Re.press, 2017). Her monograph, *Literary Infinities: Number and Narrative in Modern Fiction,* is forthcoming from Bloomsbury Academic. Her research investigates the reciprocal influences between scientific and artistic experimentation, focusing on literary modernism and the mathematical concept of the transfinite. She has published in *Textual Practice, Reconstruction, The Parish Review, Parrhesia,* and several book anthologies.

Justin Clemens teaches at the University of Melbourne, where he is working on an Australian Research Council Future Fellowship titled "Australian Poetry Today." This mainly involves interviewing local poets about their work. His most recent book is a coedited collection with A.J. Bartlett, titled *What is Education?*, with contributions by thinkers such as Silvia Federici and Mladen Dolar.

Paul Dawson's first book of poems, *Imagining Winter* (IP, 2006) won the national IP Picks Best Poetry award in 2006, and his work has been anthologized in *Contemporary Asian Australian Poets* (Puncher & Wattman, 2013) and *Harbour City Poems: Sydney in Verse 1788–2008* (Puncher & Wattmann, 2009). He is also the author of two monographs: *The Return of the Omniscient Narrator: Authorship and Authority in Twenty-First Century Fiction* (OSU Press, 2013) and *Creative Writing and the New Humanities* (Routledge, 2005). Paul is currently an Associate Professor in the School of the Arts and Media at the University of New South Wales.

Lisa Dowdall is based in Sydney, where she writes about weird and different futures. She has a PhD in Creative Practice from the University of New South Wales, and her work has appeared or is forthcoming in Paradoxa, Seizure, Spineless Wonders and Science Fiction Studies.

Luke Fischer is a poet and philosopher. His books include the poetry collections *A Personal History of Vision* (UWAP Poetry, 2017) and *Paths of Flight* (Black Pepper, 2013) and the monograph *The Poet as Phenomenologist: Rilke and the New Poems* (Bloomsbury, 2015). He is currently co-editing a volume of essays on the philosophical dimensions of Rilke's *Sonnets to Orpheus* (Oxford University Press). He is an honorary associate at the University of Sydney. For more information visit http://www.lukefischerauthor.com.

Monica Gagliano is Research Affiliate, Sydney Environment Institute at the University of Sydney and a former research fellow of the Australian Research Council. She is the author of

numerous scientific articles in the fields of animal and plant behavioral and evolutionary ecology and is coeditor of *The Green
Thread: Dialogues with the Vegetal World* (Lexington, 2015) and
The Language of Plants (Minnesota University Press, 2017). She
has pioneered the new research field of plant bioacoustics and
extended the concept of cognition to plants, reigniting the discourse on plant subjectivity and ethical standing. Her new book,
Thus Spoke the Plant, will be published in November 2018 with
North Atlantic Books. For more information visit http://www.
monicagagliano.com.

Prudence Gibson is Post Doctoral Fellow at University of NSW,
Sydney. She is author of *The Rapture of Death* (Boccalatte Publishing, 2010) and has published over 300 essays. Her 2015 book
Janet Laurence: The Pharmacy of Plants was published by New
South Publishing. She co-edited *Aesthetics After Finitude* (Re.
press, 2016). *The Plant Contract,* which addresses plant studies
and art, has been published with Brill Rodopi, Boston.

Jennifer Mae Hamilton is a postdoctoral researcher funded by
The Seed Box: A Mistra+Formas Environmental Humanities
Collaboratory at Linköping University, Sweden, and housed at
both the Department of Gender and Cultural Studies at University of Sydney and the Institute for Culture and Society at the
University of Western Sydney. Her first book *This Contentious
Storm: An Ecocritical and Performance History of King Lear*
is out with Bloomsbury Academic (August 2017); she co-con-
venes the reading and research group COMPOSTING Feminisms
and Environmental Humanities (http://compostingfeminisms.
wordpress.com) with Astrida Neimanis and keeps some research
notes at http://weatheringthecity.wordpress.com

Lucas Ihlein is an artist and academic. He is an Early Career Research Fellow in Creative Arts at University of Wollongong. His
research uses socially-engaged art to explore cultural innovations
in farming — principally in the sugar cane industry in Central
Queensland. Lucas is a founding member of Kandos School
of Cultural Adapation (KSCA), an artist collective fostering col-

laborations between artists, farmers and scientists. http://luca-sihlein.net

Tessa Laird is an artist and writer and Lecturer in Critical and Theoretical Studies at the School of Art, Victorian College of the Arts, University of Melbourne. Her book *A Rainbow Reader* was published by Clouds, Auckland in 2013, and *BAT,* is forth-coming in 2018 at Reaktion.

Michael Marder is Ikerbasque Research Professor of Philosophy at the University of the Basque Country (UPV-EHU), Spain and the Humanities Institute at Diego Portales University (UDP), Chile. He is author of numerous articles and books in the fields of environmental philosophy, phenomenology, and political thought. His most recent monograph is *Energy Dreams: Of Ac-tuality* (Columbia University Press, 2017).

Stephen Muecke is Jury Chair of English Language and Litera-ture in the School of Humanities at the University of Adelaide, South Australia. Recent publications are *The Mother's Day Protest and Other Fictocritical Essays* (Rowman and Littlefield International, 2016), a special edition of *New Literary History* ("Recomposing the Humanities—with Bruno Latour"), 2016, and a new edition of Paddy Roe's *Gularabulu: Stories from the West Kimberley* (UWA Publishing, 2016).

Dalia Nassar is a senior lecturer in the Department of Philosophy at the University of Sydney. She is the author of *The Romantic Absolute: Being and Knowing in German Romantic Philosophy, 1795–1804,* the editor of the volume *The Relevance of Romanti-cism: Essays on German Romantic Philosophy,* and co-editor of a special section of the *Goethe Yearbook,* vol. 22 (2015) on 'Goethe and Environmentalism' and of a focus section of *Studies in His-tory and Philosophy of Science* on 'Kant and the Empirical Sci-ences' (2016). She is currently working on an ARC project on Ro-mantic Empiricism and environmental philosophy.

Susie Pratt is an artist, techno-scientific muser, educator, and re-searcher. She explores how creative practice can influence social and environmental responsibility, with an emphasis on environmental health, toxic embodiment and speculative design. She currently conducts educational experiments within the Faculty of Transdisciplinary Innovation, University of Technology Sydney (UTS), as a Scholarly Teaching Fellow. Her creative work has been internationally exhibited in various forms, including digital storytelling, convergent media installations, site-specific sound works, urban design proposals, and participatory events.

Ben Woodard is a post-doc researcher in Philosophy and Art Theory at Leuphana University in Lüneburg, Germany. His books include *Slime Dynamics: Generation, Mutation and the Creep of Life* (Zero books, 2012), *On an Ungrounded Earth: Towards a New Geophilosophy* (punctum books, 2013), and *Schelling's Naturalism: Motion, Space, and the Volition of Though*t (Edinburgh Univerisity Press, 2018). He is affiliated with the Laboratory for Ontology, UK and a member of the philosophy collective P.S. based at the Performing Arts Forum (PAF) in St. Erme, France.

"The local mechanisms of mind . . . are not all in the head.

Cognition leaks out into body and world."

— Andy Clark, *Supersizing the Mind*

brainstorm books

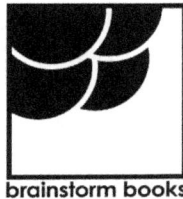

Current developments in psychoanalysis, psychology, philosophy, and cognitive and neuroscience confirm the profound importance of expression and interpretation in forming the mind's re-workings of its intersubjective, historical and planetary environments. Brainstorm Books seeks to publish cross-disciplinary work on the becomings of the extended and enactivist mind, especially as afforded by semiotic experience. Attending to the centrality of expression and impression to living process and to the ecologically-embedded situatedness of mind is at the heart of our enterprise. We seek to cultivate and curate writing that attends to the ways in which art and aesthetics are bound to, and enhance, our bodily, affective, cognitive, developmental, intersubjective, and transpersonal practices.

Brainstorm Books is an imprint of the "Literature and the Mind" group at the University of California, Santa Barbara, a research and teaching concentration hosted within the Department of English and supported by affiliated faculty in Comparative Literature, Religious Studies, History, the Life Sciences, Psychology, Cognitive Science, and the Arts.

http://mind.english.ucsb.edu/brainstorm-books/

Brainstorm Books